The
EVERYTHING.
Homeselling Book, 2nd Edition

Dear Reader:

Selling real estate in the area where I grew up is a great adventure. It is wonderful to show people how the process works and teach them what they need to do through each step of buying or selling property.

When I was given the opportunity to write this book, I knew it would be an extension of what I've done with each and every homeseller I have met since I started my career in 1988. In the process of writing, I have found this to be true, and I appreciate the opportunity to share what I have learned and taught over the past couple of decades.

As a third generation real estate agent, I discovered early in life the stresses that can upset the homeseller who does not understand what can and will happen in the process. It is my hope that the information in this book will help you avoid potential problems and lessen the stress you feel when you sell your own home. I also hope you will discover the adventure in homeselling that I have found.

Shari Maters

The EVERYTHING® Series

Editorial

Publishing Director	Gary M. Krebs
Associate Managing Editor	Laura M. Daly
Associate Copy Chief	Brett Palana-Shanahan
Acquisitions Editor	Gina Chaimanis
Development Editor	Katie McDonough
Associate Production Editor	Casey Ebert

Production

Director of Manufacturing	Susan Beale
Associate Director of Production	Michelle Roy Kelly
Cover Design	Paul Beatrice
	Erick DaCosta
	Matt LeBlanc
Design and Layout	Colleen Cunningham
	Holly Curtis
	Sorae Lee
Series Cover Artist	Barry Littmann

Visit the entire Everything® Series at *www.everything.com*

THE

EVERYTHING®

HOMESELLING BOOK

2ND EDITION

Shahri Masters

Adams Media
Avon, Massachusetts

*This book is dedicated to my clients, whose experience in selling
homes has given me the inspiration for this book.*

An Everything® Series Book.
Everything® and everything.com® are registered trademarks of F+W Publications, Inc.

Published by Adams Media, an F+W Publications Company
57 Littlefield Street, Avon, MA 02322 U.S.A.
www.adamsmedia.com

ISBN: 1-59337-396-1
Printed in the United States of America.
J   I   H   G   F   E   D   C   B   A

Library of Congress Cataloging-in-Publication Data
Masters, Shahri.
The everything homeselling book : from the open house to closing the deal, all you
need to get the most money for your home / Shahri Masters. -- 2nd ed.
p.   cm.
ISBN 1-59337-396-1
1. House selling--United States. 2. Real estate business--United States.   I. Title.
HD255.R4432 2006
643'.12--dc22

2005029890

This publication is designed to provide accurate and authoritative information with regard
to the subject matter covered. It is sold with the understanding that the publisher is not
engaged in rendering legal, accounting, or other professional advice. If legal advice or
other expert assistance is required, the services of a competent professional person should
be sought.
  —From a *Declaration of Principles* jointly adopted by a Committee of the
American Bar Association and a Committee of Publishers and Associations

Many of the designations used by manufacturers and sellers to distinguish their products
are claimed as trademarks. Where those designations appear in this book and Adams
Media was aware of a trademark claim, the designations have been printed with initial
capital letters.

*This book is available at quantity discounts for bulk purchases.
For information, call 1-800-872-5627.*

Contents

Acknowledgments

Thank you: To Margie, for introducing me to the idea of writing, and to the people who brought this book to life. To June, my agent, and to Gina at Adams Media, the most patient women I know. To my assistant Lauren, my best friend Linnea, and my broker Bill for helping me and for keeping this book a secret. To my special friend Maureen, for proofing the final draft. To my husband David and my daughter Abby, for their love and support as I wrote diligently for hours, both at home and abroad. And to the family of Hotel Francis in Luxembourg, who tended to me as I wrote and even added wireless Internet to their hotel just for me.

Top Ten Things for Homeselling Success

1. Understand your motivation. Knowing why you are selling your home and what benefit you expect to gain will help you throughout the entire process.

2. Create order in your home. A high level of organization is a key component in any successful endeavor.

3. Make repairs and freshen up. Buyers will notice. Even if your house is getting on in years, it'll attract attention if it's well maintained.

4. Understand the market. Knowledge of your market will teach you volumes about what to expect as you move forward toward a sale.

5. Price your home appropriately. Determining the right price is the most significant factor to assure success.

6. Choose an agent or decide to sell yourself. Carefully weigh the pros and cons of this important decision.

7. Learn about the paperwork. There is plenty of it, and knowing what to expect will keep surprises to a minimum.

8. Keep your emotions in check. When things get frustrating, a cool head and steady hand are your best allies.

9. Work with your financial consultant to discover areas where you can be flexible or even accommodating with your buyer. Be sure you understand your tax consequences, too.

10. Be patient. From preparing your home for sale, showing the house, and dealing with strangers, offers, negotiations, and the actual sale, there are a lot of chances to lose your cool. Remember your motivation and keep your eyes on the prize.

Introduction

▶ Welcome to the world of homeselling! Your decision to study the subject shows that you already realize a very important fact: There is more to the process than putting a sign on the lawn and waiting for a big check.

Perhaps this is your first house and you have never sold a home before. Perhaps you have some experience at this, but you have not sold a home in several years. Whatever your situation, you have chosen to arm yourself with knowledge of what lies ahead. This book will help you with all of the big decisions and most of the little glitches that arise as you undertake the sale of your house.

The first thing you should keep in mind is that right now this house is your home. It is more than a financial investment. Your home is a very personal space. Whether or not it meets your present needs, you are probably accustomed to it and somewhat comfortable there. Your home holds your personal things and your private life and provides sanctuary from the outside world.

Over the years, it may have become too small or too old. You may still love it but need to move out of the area to take a new job or start a new life. Whatever your reason for selling may be, once your home is on the market, all that privacy and comfort will be compromised—at least sometimes.

Selling your home can be an intense and complicated process. It involves your personal finances, personal style, personal time, and personal space. Knowing that potential buyers will be tromping through and judging the home that has been your own all these years can be an emotional roller coaster. Before you board the roller coaster, it will be helpful to know what to expect at every loop and turn. Knowing how the process works will steady your emotions and allow you to ride through the adventure swiftly, with as little stress as possible. You may even enjoy it.

From necessary repairs and fix-ups to making it look like a model, you will learn how to prepare your home for sale. You will learn how to turn your home back into a marketable house. You will understand how buyers think, what they value, and what makes a house look like a welcoming home for someone else. You will discover the pros and cons of selling on your own, as well as the pros and cons of working with an agent. You will learn how to choose an agent and how to market your own home if you decide to go it alone.

You will also learn how to assess the real estate market in your area and find your place in it. You will understand the importance of proper pricing and how to determine the right price for your house. You will know what to do when you receive an offer and how to deal with negotiations, paperwork, and all the legalities involved in selling your home. Finally, you will be aware of how to protect your interests, and you will be alerted to the little nuances that can make or break a sale.

Many people who decide to sell their homes are shooting in the dark. They may hit something, but without a little training, they might just make a lot of noise. This book will turn on the light for you. The information will enable you to see more clearly, hit the mark, and get the best possible price for your house, in the shortest amount of time.

Chapter 1

The Big Decisions

The decision to sell your home is an important one, and before you do anything else, you need to determine why you are selling. You may need to sell, or you may want to sell. It may even be a combination of both. This chapter will help you determine your motivation. If you really want to sell, the information in this book will help you move forward with your decision. If you're leaning the other way, this book can help you make the final choice that's right for you.

Why Are You Selling?

Every seller has a different reason for selling a home. When a move is necessary, the motivation is clear. Getting a job transfer and outgrowing your house are obvious reasons to sell. But when you're thinking about making a profit or just feeling like it is time to sell, such as to scale down after your kids have moved out, the motives are less apparent. Whatever your situation, your motive for selling is significant and requires careful consideration.

Selling to Make a Profit

In some areas, there are people who are selling because the market is good and they want to make some money. They believe that if they sell their home they will be rich. This is not usually the case. If you sell in a good market, chances are you won't be able to purchase in the same market. You may have to buy someplace else.

In a seller's market, the demand outweighs the supply. There are more buyers and fewer available properties. Prices are driven up. When it is a buyer's market, supply outweighs the demand. There are fewer buyers and more available properties. Prices are driven down. It is great to be a seller in a seller's market, but it's not so great to be a buyer in a seller's market.

Remember, you will be a buyer after selling your house. If you are willing to leave the hot market area to make money, then selling may be an option for you. If you don't want to leave, you may decide not to sell.

Selling to Scale Down

Perhaps you are selling because your kids are moving out and you want a smaller place. At this stage of life, many people plan to rid themselves of furniture, simplify their lives, and scale down. However, this is often much easier said than done.

Selling to scale down might seem like a great plan, but are you willing to do what it takes to make it happen? It's wise to look at some smaller homes and see if you can really live in significantly less space before making the final decision. For example, will there be room for your grandmother's piano with which you couldn't stand to part? Can your six-piece antique bedroom set fit in a smaller bedroom? Are you hanging on to numerous items for their sentimental value? Can you cram all these things into a smaller house and still have a place to eat your dinner? Address these issues before you even consider scaling down.

ALERT!

Your reason for selling may be vague. Perhaps you want to sell, but it's not because of a job transfer, financial problems, or a pending divorce. Brainstorm to discover why you want to sell. Write down all the reasons that come to mind and ask yourself what you expect to achieve by selling. Do your goals seem attainable?

When to Move

Once you decide to sell, you need to determine how fast you want to sell. Though you do not have control over the market and your house may not sell in the time frame you choose, there are certain things you can do to improve your chance of selling according to your schedule.

Determining Average Market Time

Market time refers to the length of time your home may be on the market before it sells. The length of time depends on many factors including the price, location, and condition of the house, plus the ratio of buyers to sellers.

First, you need to find out the average market time in your area. If possible, it is also helpful to discover the average market time for homes in the same price range as yours. Homes in higher price ranges traditionally take longer to sell than homes in lower price ranges. Remember that determining an average market time means there are above average market times and below average market times. Be willing to work within a range.

Information on average market time can be found in a number of different places. It may be published in your newspaper, usually in the real estate section on a quarterly or monthly basis. You may be able to find the average market time on the Internet, but information for larger metropolitan areas can be found more easily than rural areas. Some smaller regions have no statistical information on the Internet. In smaller areas, your local Chamber of Commerce may have statistics that can help you. A real estate agent is a good source, as is the local Board of Realtors®. The most unreliable but easily available option is local gossip: "John's house sold in only two weeks!" "Sarah's house was on the market for a year!"

The Best Time of Year to Sell

Every region has a favorable time to sell property and a slow time to sell property. Is your market dictated by the school schedule? How about weather? Is it best to sell in the spring? Does the ski season bring buyers, or do they come for the beaches? Is there a local factory that gears up at certain times? How about a new business coming in or an old business leaving?

Of course, you can't always choose to sell at the most optimal time. Sometimes you have to move now and the market isn't ready for you. Having a less urgent need to sell is always helpful. Once you know the average market time and the right time to sell in your market, you can start the preparations with realistic expectations.

To find out the best time to sell, ask your real estate agent. If you do not have an agent, check the county records. Look through sales of the past several years to determine the average number of sales per month. Count backwards for escrow time and market time to get a general idea of the selling season or seasons.

Can You Afford to Sell?

There are dangers in thinking you can make the money you want or need instead of what your house is worth. Of course, you're probably fantasizing about all the things you would do if you made some money off the sale of your house. Perhaps you imagine paying off credit card bills, paying back student loans, and getting a new car, while still having money left over to buy another house. If all goes really well, maybe you're even considering a vacation. Unfortunately, the chances of you making that much money off the sale of your home are very low. You may be able to do one or two of these things, but in a tough market, you may not be able to do any of them.

Determination of Value

It is important to get an educated picture of what your house is really worth, not just what you want for it. Getting a comparative market analysis (CMA) from a trusted real estate agent will help you to determine the real value. Sometimes a real estate agent will want to please you and will give you the highest value possible; take that into consideration when you are making a final determination of value. Real estate agents perform CMAs as a courtesy and rarely charge for the service. They are hoping that you will decide to use them to sell your home when you are ready. A licensed appraiser can also give you a determination of value. Appraisers charge a fee for this work, usually in the $300 to $500 range. (See Chapter 13 for more about CMAs and appraisals.)

What's Left After All the Costs?

Once you discover what your house is worth, you will need to subtract the cost of selling the house and the cost of your loan. Real estate fees and/or attorney fees, title fees, escrow fees, any repair or fix-up costs, the current loan, and a potential myriad of other expenses need to be taken into account. Each area has different customs as to which costs are assigned to the seller and which are assigned to the buyer. The following table will give you an idea of the type of costs you may have, either with a real estate agent or when selling yourself.

Average Seller's Costs

Seller's Cost	Description	Average Amount
Purchase Price	How much the buyer is paying	$200,000
First Deed of Trust	Mortgage	$100,000
Second Deed of Trust	Second Mortgage	$20,000
Line of Credit	Line of Credit	$10,000
Any Other Liens	Such as mechanic's liens for unpaid contractors' work	$1,000
Reconveyance Fees	What each loan company charges to take loan off title to the property once it is paid in full	$100 each
Prorated Interest, Taxes, and Insurance, Prorated Rents, Prorated Homeowner's Association (HOA) Dues	Nearly a month's worth of costs, depending on day of the month the property closes escrow and when payments are due	$900
Bonds and Assessments	County or municipal bonds or HOA assessments	$500
Appraisal Fee	In many cases, a cost borne by the buyer; with some types of financing, the seller's responsibility	$300
Attorney Fees	The cost is higher when not using a real estate agent because the attorney checks the contract to be sure it is in order and you are protected.	$750
Escrow Fees	Some areas of the country use an escrow company to hold monies and transfer the property; other areas use attorneys. Traditionally the East Coast uses attorneys, and the West Coast uses escrow.	$1,200
Brokerage Commissions	Your agent gives a portion of this, usually at least half, to the agent who brings a buyer.	$14,000
Building Department Reports	This is a cost in some areas of the country.	$100
Document Preparation	Such as preparing the Grant Deed	$75
Home Protection Contract	A little insurance policy that protects the buyer against repairs of major systems such as heating, appliances, plumbing, etc.	$250–$300

Inspections Not Paid by Buyer	In some areas the pest or septic	$200
Transfer Taxes or Tax Stamps	The county may charge for transferring the buyer's name onto the tax rolls; a revenue generator for the county.	$800
HOA Documents	To give to the buyer for approval	$100
Transfer Fees for Condominium Associations	Association charges to put the buyer's name on the condominium HOA rolls; a revenue generator for the HOA; used to accomplish any HOA-related work that needs to be performed to transfer the property, such as pest control.	$250
Loan Costs for VA and FHA	Some loan programs require the seller to pay the loan fees.	$1,800
Notary Fees	Transfer documents need to be notarized.	$25
Fix-up Costs	Done in advance of placing your home on the market	$4,000
Repairs Determined by Pest and Physical Report	Requested by the buyer	$500
Security Deposits	Most often from tenant occupied property	$1,500
Title Insurance	To prove to the buyer that you own the property and can sell it, it is not overencumbered, and there are no easements or other judgments against the property with which they cannot live	$2,000
Recording Fees	What the county requires to record the transfer (Grant Deed)	$50
Wire Fees	Send money to the lender for payoffs	$50
Federal Express Fees	Send money to the lender for payoffs	$25
Moving Expenses	Costs will vary, self versus professional	$5,000
Cleaning Expenses	Professional cleaning including carpets and windows	$500
Holding Costs of Two Properties	If you are not buying before selling	$1,800
Reimbursement of Advertising, Signs, etc.	If you are an FSBO (For Sale by Owner)	$1,000

Use the previous chart as a guide. Costs associated with your sale will vary according to the region you live in and the price of your house. Some costs are a percentage of value, some are a fixed amount, and some costs may not apply. None can be exactly determined here. To get a clear estimate of sale costs in your area, check with your real estate agent, title company, attorney, and/or county.

Buying Before Selling

Will you be in a financial trap if you buy your next house before selling the present house? The biggest issue in buying a new house without selling the old house is cash flow. What is the cost of carrying two houses on a monthly basis? Remember that it's not just an extra mortgage payment. There will be two tax bills, two insurance bills, two sets of utility payments, and two houses to maintain (swimming pools, gardens, snow removal, etc.). How long will it be before that change in cash flow interrupts your lifestyle? How long will it be before you panic because you are uncomfortable and drop the price of the old house below market value, just to sell it?

This doesn't mean it can't be done; it just takes careful planning and full knowledge of the real costs on your part. If you can afford it, it can be an ideal situation. Not having to sell your old house makes you a stronger buyer on the new house. Moving before you put your old house on the market eliminates the problem of keeping the old house in showing condition. The unoccupied home will stay in showing condition pretty easily.

If Your House Sells Tomorrow

You should be prepared for the fact that your house may sell quickly, especially if it is a good market and priced correctly. You need to be mentally prepared for the possibility of putting your house on the market today and having it sell tomorrow. To avoid the requirement of moving immediately, there are a couple of things you can request when you first put your house on the market. For example, set a close of escrow date in the future, such as "no close of escrow before October 15," or request to rent your home back after the sale, such as "seller requests a rent back for up to thirty days after close of escrow." If neither of these works and your house does sell tomorrow, it does not mean it will close tomorrow. There is still the escrow process to go through, and that takes some time, usually thirty to ninety days.

Putting requirements on the sale may be okay for you, but they may not work well for the buyer. Would you move immediately if you got your asking price? If you are not ready to move immediately, you may not really be ready to sell. If you are planning on just winging it, you may panic when you get a good offer and respond unfavorably. It is important to be prepared to move.

QUESTION?

Moving is such a daunting concept. Where do you start?
The best way to begin preparing for a move is to get rid of everything you don't need or want. Have a garage sale and donate unwanted items to thrift stores and charities. Once you've eliminated some unnecessary baggage, you'll be able to pack in a more organized fashion.

One of the first things you should do as you prepare to move is to get a quote from a moving company or determine the cost of renting a self-driven moving van, plus a couple of laborers. Start getting rid of the things you don't need and don't plan to take with you. Go room by room and make three piles—one pile to keep in the house (things you use all the time), one pile to pack for the new house, and one pile to purge. Packing things up in advance and stacking them neatly in the garage or taking them to storage will make the whole process seem less ominous. This will also mentally prepare you for the move and make it easier if you get a fast sale.

Determine Your Destination

Before you put your house on the market, you will need an exit plan. Part of the selling process is knowing what you will do after you sell. Are you moving to another area? Are you trying to get on your financial feet and start over? Are you going to buy another house? Will you rent? Will you move away? If you are moving, what is the market like where you are going? Don't just guess at the market conditions in the new location. Do some research.

Visit the area and look at properties. Can you achieve your home ownership goals there? If you're hoping to find a smaller house but you're looking in pricey areas, you could end up spending more money on a smaller house. This is something to be aware of before you get too far into your search.

You may decide to sell your home and rent for a while. If that is the case, do the research on rentals in your intended area. How much are they? Will they take pets if you have them? How much lead time do you need? The places available today may not be available when your house sells, but the research should give you a basic idea of what to expect.

FACT

It's sad but true: Not all houses sell for the asking price. The good news is that all houses will sell at the right price. Ask yourself how low you'll go. Are you willing to sell at any price? Are you willing to take a loss? Are you willing to sell for less than you owe and come to the closing table with money? If the answer is no, there are other options to consider. Some of these options are covered in Chapter 17.

Making the big decision to sell your home will subtly change some of the things you normally do every day. You will make your bed more often and throw out junk mail instead of letting it pile up. You may purchase less at the warehouse store, since stocking up on groceries and toilet paper means you have more to move. You will check your telephone messages more often in case someone wants to see the house. You may feel like you are at a crossroads, a temporary place. You are! But with the right tools and a little luck, you won't be in this transitional phase for long.

Chapter 2

The Selling and Buying Process

There are times when you want to move, and there are times when you have to move. If you want to move, you can decide when to put the house on the market, and you can be more discerning about which offer you accept. If you have to move, you cannot always take advantage of market timing. You may even take an offer that would otherwise be unacceptable, just to go forward with the move. Then, once you've sold, you need to worry about buying.

Plan of Action

In an ideal world, you would not have to sell one house before buying another, but in most cases that is the only way. When you are negotiating the sale of your house, see if you can have a few days of rent back, which will allow you more time to move after close of escrow. If that is not possible, be sure that you can rent a moving van for several days. Allow enough time to move everything out, clean the old house, and park the van in front of the new house while you move in. The expense is usually worth it. Even if you have to spend a night or two in a hotel or with friends, it will be easier than trying to move, clean, get to the new house, and unpack all in one day.

After all the contingencies of the sale are removed, be sure that your plan includes enough time to accomplish your move. You don't want to move out and then discover that the sale has fallen apart because of poor timing. Use a timeline to keep yourself on track.

The first thing to do in your timeline of action is realize that you are selling. This may sound simple, but many people have trouble with the process because they have not truly recognized everything involved with their decision to sell. There's a lot to do, and figuring out a plan from the start will serve you well.

Becoming acquainted with the place you're moving to is a good start. Once you have that covered, you can deal with packing up your current home. It will help if you sort all your belongings into categories:

1.   Keep (two methods)
1.A. Pack up now
1.B. Still in use
2.   Get rid of (three methods)
2.A. Give away
2.B. Sell
2.C. Throw out

Research the cost of moving companies and/or the rental of self-moving vans and the cost of a couple of laborers. Find out what it costs to keep the van for several days. If you'll be moving far away, you might need to hire movers and/or rent storage space. Getting rid of unwanted items early will help you more accurately judge how much moving and/or storage costs will be. Most movers and storage companies charge by weight, and many will offer a free estimate. If applicable, negotiate with your new employer to see if any moving costs will be covered.

Interview real estate agents and then choose an agent or decide to sell on your own. If you choose an agent, you'll sign a listing contract. If you decide to sell on your own, you can choose from several methods: buy a sign for the yard, put an ad in the newspaper, and/or create a flyer.

Speak with a lender to see if refinancing or taking a line of credit will enable you to buy the new home without selling the existing one. If you have the financial means, you can purchase the new home once your current house is on the market. Meanwhile, continue to sort through your belongings and pack them. Finish up any necessary repairs on your current house and start showing it. You will receive offers, and you will need to respond to them. Negotiate until acceptable price and terms are reached and accept the offer. Subject to the closing of the old home, purchase the new home if you have not already done so. If you are not planning to buy right now, secure a rental at this time.

Have the buyer do inspections and go through the loan process, if applicable. Do any fix-ups required by the buyer's inspections. Schedule movers or the self-moving van to start a few days before closing. Plan for a place to stay for the few days before closing. Pack a suitcase for each member of the household and keep out a few essentials (dishes, pots and pans, etc.). Everything else should be packed to move.

A day or two before the closing pack up the van and take everything with you. Notify the utility companies that you are moving and have service removed from your name as of the day after the closing. (Don't do this the day of the closing in case there is a delay.) After you have moved out, clean the house. Once the closing occurs on the old house, have the funds sent to the closing company for the closing of your new house. If you are moving into a rental, have the funds sent to your financial institution to be invested or saved until you find a house. Close on the new house and move in.

Corporate Transfer

Employers transfer employees for a number of reasons. A transfer often comes with a promotion, but occasionally the company is closing some of its offices and moving its best people to another location. Sometimes, the only way to keep your job is to move.

Here are some good questions to ask about the transfer.

- Why are you being moved? Is the move optional or mandatory?
- If the transfer is optional, how much time do you have to decide whether to take the transfer before you must move?
- Is the company paying for your move?
- Is the company guaranteeing the sale of your house?
- Is the company picking up any costs related to the sale of your home?
- Will they pay for a rental in the new location while your house is on the market?
- How much time will you have to get the house ready, sell it, and find another house before the job starts in the new location?
- If you are moving to a more expensive community, does the promotion make up for the higher cost of living?

By getting answers to these questions, you can better position yourself for the sale of your home and the move ahead. If the company is paying for the move, guaranteeing the sale of your house and/or paying costs will eliminate some of the stress of moving. If you plan to purchase a home in the new location, these guarantees will also help to give the seller of that home faith that the purchase will go through.

Know the Market in the New Location

It is ideal to know the market in your new community before you decide to take the transfer and before placing your existing house on the market. If you need to move quickly, finding a rental in the new community while your house is on the market may be the best option for you. If your home does not sell quickly, being able to afford two places can be tough, but it makes for a smoother transition. Optionally, when there are two or more people in a household, one may stay to sell the house while the other heads to the new job. When this happens, the person leaving can usually rent inexpensive, temporary quarters, while the rest of the family stays at the old location to sell the house.

Time the Transfer for the Selling Season

Some areas have a selling season and a nonselling season. It could be based on the weather, school schedule, or economy. It is important to time your sale for the selling season if you live in this type of area (see Chapter 1).

Here's an example: Perhaps you are being transferred, but the transfer is not going to happen for several months. Let's suppose the market is at the beginning of the best sales season when you first find out about the job transfer, and you decide to list your home immediately. When your home sells, you move to a rental and wait for the job transfer to go through. This strategy will work in your favor. By selling your home during the season, you are able to get a better price than you would have received if you had waited for the transfer paperwork. Now, you will have cash in your pocket when the transfer takes place, making you a stronger buyer in the new market.

Changing Jobs

Moving because you are changing jobs is similar to moving due to a job transfer except you will be responsible for the expenses that the company may have picked up if you were being transferred. A job change may occur for several reasons. Being offered a better position or becoming a casualty of corporate downsizing are the most common.

Recruited to a New Company

Companies are always looking for ways to improve business and therefore improve profits. If you have a skill that few others possess or if you are well positioned in your current company, you can be a target for headhunters. Headhunters are hired by companies that are looking for good employees, and they often look to the competition. By hiring a good employee away from the competition, they get someone who makes their company stronger plus the added benefit of making the competition weaker, due to the loss of that employee. If you receive an appealing job offer in a different community, do the research on the new community before accepting the position. You can treat this opportunity like a job transfer. If the new company wants you badly enough, it may be willing to pay your moving expenses or guarantee the sale of your house.

Corporate Downsizing

Looking for ways to cut costs, companies are sending jobs overseas or eliminating positions altogether and requiring remaining staff to pick up the extra work. If you lose your job due to downsizing, you will be looking for work elsewhere. In many cases, you can find work in your own community, but in some cases you cannot. Even if you do find work locally, you may experience a cut in pay that makes your house payments a financial burden.

Improved Lifestyle

The easiest time to sell is when your lifestyle has improved. You are making good money, and your home, which has always seemed small, has shrunk to uncomfortable proportions. In this situation, you can often buy a new house before selling the old one. However, if you have too much equity tied up in the old house and need to sell it, spend some time sprucing it up before putting it on the market.

With an improved lifestyle, you may want to sell one house and buy two houses: one for the summer and one for the winter. If this is your plan, there are several different ways to approach it. One way is to purchase both new places simultaneously so that you can divide your belongings and move them to the appropriate spots. The other option is to purchase one place at a time. If you do this, it is best to purchase the larger of the two houses first. This will allow some space to store the belongings that will go to the other house, once it is located.

ALERT!

If your improved lifestyle has resulted in treating yourself to new toys, rent a storage unit to stow those items. When a buyer sees a boat and a sports car in the garage of a starter home, she may think you have too much money and make a low offer.

Although this kind of abundance is pleasurable, contemplating a move can still be a difficult time for some people. The little house you're planning to sell is special. It is sometimes hard to let go, even if the home is too small or in a neighborhood that has gone downhill since you purchased. You may find that your sentimental attachment is too great to allow the house to be properly priced. Be sure to think about why you are moving, determine your motivation, and then focus on the bigger and better place.

Empty Nesters

Empty nesters often have an emotional time selling their homes, especially if they have lived there a long time. The memories of raising a family seem to live in the walls, and leaving the house can feel like you are leaving the memories as well. Scaling down often means getting rid of furniture; Mom's hutch won't fit in the new condo. The kids' furniture is too good to get rid of, but they don't want it.

To ease your mind and help cement the decision, do a little research on the smaller places. Think about what you will keep and what you are going to sell or give away. Be sure to take lots of pictures to remind yourself—for example, "This is the tree we planted when Billy was born." The memories will make the move with you.

Here's a fun idea: If you're marking your growing children's heights on a piece of door trim, why not take the piece with you? Replace it with an identical piece of trim and put the marked one up in your new home. Perhaps someday your grandchildren will get a kick out of seeing how tall their mother was when she was their age!

If there are things you can't part with yet, rent a storage unit. Once you have paid on that for a year or two and never visited your stuff, it will be easier to pass it along.

Divorce

One of the hardest reasons to sell a house is because of a divorce. It is often the only way to divide up the assets of the relationship, and it can be very stressful. Each person wants the most they can get from the sale to give them a nest egg for a new beginning. Everything, from picking a real estate agent to deciding on a price, can become a new reason to argue.

QUESTION?

In a divorce situation, who handles the sale of the house?
In some divorces, each spouse will choose a real estate agent. They put the two names in a hat and have a mutual friend draw one. That helps eliminate one point of argument. If they agree to price the house as the agent recommends that helps to squelch another potential argument.

Sometimes the parties can't even come to an agreement on very basic decisions. If that is the case, the court will often step in and make some of the decisions for you. A judge may require that you reduce the price of the house by a certain amount every thirty days. One person may be granted permission to live in the house while the other person pays for it. In all likelihood, there will be a lot of things that don't seem fair to one party or the other.

If one person has already moved out with half the furniture, having the home staged will help with the selling process. Be aware that if it looks like a divorce sale, in the mind of the buyer it looks like a bargain. (See Chapter 12 for information on staging your home for sale.)

Disease and Disability

Selling because of a health hardship, disease, or disability usually means that you must sell quickly. To get the house sold now, aggressive pricing is more important than getting the most money possible. Your health is the biggest asset you have. Anything you can do to keep or improve it should be a priority.

Often, the infirm must retrofit a house to accommodate special health conditions. Ramps to the front door and grip bars in the bathrooms will make your life easier but may make the buyer uncomfortable. Keep what is necessary, but try to avoid having a bed in the living room. Within reason, make the house as healthy-person friendly as possible.

It is unfortunate, but many buyers will see a bargain when they see a health issue. Even if the home is priced competitively against other houses in your market, you may need to take less money. Try to be comfortable with this difficult fact. Your health comes first.

Imagine that within a few weeks of buying your house you are diagnosed with a disease that requires a transplant. In a town where you know no one, with a condition that is life threatening, you realize you need to sell immediately. There is a hospital with the facilities to perform the transplant in another community, and this other community also has family members who can help and support you. With a great surge of hope for the improving market, you ask to price the house to cover the expenses of purchasing and selling, as well as give yourself a little profit. It does not sell, and your condition begins to deteriorate quickly. You begin to realize that your life is more important than any money the house can bring. You finally reduce the price to allow for a quick sale and take a financial loss. More importantly, you lose time that could have been better used for healing, rather than waiting for a profit. Don't let this scenario become your own experience. Remember that financial loss is not as serious as loss of life.

Building Your Dream House

One of the greatest joys is building your dream house. If you are building at a new location, wait as long as you can before selling your present home. Ideally, you should finish the new house and move in before putting the old house on the market. If that is not financially possible or you are tearing down the house you live in to build your dream home, you may need to rent until the new house is ready.

In some areas, the building department or the health department will allow you to park a motor home on the site, which will give you a place to live during construction. Some building departments allow you to move into your new house before it is totally complete. They may only require a working heating system, working kitchen, and working bathroom. Other regions require everything, including shower enclosures and floor coverings, to be completed before the home is approved for occupancy. Check with your local governmental agencies to see what possibilities are available to you.

Chapter 3

Ten Common Homeselling Mistakes

As you go through this process you will discover that selling your home can be stressful. You have to keep the house in order, get a handle on your finances, and pack up everything you own! Just thinking about all these things can cause some people to make mistakes. Up front, you should understand that inconvenience is part of selling. This chapter will explain ten common mistakes that homesellers make and how to avoid them in your own experience.

Mistake 1: Comparing Your House with Others

Your house may be your castle, but it isn't everyone's castle. Buyers looking at your house have no emotional attachment. If they hear about your emotional attachment, they may subconsciously feel you are not ready to sell, and they won't make an offer.

Sometimes your emotional attachment comes out like this: "John up the street got $250,000 for his house. Mine is much better!" For one, John may not have gotten $250,000; he may just tell you that because he is too embarrassed to admit that he took far less than the asking price. Secondly, maybe John's house is a better house in the eyes of a buyer. True, John didn't hand pick the chandelier at the art show after months of looking, but there was something about John's house that was worth $250,000 to his buyer. That something may not be true of yours.

FACT

Knowing the true value of your home, not just by rumor but with a market analysis by a real estate agent or an appraisal by a licensed appraiser, will keep you focused. Don't try to guess the value of your house based on other houses you have lived in or seen. The market is constantly changing, and beauty truly is in the eye of the beholder.

It is a good idea to spend some time looking at the competition. If you think your house is worth $250,000, go shopping with an imaginary $250,000 and see how you measure up. Be as unbiased as possible. This can work especially well if you look at the other houses with a friend. Be sure to pick someone who will be honest about how she thinks your house stacks up against the competition. Consider these questions:

- Do the other houses have a better location?
- Do the other houses have a better setting?
- Do the other houses need less work?
- What are the pros and cons of each house?

Don't look under the house or in the attic to check the quality of construction. Most buyers are looking at the things they can see and understand easily, such as older style bathrooms. The amount of insulation is not as important. Remember, not everyone has the same tastes or the same needs as you have; ignore the fact that certain details may not fit your taste or lifestyle.

Mistake 2: Laziness About Repairs

Not everyone is handy at home repair. Experience reveals that even people who are handy are not interested in doing handy work at home. It is also true that most people, when they see that something needs to be done, see it as a much bigger deal than you do. The hassle of fixing something will come off the price that a buyer offers. If a buyer observes something that obviously needs to be fixed, he can assume that there are less than obvious things that need to be fixed as well. The cost of needed repairs comes off the sale price, and the impression of poor maintenance can reduce the offer.

Of course, some things are difficult to fix when you are occupying the house, and sometimes cash flow does not allow for certain repairs. In these cases, make things as easy as possible on the buyer so they will not see repairs as a deterrent.

Carpet

The most common repair is replacing old carpet. While this is technically maintenance rather than repair, replacing carpet is a difficult task that is rarely undertaken until it's absolutely necessary. Everything from each room has to be packed and moved into another room, as old carpet is removed and new carpet is laid throughout the house. Naturally, the process takes longer when a house is occupied than it does when it's vacant.

If you have a pet, you may not even want to replace the carpet. If the new owner is allergic to pet hair and has to replace the carpet anyway, it will be a waste. You also don't want to leave any opportunity for your pet to have an accident on the new carpet before the new owner moves in. In the instance of cats that spray, the floor boards may need to be sealed or replaced. In lieu of replacing the carpet yourself, you can offer to give the buyer a credit on the purchase price toward the cost of replacement.

There are times when replacing the carpet is important. Whether you offer a carpet credit or not, threadbare or very badly stained carpet will put people off. If this is the case, you should consider replacing it, even if you have pets and are worried it will get ruined again.

Many carpet stores stock reasonably priced yardage that they sell for use in rentals, where carpet might be replaced after each tenant. These are often of only fair quality in a neutral/dark beige color. The carpet may not last a decade, but it will be clean, new, and last long enough to get your house sold.

If the carpet is damaged only in certain areas, some well-placed area rugs may be the best solution while the home is on the market. You can even take them with you when you move! Room-sized area rugs are available for reasonable prices at home improvement warehouses and discount department stores.

There are also times when the carpet in one room is really bad but the rest of the house is okay. If you can't afford to replace all of it, at least replace the really bad room. When doing just one area, be sure the new carpet matches the original as closely as possible. If the carpet will be replaced in a room that adjoins hard surface flooring, the match will be less critical.

Roof

The roof is one of your home's biggest features and one of the first things a buyer will notice as they approach your house. Even if it is not leaking, an older roof can cause a buyer concern. It is an expensive fix-up, but replacing a roof can often mean the difference between having a sale and not having a sale. This is especially true of older roofs. Buyers will be worried about potential leaks, which may mean mold. They need to be reassured that this is not an issue.

If your roof is in poor condition, you need to address it. The best solution is to replace it. If that is not possible, replacing damaged tiles or shingles is the next best solution. The very least you should do is get a quote for repair or replacement and have it available for potential buyers. If a buyer knows how much the roof will cost, some of their fear will be dissipated.

Many insurance companies will not insure a shake roof because of fire danger. If you have a wood shake roof, you may have to replace it before you close escrow to satisfy the insurance company. Scheduling the work during escrow and having it paid for at closing will solve this situation.

Sometimes your roof is not leaking, but it has leaked in the past. There may be evidence of those past leaks in the ceiling of the upper floors. Even if you have a new roof, the evidence of past leakage will be of concern to the buyer. They will wonder if a leak wasn't fixed when the roof was being replaced. They will wonder if this is evidence of another problem, aside from the roof.

Repairing areas of the ceiling that show evidence of past leaks is an important part of getting the house ready. Retexture the plaster or sheetrock and repaint. Be sure to use a primer that will prevent the stain from reappearing. Not all primers are designed to hold back such stains, and many show through after awhile, if not treated properly. The process of removing stains from a wood ceiling is more involved. If you have a wood ceiling, check your local hardware store or home improvement center for information and products to help you with this.

Paint

A fresh coat of paint can make your house look well cared for in the eyes of buyers. Most people fret about the idea of painting, but it does not have to be that difficult. For maximum ease, hiring a professional is ideal. If that's not in the budget, you can do the work yourself without too much trouble.

To begin, break up the big job into reasonably sized jobs and start with something small. Since the front door is a first impression item, start there.

Be sure to mask off the doorknob, hinges and trim, and put some drop cloths on the floor. Select a quick drying paint, with help from your local hardware or paint store, and pick a sunny day so you can leave the door open until it dries. Once you see the results, you'll be eager to continue.

Expensive repairs are often put off because of cash flow. If cash flow is an issue, you may want to consider a line of credit on your home. This is a loan that can be borrowed in increments as needed. You only pay interest on the money you actually borrow.

For your next painting project, select just one room. Move everything away from the walls and take everything off the walls. Remove the covers from all the electrical outlets and mask everything you don't want painted. Move furniture to the middle of the room and cover the furniture and floors with plastic drop cloths. Start with the ceiling, then paint the walls, and end with the trim.

Detailing

There are a lot of things you can do with inexpensive materials and a little time. Go room by room and make a list of every little detail that needs fixing. Replace broken light fixtures and be sure there are working bulbs in every light, both inside and out. All doors should close and latch well; windows should open and close easily and have functional locks. Be sure there are screens on the windows as well.

Are the door stoppers intact? This is a $1 item and can easily be replaced. Are there chips in the sink? If you can't replace the sink, check your Yellow Pages for enamel repair companies that will patch and resurface your sink or bathtub. Are there knobs missing from the stove? Find out if you can get replacement knobs. Caulk any chipped or damaged grout. The more little things you can repair, the better. Check them off your list as you progress. Enjoy the satisfaction of knowing that each effort reduces the risk that the bigger things (like carpet and roof) will scare a buyer.

Sometimes, a fresh new look can be achieved with very minor changes. New cabinet knobs or even bright new bathroom towels can revitalize a tired room. New bedspreads, a new tablecloth, and a good deep cleaning also make a world of difference.

Mistake 3: Disregarding the Exterior

If a buyer is not coming inside, chances are there is work that needs to be done to the outside. Start by making the exterior appealing. Paint the front door. Pull up weeds and trim back trees or bushes, especially if they are hiding the front door. Plant some colorful flowers. In the winter, be sure that the snow is shoveled and the walk is treated with ice melt to keep it from being slippery. On the porch, a planter or two with brightly colored flowers will look welcoming. You can even use silk flowers in the winter. The inviting spot of color will attract attention. Buy a nice welcome mat and a seasonal wreath and keep the area well lit. Repair the siding or stucco and repaint if you can. If you cannot afford to fix the siding on the entire house, at least spruce up the front. All these touches will make the outside more appealing and inspire people to venture inside.

The little things matter! Be sure your front door lock works well. If a buyer comes to your door and it jams or doesn't open properly, the first impression is that he can't get into the house easily. This negatively impacts everything else.

Some of the more distinct exterior features are not so easily changed. For instance, people are not used to the idea of a dome-shaped house, and many wonderful homes are overlooked because no one comes inside. If your home has unique exterior design features, you may want to advertise with interior photographs or photographs of the view, setting, or yard instead of an exterior photo. If you have a flyer box posted outside, put some interior pictures on your flyer. Someone may fall in love with your fireplace or kitchen, and then you can get him in the door.

Holding an open house can often lure people into homes they might not otherwise see. Be sure to make the open house inviting. Place balloons at the street corner and post a nice sign or banner. (Learn more about holding a successful open house in Chapter 14.)

Mistake 4: Dark Equals Cozy

Dark houses portray a few things, but cozy is not one of them. If the blinds are pulled, buyers often assume you are hiding a bad view such as the neighbor's garbage cans or a brick wall. In areas of the country where there is cloud cover for months at a time or where it snows or rains throughout the winter, available sunlight can be a very important feature for a buyer.

If sunlight in your area is very intense and you don't want it to fade the furniture or the carpet, keep the blinds closed except when you have a showing. Open them up when people are going to see the house to let them know that you are not hiding anything. Also, most buyers consider lots of sunlight a selling point, not a detriment.

Dark can also mean dated. Dark paneling, a popular feature years ago, has gone out of vogue. Dark carpeting, originally picked because it does not show dirt, is thought to be dirty even when it is clean. Painting a lighter color over dark paneling can help, but there are circumstances where you may not want to do that. If the paneling is made of mahogany or some other valuable wood, painting it will diminish its value. You might consider hanging a light colored painting or tapestry on the wall instead. If that isn't possible, purchase some floor lamps and position them to give the wall some upward lighting. Light colored throw rugs or area rugs can help to overcome dark carpeting that you do not want to replace.

FACT

Fixing up the house is important, but adding an unnecessary feature, like an elevator, is usually just a waste of money. Doing the necessary repairs will help you sell your home, but excessive improvements and renovation may not earn you any return on the investment. They may even personalize the house too much. Be judicious about incurring expenses that a buyer won't be willing to pay for and may not care about.

Mistake 5: Inflexible Financing

Conventional loans are based on interest rates that fluctuate with the economy. There are times when rates are high and times when rates are low. Certain economic conditions make obtaining a conventional loan easy, and other economic conditions can make obtaining a conventional loan more difficult. Sometimes, selling your home may depend on a bit of financial flexibility.

Let's say you have a buyer with less than perfect credit. This buyer has a substantial down payment but cannot qualify for a loan with a decent interest rate. If you own the home free and clear, you may want to consider loaning the buyer the money to complete the purchase of your house. In essence, you become the bank. The down payment is your insurance against the buyer defaulting.

If the buyer does default, you get the house back to sell again. Perhaps you will not have to be the bank the second time. If necessary, you can use a portion of the down payment for fix-up costs, and you may even get a better price the second time around. Some savvy sellers will not sell unless they can carry the mortgage. Those monthly payments are their income.

Mistake 6: Being Present During Showings

Buyers are uncomfortable about having a seller in the house when they are touring it. They feel like they cannot look inside closets or speak openly with their agent. They become very aware that they are in someone else's house and have a harder time picturing it as their own. If it is possible, you should leave the house whenever a buyer arrives.

Concern About a Buyer's Honesty

Are you afraid that a potential buyer will take something? If you are, the first thing you need to do is store your valuables in a safe place. If you imagine that your buyer will bring a four year old with a penchant for shiny objects or if you imagine your buyer as a big, clumsy person who will knock things off tables, you will automatically put away a lot of items that could accidentally be taken or broken. While it is unlikely the buyers will take anything, it is worth putting things away to allow you the comfort of letting a buyer view your house without being followed around. It may not look as pretty without your objects displayed, but you will feel more secure in allowing your house to be shown in your absence.

Attempting to Hard Sell the House

Another reason sellers like to hang around is to sell the house. They may not think of it as hard selling, but a buyer usually sees it that way. Of course, you know the house better than anyone, but does that mean you are able to sell it? In fact, a seller's knowledge can actually hurt the sale. Giving a buyer all the details of what you did when building or remodeling makes them feel like you put your heart and soul into the property. They would not want to take your heart and soul away by buying it. Sellers have a tendency to oversell and turn off the buyers.

ALERT!

People can't visualize themselves in your house if it's so full of you that there isn't room for them. Start by packing up your trophies and hobbies. Pretend you're camping. Decide you will be camping without your personal stuff until your house sells. Box it up and put it in storage. Besides making your home look more spacious, you will make it easier for buyers to envision their treasures in the house.

The details of every hand-laid block in the foundation and every hand-milled piece of trim may be interesting to you, but they will usually just bore the buyer. Not every buyer thinks like you do. Solid construction may not be as important as closet space. Each buyer has her own hot buttons, and days spent showing property to this buyer has educated her agent as to where those buttons are. A few minutes with this buyer in your house is not enough to educate you. You may be selling a feature that doesn't thrill her or overlooking one that she really cares about.

Mistake 7: Everyone Loves Pets, Right?

Wrong! Even people who love pets may not love your pet. Buyers and/or their agents may be dressed up when viewing property and may not want to have dog hair or dog kisses on their clothing. Many people are allergic or even afraid of animals. When your house is being shown, the best place for your pet is out of the house. Take the animal on a walk if she cannot be kept at a friend's house or a kennel during your showings. If this cannot be accomplished, at least keep her in the yard or, better yet, in an outdoor pen so that the potential buyers can appreciate the yard.

Dogs

If your dog is barking the entire time the house is being shown, the amount of time the buyer will spend is going to be much less than if the dog was not home. Even dogs that don't normally bark may do so when the house is on the market. The stress of strangers coming through the house, the break in the routine, and the fact that you are not home can make a good dog turn bad.

Also, pick up food and water dishes so they don't get accidentally tripped over and spilled. Cleaning up dog droppings will allow people to walk through the yard comfortably, and daily vacuuming of the carpet and furniture will keep the hair down.

Cats

It seems that more people are allergic to cats than any other animal. Vacuuming up hair is very important in a house with cats. Be sure the cat box is in an inconspicuous place and cleaned out several times a day, including sweeping up around the box where litter may have spilled. If you do not want your cats outside, put a note on all the doors warning people not to let the cats out.

Cats can become very skittish when strange people are in their house. A normally friendly cat may hide or even bite if he receives unwanted attention. Another sign asking that no one pet the cat may help prevent this.

Fish

Fish tanks can be an attractive feature—when they are clean. Watching live fish swim around in an interesting aquarium can be soothing. However, if your tank is not clean, a buyer may assume that there are other things you haven't maintained. A dirty fish tank can also smell bad. It can even smell like mold. The smell of mold will turn a buyer off. Even if it is coming only from the fish tank, the smell may stay in the buyer's nose as they walk throughout the house, and they will assume the smell is everywhere. If it is a large tank, especially if it is sitting on the floor, a buyer may also be concerned about potential water damage to the floor underneath.

Reptiles

Reptiles have a particular odor that cannot be hidden. While your house is on the market, the best place to keep your reptiles is at someone else's house. If you cannot do this, be sure you clean the cages daily or more often if possible. Keep good ventilation in the room where they are located. Because many people are afraid of reptiles, it is best to ensure that they are in a secure location and not allowed to roam the house when it is being shown. Cover the cages when you can.

Birds

Clean cages and a clean floor around the cage are very important. If your bird is on a perch, you may want to consider a tether to keep it from flying at a potential buyer or jumping from the perch to someone's shoulder. Many people, especially children, will stick their fingers into birds' cages. This can be a liability to you if someone is bitten. A warning sign adjacent to the cage will help prevent fingers in the cage, and if it happens anyway, the sign is protection against lawsuit damages.

Mistake 8: Pricing High

Sellers often want to set a high initial price, reasoning that they can always drop the price later if the house doesn't sell. In fact, an overpriced house will often just sit on the market. There will be showings, using your house to sell other houses that are similar and more reasonably priced. Those showings may give the seller a sense of activity. Activity does not always mean offers; it may just mean showings.

Most sellers worry that they will price their house too low. If their house sells fast, they are sure of it. Houses can sell fast for several reasons.

The Ready Buyer

This person has been looking at homes for a period of time, and they may have missed out on other properties. They are educated on the fair market values, prequalified for a loan, and ready to move now! As soon as your home hits the market, this ready buyer will look at your house and make an offer. Most agents have a ready buyer or two that they are working with, and one of these may be the right buyer for your home.

A Seller's Market

During a seller's market your house may sell fast. If it is a frenzied seller's market and your house is priced too low, there will be more than one offer, and the sale price will adjust upward.

Don't Get Stale

One of the first questions a buyer asks is "How long has this property been on the market?" Houses that stay on the market too long get stale. If there is nothing wrong with the house, buyers will still assume there is a problem if it has been available a long time. Even if there have been several price reductions and the property is finally priced correctly, it is stale. The ready buyer does not look at price reductions; he looks at newly listed properties. It is the bargain hunters that look at price reductions.

Mistake 9: Stubbornness About Price

Is it a matter of principle? Sometimes the indignant person with his matter of principle loses out on a deal that could really work. When the stock market took its fateful dive in 2000, many of the high-end properties owned by overencumbered investors went on the market. They hoped to make up for their stock market losses by pricing their houses accordingly. One home, originally purchased just one year before for $2 million, was listed for $4 million. The owners angrily rejected an offer of $2.2 million, which would have saved them their $1 million in equity and paid off their mortgage. Months later, they begged the buyer to come back, but the buyer had purchased elsewhere. The seller eventually lost the home to the bank.

If you are not going to budge on the price, is it because you do not have to sell? If you do not have to sell, why go through the hassle of having your house on the market? Think about why you are not willing to budge on the price. If you are just looking for that one person who is uneducated on home values and willing to pay too much because they like the house as much as you do, you may be waiting for a long time.

Mistake 10: Waiting for a Better Offer

As the saying goes "It's okay to be a pig, but don't be a hog because hogs get slaughtered." Don't get greedy. The first offer is often the best offer, and sitting on it may cause you to lose it. Buyers want to be respected and will often walk if they think they are being shopped. They want you to respect the fact that they are putting up money. If they think you don't appreciate the offer, they will not want to do a deal with you. Be grateful for every offer. If you do not like the offer, counter it.

If you receive an offer that has acceptable features but there are portions of it that you do not want to accept, you can present a counteroffer to the buyer. A counteroffer basically says, "I accept this offer with the following modifications." Both parties sign the original offer, subject to the counteroffer, and the modifications are outlined and signed by both parties as well.

Chapter 4

Fantasy Versus Reality

There is a story about a golfer who got a hole-in-one. When a journalist interviewed her, she said something along the lines of "I don't get what the big deal is. Isn't that the point?" It turns out that the day she got the hole-in-one was the first time she had ever played golf. The hole-in-one spoiled her into thinking it was easy. It's tempting to assume that you'll get a hole-in-one as a first-time homeseller, but it's in your best interest to be more realistic from the start. This chapter will let you in on the realities of the decision to sell.

Is It a Dream?

A hole-in-one is the fantasy of many homesellers. They have heard about hot markets in which homesellers receive multiple offers and dollar signs appear in their eyes as they reap great profits in no time. They may have even experienced a hot market firsthand. Stories about friends or neighbors who had a knock on the door and sold their house for an outrageous sum make it sound like this will happen to everyone. They won't have to prepare the house, and everything will go their way. Like the new golfer, whose first try resulted in a hole-in-one, they assume their houses will sell immediately. But if selling a house was that easy, people would do it all the time, right?

Okay, so it's not as simple as you hoped. But there are ways to make the realities of homeselling easier to bear. One is marketing. Marketing gets the word out that your house is for sale. Two other things determine whether or not your house will sell: price and condition. Here are some guidelines:

- If you don't market your house, no one will know it is available.
- If your price is right and your house is in the condition buyers expect for that price, your house will sell.
- If your house is overpriced, no one will consider purchasing it.
- If your house is in poor condition, chances are it will take time to sell, if it sells at all.

Know the Statistics

Before you put your house on the market, you should know the statistics in your area. How many houses are currently on the market? How many houses sell each month? There is a turnover rate for homes that can help you to determine market time. Start by taking the number of houses on the market and divide that by the number of sales per month to determine the turnover rate.

For example: There are 210 houses on the market with an average of twenty home sales each month. The turnover rate is ten and one-half months. This means it could take as many as forty-two weeks to sell your house. You will need to price aggressively or wait nearly a year to sell your house in this market.

If there are 210 houses on the market and an average of 140 sales per month, the turnover rate is only one and one-half months. If your house takes longer than six weeks to sell, you have either overpriced it or you need to look out for problems with your home's condition. You may also want to determine the turnover rate for homes the same size as yours, the same age, or in the same school district. If you dissect the statistics from every direction, you will see a trend.

FACT

You can find homeselling statistics in a number of places, such as the newspaper or the local Board of Realtors®. You may want to meet with a real estate agent and have him give you the information you need. Remember though, statistics can be manipulated, and they can be skewed by outside influences. To be sure you are getting a true picture, check several sources to see how many houses have been on the market and how many have sold.

It is not only how many houses sell, but also how many houses do not sell that matters. There are a number of homes in every market where the sale just doesn't happen and the seller gives up. In real estate terms, these houses "expire." These statistics are just as important as those for the houses that do sell. How many houses in your market have expired? Did ten drop off the market this month? Did they come back on at a different price, or are they gone completely?

The more you can discover about the terms of the sales, the better. If there are extenuating circumstances on any particular property or group of properties that may sway the statistics, you'll be better off knowing about them.

New Developments

If there is a market trend where buyers are purchasing newly constructed homes before they are completed, these sales can skew the statistics. It is best to take this type of sale out of your calculations to get a truer picture.

Here's an example: There was a subdivision with fifty homes where prices were set before construction. The market was on the upswing, and there was a sudden frenzy to purchase these homes because the market had risen above the asking price. Most of them were sold before the development company broke ground, and this situation really skewed the statistics.

Properties That Can't Sell

There may be problems with certain homes that delay their ability to sell. This can skew the numbers as well.

For example, consider the condominium association that was suing its builder for incorrectly installed siding. Water was condensing behind the siding, and mold began to form. Most lenders would not lend on these units with a lawsuit in progress. The units were not selling, and prices dropped. Buyers were concerned that there would be additional assessments and did not want to make a commitment. This situation skewed the statistics for similar condominium projects. Once the suit was settled and the siding was replaced, the prices made a strong upward adjustment, higher and faster than usual, due to the pent up demand. Now, the statistics are back on track.

Time Required

The time required to sell your house may be different than the time you have in mind. Some people want to sell during a certain tax year or before a certain event. This can be accomplished, but sometimes the market does not cooperate with your needs.

Market Time

Start out by determining the average number of days a home is on the market. Figure out the average market days for homes in your price range, the average market days for homes in your area, and the average market days for homes of a size comparable to yours. This will give you an idea of how much time it will take to sell your house. Starter homes usually sell faster than expensive properties, since there is a larger pool of buyers in the lower price ranges.

Escrow Time

The timing from the day you receive an offer until you close escrow should be counted as well. Escrow time varies with the traditions of the market, the amount of time it takes to get a loan, the amount of time it takes to get an inspection, and other factors. Here are some helpful timeline points:

- Receiving an offer and accepting it starts the clock. From that day forward there are things that need to be accomplished.
- The buyer submits a loan application in the first few days. This should be outlined in the contract.
- The loan process can take a month or more. An appraisal must be scheduled and, depending on how much work the appraisers have, can take from a week to more than a month.
- Simultaneously, a title search is commenced, and inspections are ordered. Once again, several others have schedules that affect your timing.
- Most title companies can run a search rather quickly. A preliminary report can be accomplished in just a few days.
- An inspector may take longer due to coordinating his schedule with the buyer, if the buyer wants to attend, and with other inspections that need to be accomplished. After the inspections are done, a written report must be prepared. The timing on these items is usually in the three-week range.
- There may be other contingencies, such as a survey, leach field test, mold test, or a review of homeowner's association documents. If everything is run concurrently, it is likely that most items will be complete within thirty days.
- The buyer's down payment must be submitted, and funds need to be transferred from the lender.

From start to finish, the process takes about forty-five days. Naturally, if there are no delays, it can be accomplished more quickly. If there are delays, it can take longer. Circumstances, such as the need to close after a certain date by either party or a contingency on the sale of the buyer's house, can extend the time frame by days or even months.

Answering Inquiries

If you are selling the house yourself, you will need to answer inquiries from prospective buyers. However, an agent will typically handle this type of call for you, if you're using one.

Usually people who call about a home are looking for a way to eliminate it from their list of properties to see. They are often calling a list of hundreds of potential properties found through the newspaper or the Internet. They rarely know where to begin, and so they begin by eliminating some of the options. They ask a lot of questions that are designed to get a "no" answer at some point. That "no" is their cue to move on. A conversation may go something like this:

Buyer: "I'm calling about the house in George Washington School District listed for sale in the paper. May I ask you some questions?"
Seller: "Yes."
Buyer: "Does the house have a garage?"
Seller: "Yes."
Buyer: "Does it have a pantry?"
Seller: "Yes."
Buyer: "Does it have a walk-in closet?"
Seller: "Yes."
Buyer: "Does it have double ovens?"
Seller: "No."
Buyer: "Thank you very much. I'll get back to you."

A better conversation might go something like this:

Buyer: "I'm calling about the house in George Washington School District listed for sale in the paper. May I ask you some questions?"
Seller: "Yes, of course."
Buyer: "Does the house have a garage?"
Seller: "Yes. It has an extra deep two-car garage. Would you like to come and see it?"
Buyer: "Does it have a pantry?"
Seller: "Yes. The pantry is very large. It's great for buying in bulk."

Buyer: "Does it have a walk-in closet?"

Seller: "There is a walk-in closet in the master bedroom. Would you like to come and see it?"

Buyer: "Does it have a fenced yard?"

Seller: "Yes. The entire yard is fenced."

Buyer: "Does it have double ovens?"

Seller: "Do you entertain? The kitchen is a nice size, and there is room for a double oven. Would you like to come and see it?"

Buyer: "I get home from work around 6:00 P.M. Could I come see it then?"

Repeatedly asking if the person would like to come and see it may seem excessive, but it will plant the idea in the caller's mind that seeing the house will answer all of her questions. By avoiding "no" as a response and repeatedly offering to show her the property, you are keeping the conversation positive and avoiding being crossed off the person's list.

Even if you have an agent, you may have to set up showings for other agents, especially if you live in the house. These other agents may ask you the same types of questions that a buyer will ask, particularly if they have not previewed your property in advance. They may believe that they know everything for which their buyer is looking. "My buyer won't look at anything without double ovens." If your house has nearly every other feature the buyers want, the buyers will often compromise on the hot button they told their agent, such as double ovens.

Qualifying Buyers

Qualifying a buyer means being sure a potential buyer has the ability to purchase your house. Your real estate agent should do this for you, but if you are selling the house on your own, you will need to qualify buyers yourself. Do not try to qualify the buyers if you have an agent to do this for you. You may insult the buyers, and they will lose interest in your house.

If you are a "For Sale by Owner" (FSBO) offering cooperation to agents who bring a buyer, work through the buyers' agent to get your questions answered. Give their agent a call before or after the showing. Chances are the agent has qualified them already because no agent wants to waste her time showing property to a person who is not qualified to buy.

If you are an FSBO with no agent cooperation or if you find the buyer on your own, you will need to ask the right questions.

- Are you working with a lender? (If the buyer is interested in your house and has not met with a lender, you may want to give him a list of preferred lenders, especially if he is from out of the area.)
- Have you been prequalified for a loan?
- Do you have another house to sell?
- Do you have to sell the other house in order to purchase this one?
- How soon do you need or want to move?
- If you are not planning to move soon, are you ready to buy a house now?

Legal Requirements

The number one requirement is disclosure! This is no longer a "buyer beware" country. As a seller, it is your obligation to let the buyer know everything you can. Most states have a seller's disclosure statement that must be filled out and presented to the buyer. This statement is usually designed with an outline of items in the house. The way it is designed helps you to remember as much as possible about the house, which will enable you to disclose everything.

Federal law requires a lead-based paint disclosure for every house built before 1978. There are community disclosures, regional disclosures, and state disclosures. Are you in a flood plain? Are you in an avalanche area? Are you subject to Mello-Roos? Are there hazardous materials? Every area has different paperwork, and knowing what is required in your region is critical. If you are working with a real estate agent, he should be able to guide you through the legal requirements. If you are not, you will need to do some research to be sure you have everything in order.

If you have an agent, paperwork is the task that really helps her earn her commission. There are places in the country where the contracts, with all the disclosures, can be as many as fifty pages!

FACT

Mello-Roos are special, districtwide taxes that have become common in California. These taxes are in addition to the taxes assessed for your property. They may be on your property tax bill, or they may be sent in a separate bill.

If you are an FSBO, standard contracts that can get you started are available through office supply stores. Your escrow or title company may be able to guide you toward some of the necessary paperwork. It is also a good idea to hire an attorney to review everything. As an FSBO, you will want to be sure that every blank in the contract is filled in. If a portion of the contract does not apply, place N/A (for "not applicable") in the blank space. Each and every page of the agreement must be copied for all parties involved. One copy for you, one for the buyer, one for the lender and, often, one for the appraiser as well, one for the escrow company or attorney, one for the title company, and one for the buyer's agent, if the buyer has an agent working for him.

Any changes to the contract need to be in writing and signed by both the buyer and the seller. All changes need to be copied to the parties involved. All contingency removals need to be in writing and signed by both the buyer and the seller. Once again, copies need to be given to all parties involved. There are places where the lender, escrow, or title companies do not care about contingency removals, but it is better to provide copies when they are not needed than to find out later you should have and didn't (see Chapter 18 for more information).

Ensuring the Closing

Sometimes getting the contract is the easy part. Keeping it together is where the work comes in. Here's an example: There was a happy buyer and a happy seller. The seller got the price he wanted with a limit on repairs of only $500. The buyer felt he had gotten a great deal on a house that appeared to have very little work to do.

Inspections were ordered, and things seemed to be going along as hoped. The inspection report came back with lots of little items that needed to be taken care of, nothing serious or expensive, but there was a glitch. The heater was undersized for the house. The buyer requested all the little items be accomplished and that the seller replace the heater with one that was more appropriate for the size of the house. This was going to cost $3,000. The seller was willing to fix the little items; the price to fix them was about $560. He was even willing to pay the extra $60 for those little items, but he was not going to replace the heater. They had lived in the house for five years with that heater, and in their opinion, it was fine. The buyer wanted a new heater and was not going to go through with the purchase unless the heater was replaced. No one budged.

There are times when the buyers' requests are unreasonable and expensive. When this happens, it may be time to back out of the sale. Most of the time the buyers' requests are little things that are important to them and are reasonably accomplished for a small amount of money. Think about how much those requests will matter a month or a year from now. If they won't matter much or at all, consider a compromise.

The buyer asked for cancellation instructions to be drawn up. The seller's agent urged the seller to reconsider. At first, the seller stood on principle. The agent suggested calling back the heating contractor to find out if there was another solution. Finally, the seller allowed the heating contractor to be called. After much consideration, the heating contractor determined that although the heater was undersized that it was in good working order. He suggested adding another smaller heater and tying into the same ductwork, easily accomplished at this house and at a cost of half of the original bid. The buyer found this to be an acceptable solution and continued with the purchase. The seller was able to save the sale for less money than the cost of another month's mortgage payment.

Think about what it costs to keep a sale together. Even if the buyer's request is unreasonable in your eyes, it may not be expensive. Why fight it just because it doesn't make sense to you?

Here's another example: A married couple had their house in escrow. During the inspections, mold was discovered. The mold remediation company said the repairs were going to cost $30,000. The repair limit was only $1,000, but the couple wanted to make the deal work. They were moving to another community and needed to sell the house. They figured out what they could do and agreed to pay $7,000 toward the remediation. The buyer wanted the entire $30,000 or they were going to cancel the contract. The sale was lost.

When the next potential buyer came to view the house, the agent had added a note to the flyer. It said, "This house has been found to have mold. Seller will pay up to $7,000 toward mold remediation." The new buyer made the statement that "Every house has mold." They were thrilled to receive $7,000 toward mold remediation, and the sale went through without a hitch.

 Local Market Conditions

Being aware of local market conditions and trends will help you to make your home competitive with others for sale in the area. Market conditions include prices and market time, as well as the style of home that is popular in your marketplace. This chapter will teach you how to evaluate the market knowledge you already have and expand upon it with information about different types of markets, timing your sale, and your role in the process.

Your Market Knowledge

Have you ever met people who appear to be real estate junkies? These people read the entire real estate section of the newspaper every week. They call their real estate agent friends with questions on certain properties. They remember a particular house that sold two years ago and want to know why the new owners are selling. They notice if a house is being spruced up for sale and can guess, fairly accurately, when it will go on the market. They have great market knowledge because they follow it consistently every week.

If you are a real estate junkie, you have a head start, but there are things you can't track easily, such as sold prices. So, you still have to do some research. Check with your favorite real estate agent or the assessor's office to get the sold prices for homes in your area. Determining sold price and market time will give you a better evaluation of what is happening in the real estate market.

Reading the real estate section of your local newspaper is the best way to start. You should also check with your local Chamber of Commerce, your favorite real estate agent, or the local Board or Association of Realtors® for information about the market. The Internet is also a good source for abundant, up-to-the-minute articles explaining what is happening in the real estate arena. Get yourself as well acquainted with market conditions as possible. Familiarity with the current climate will help you market to the widest audience.

Most people don't have the real estate junkies' level of interest. Typical people only pay attention to the real estate market when they plan to be part of it. Even then, it is not something they understand well, and it can be overwhelming. For these people, real estate is not a hobby or an obsession; it is just a necessary thing at a certain time. If you fall into this category, it is still important to understand the market when you plan to sell or buy.

Seller's Market

It's likely that, over the years, your area has alternated between being a seller's market and a buyer's market. In a seller's market, demand outweighs the supply. There are more buyers than there are houses for sale. This doesn't mean that every property on the market will sell. Even in a seller's market, there are houses that are overpriced or that do not appeal to buyers. However, it does mean that sellers have the advantage. When positioning yourself in a seller's market, be ready to move quickly.

FACT

Pricing your home correctly in a seller's market is critical. There may be time for price reductions in a buyer's market, but in a seller's market, your home will get stale long before a price reduction can take effect. Homes get stale quickly in a seller's market.

In a seller's market, there are buyers waiting in the wings for homes to come on the market. Often, they have been looking for houses in your marketplace for some time, and they know what they want. They usually have an agent checking new properties every day to see what fits their parameters.

These buyers are educated on market values. They know if something is priced too high or if a property is priced right and worth making an offer. These buyers are often prepared with a preapproved loan, and their down payment is in cash, not tied up in another property. In a very strong seller's market, they are even willing to purchase your home without inspections or other contingencies. They know they could be in a multiple offer situation, competing with other buyers. In a seller's market, buyers have usually missed out on other properties and are ready to move fast. You may have to move fast, too.

Some seller's markets are famous. California was known for quite some time as the land of multiple offers. People were submitting biographies and photographs of themselves to sway the seller into accepting their offer over the other offers the seller received. Some sellers received ten or more offers, but everyone got at least two. Properties were selling for more than the asking price after just a few days on the market.

Multiple offers can sound like a great thing, but they can also become a nightmare. When faced with a buying frenzy, sellers will often get greedy and forget they were willing to take a lower price when they signed the listing contract or, in the case of FSBO, started the marketing program. They may start asking for special terms or more money than the highest offer and, thus, lose their buyers. A frenzy also makes it easy to miss things in a contract and increases the possibility of a lawsuit.

When presented with multiple offers, you will read over several different contracts at once. It is easy to get the terms mixed up or to be unaware that an important factor is missing. To avoid confusion, create a table with all the different parts of the contract side by side so that you can look across and compare. Have your agent help you to be sure you don't miss anything.

If people feel they have not been treated properly, it gives them another reason to call an attorney. Take this story, for example: A couple put their house on the market on Friday, and on Saturday they received an offer. They had actually seen the buyers as they were leaving the house and felt they were the perfect buyers for their home. When the buyers' agent presented the offer to the couple, they expressed this sentiment to her. The agent went back to the buyers saying she was sure they would get the house. Within an hour, two other offers were presented. Both of the new offers were better than the first. One of the offers was perfect. It was more than the original asking price with a quick close of escrow and virtually no contingencies. The couple accepted this offer and rejected the other two, including the initial offer from the "perfect" buyers.

The "perfect" buyers felt they were misled. They were sure they were going to get the house. They quizzed their agent to find out exactly what the selling couple said, and they hired an attorney. They claimed a verbal contract had been made and that the house should be theirs. Although the "perfect" buyers lost the case, the house was tied up in litigation for some time, and the selling couple lost the buyers with whom they were under contract. The couple could have countersued for the loss of the contract, but they just wanted to move on. So, they put their house back on the market and started again. The lawsuit cost them some time and money. Luckily, they were still in a seller's market, and the house sold quickly the second time around.

In a multiple offer situation, there is also the risk of opting for a buyer who doesn't complete the sale and losing buyers who have moved on to other properties. By then, your property could be stale, or even worse, the market could have changed. A house that goes stale in a very frenzied seller's market is even worse than a house that goes stale in a balanced market.

Buyer's Market

In a buyer's market, supply outweighs the demand. There are for sale signs coming up like dandelions in every front yard and a very limited number of buyers. Those few buyers who are looking for homes are also looking for a bargain. Their experience in the marketplace has taught them that they are in the driver's seat. They know how many homes are for sale. The buyer will look at other properties that are almost certainly similar to yours, and there is the chance that the buyer will never see your property because they will find something before you get to the top of the list.

QUESTION?

What causes a buyer's market?
Sometimes the situation is created by the local economy. In that case, you may have to price aggressively (perhaps below market value) to sell your home. If an abundance of newer properties creates competition for resales of older homes, sprucing up your house can help you to be competitive.

Even if your price is competitive and your home is in excellent condition, you may still not get any showings. In a buyer's market, you have to be creative just to get people in the door. When there are a lot of properties to look at, the agent and the potential buyer will be selective about which properties to see and the order in which to see them. Homes that meet the buyer's needs will be at the top of the list. Starting with the most likely candidates, they will probably find a home before they have seen everything that meets their budget and style parameters.

Holding open houses can attract buyers who would not have otherwise noticed your home. While driving around looking at other properties, people will often stop at an open house just out of curiosity. It may not have been a house they would have considered, and it may not even have been on their list. They may like the location, your landscaping, or the color of your paint. It could just be the opportunity to venture into a place that would otherwise be off-limits to them. Somehow though, the open house sign entices people. This includes real buyers and people who are just passing by.

Another incentive to get people in the door is to offer them a gift. Enter every agent who shows the house into a weekly drawing for dinner at a local restaurant, a massage, movie tickets, or some other gift that they might use or give to their clients. When offering incentives, it's important to get the word out. They will only help increase showings if the agents know about them.

More commonly, for any agent who brings a buyer who purchases the house, a vacation or commission bonus can be the extra push needed to get your house on the list of must-see properties. In most states, the law requires that agents disclose any fee or bonus they receive. Because of this, some agents will end up giving their bonus away. Take that into consideration when offering agents a bonus or incentive.

You may offer the buyer an incentive to buy your property. The best incentive is to price the house lower than competitive properties. Even with a lower price, not all buyers will see your house. Offering a few months of maid service or a credit toward moving costs can help.

Balanced Market

Distinct seller's markets and buyer's markets do occur, but many markets are actually fairly balanced. The balanced market may be slightly geared toward either sellers or buyers, but the leaning is not so dramatic as to be noticed readily. Because every market has lower and higher budget properties, older and newer homes, larger and smaller properties, and other divergent factors, sections of the market will be a buyers market, and sections will be a sellers market. The balance is usually rather close.

FACT

If small homes with large yards and old growth trees are in a seller's market and large homes with small yards and no trees are in a buyer's market, the statistics may show a balanced market. This is especially true if the different types of properties are in the same price range.

In a balanced market, you may only need to do a few things to move your home toward the seller's market category. As the seller with no trees and a small yard, doing some planting may tip the scales in your favor.

Is There a "Best" Time to Sell?

The good news is that any time you want to sell can be the best time to sell if you are willing to work within the market that exists at the moment. Success will come from preparing yourself, your home, and your marketing to accommodate current conditions. So, again, awareness of your market is critical.

If it doesn't matter when you sell and you can make a choice on timing, you can position yourself for optimum market conditions. Every market has its selling seasons. Some are well defined, and some are less defined. Many markets are based on the school schedule. People want to move their kids during summer vacation and be in their new home by the time school starts. This is less cyclical in a year-round school area but may still be a factor if buyers are coming from conventional school systems. School year timing may be less relevant in a retirement market, but old habits die hard. Retired couples often retain the leftover perception of a school schedule, believing it is best to buy in the summer and settle in before fall.

In a seasonal market, virtually everyone is selling at the same time. It might be better to be on the market during the quiet time and be one of the few properties available. There is a smaller pool of buyers, but you have less competition, too.

Selling seasons can be based on climate conditions in areas of the country where weather plays a prominent role. The warmest areas of the country, where summer is miserable, traditionally have more sales in the winter. In beach towns, people buy homes more often during the summer. In ski towns, winter can be a good time to sell. In areas where the humidity is high, spring and fall are less humid and often better times to sell.

The Importance of Style

Each region has different home styles that are popular in that area. You may live in a place where a modern home is fashionable or in a place full of log cabins. There are regions where the majority of houses are made of brick and other regions where they are covered with stucco. A Tudor style home may be the choice in your neighborhood, but in another, it may be a craftsman style home. Popular home styles follow trends, and you can't easily remake the style of your home. So, if yours is not "in fashion" at the moment, just be sure it shows as well as possible. Take the popularity of its style into consideration when pricing the house.

No matter how attractive your home is, if it is too unique, the average buyer will not consider it for purchase. Maybe you live in a geodesic dome home or you have an unusual floor plan. Drive around and look at the homes in your area. If your home does not fit the mold, you will be looking for a special type of buyer. Marketing to that special buyer could take extra time and effort. You were likely that special type of buyer when you purchased your unique home, and so you have an idea of what might appeal to your buyer.

To come up with ideas of how to market your unique house, think about what intrigued you about the house when you were a buyer. Since you will have a smaller pool of buyers, you may have to compromise more on the price than you would with a home that fits the expected standards of the environment. Not everyone is looking for unique.

Winning in the Game of Real Estate

Your responsibility with regard to market conditions is to be flexible. Be ready and willing to move with the flow of the market. On a national scale, the market can change dramatically. During election years or during a terrorist crisis, the pendulum can swing spectacularly from a seller's market to a buyer's market. The threat of a spike in interest rates can create a swift turn from a buyer's market to a seller's market, as buyers make the decision to buy before rates actually soar.

FACT

In addition to national factors, many local factors can shift the market as well. Extreme weather conditions, a fire that destroys many homes in an area, a factory closing, or a new company moving to town can move the market unexpectedly. The development of a new subdivision or a moratorium on construction can also move the market in one direction or another.

Real estate is big business. It is a complex and ever-changing industry. You can learn what you need to know in just one book and yet take a whole lifetime of actually doing the work to perfect your skills. Amateurs play with professionals, and professionals play with other professionals. Sometimes, amateurs will play with other amateurs, a situation where no one really understands the process and trouble can be the name of the game.

Some real estate agents have a lot of experience, assist in making good decisions, and can help those sellers or buyers who are less experienced.

Other agents are as inexperienced as any novice in the marketplace. They may know the rules from their schooling, but they don't know how to apply them. Real estate school helps agents learn the laws of the game—the rules and regulations attached to real estate. Learning how to artfully *play the game* comes from actually doing it. Just like any other sport, learning comes with practice. You can read all the books in the world about figure skating, but you will never know how to skate until you get out on the ice!

ALERT!

Most buyers and sellers are not as experienced at the game as real estate agents. Buyers also have a higher stake in it and commit to a long-term debt to acquire a home. Sellers commit to signing over their largest asset, a home, for what is hopefully the right amount of cash.

Buyers often enter and exit the game at will. They may change real estate agents to be sure they have a true professional on their side. Sellers often enter the game and wait. If the home doesn't sell, is it the market or has some other factor come into play? The more you learn about being a seller, the better chance you have of winning the game. The rules for winning include understanding the first-string players—namely *market conditions*—and being flexible about price. The second-string players are important too; they are *condition*, *style*, and *marketing*.

It is not a requirement to be in a win-lose situation. A win-win situation is always best, and there are plenty of them. In the best deals, no one feels taken advantage of because everyone feels good about the sale. Any problems that may arise can be handled easily and may not be looked on as problems at all.

The best news is that everyone can win in the game of real estate—and it's a game worth playing. It has traditionally been the best investment that people make. It has outperformed all other investments in the long run, including the stock market, and it has the added benefit of being one of the safest investments. This does not mean that you will always make money in real estate, but if you are willing to wait for the right conditions, you can.

Chapter 6

Important Financial Considerations

Every sale has different money issues to consider, and you need to understand what these are before you put your house on the market. There may be tax consequences on your sale. You may have more than one mortgage for a period of time. You need to be comfortable with paying for both of them. If you decide to do all or a portion of the financing, you may have the opportunity to make more money than just the value of your house.

Exploring Financing Options

Before you place your house on the market, it is a wise move to talk to your CPA or tax adviser. You may also want to get a second opinion from another CPA or financial consultant. Sometimes your personal consultant gives the best advice, and sometimes she is too close to your situation to see additional options. Getting a range of ideas can help you make the best possible decision.

Most people are aware of The 1997 Tax Reform Act. Unless there was something in the tax reform act that applied to you at the time, you may not know how it can benefit you today. The 1997 Tax Reform Act was one of the largest and most sweeping alterations to the Internal Revenue Service's tax code.

ALERT!

To avoid surprises at tax time, be sure to consult your CPA or tax adviser for current information on your specific situation. As of this writing, if you sell your personal home at a loss, the loss is not tax deductible.

For years, the amount of gain, or profit, on the sale of your primary home (the home you actually live in) was subject to capital gains tax. Unless the profit was reinvested in a more expensive home or you were over the age of fifty-five and could receive a one-time exemption, you would have to pay capital gains tax. In 1997, all that changed. It is now possible to sell your primary home every two years and be exempt from capital gains tax on the first $250,000 for an individual or the first $500,000 for a married couple. The exemption is allowed, regardless of age. You don't have to be over fifty-five to take advantage of the new law.

The IRS code still changes every year, so check with your CPA for additional details on the law. The rules are applied differently to houses that are inherited. There are also important financial considerations for properties sold by someone who is widowed. Special consideration is also given to people who must move for health reasons.

Knowing what financial options are available to your buyer will provide additional fuel with which to market your property. Meet with a mortgage broker or a banker to find out what types of loan programs are available. Ask how the loan process works so you will know how to accept an offer. Of course, the financial ability of the buyer will determine the loans for which they qualify. However, having an idea of what is available and how the loan process works will give you marketing ideas and a better understanding of the financing the buyer plans to obtain when an offer is presented.

Some houses qualify for FHA or VA loan programs, and some houses do not. If your house does qualify, you can add that benefit to your flyers and marketing materials. If your house does not qualify, you may be able to get it qualified before you get an offer. If this is not possible, you will want to research other loan programs and find one that can work for the majority of buyers, adding that to your marketing materials.

If you are working with a real estate agent, this is one of the jobs you can cross off your list. Most agents have a working relationship with a couple of lenders and will know what type of financing will work for the majority of buyers.

Most lenders are happy to cooperate with sellers. This gives them a chance to be the lender that your buyer chooses. Ask the lender to create a table showing the down payment, interest rate, and monthly payment for several different loan programs. You can attach this table to your flyer.

Full Seller Financing

As a seller, you may want to consider financing the sale of your house. If you own your home free and clear and you do not need the cash to purchase your next home, financing the sale could offer you a better rate of return than if you were to deposit the proceeds from the sale in a bank or savings and loan account. With seller financing, you delay receiving the equity you have in your home. Instead, you receive interest on that equity. As security, a document is recorded with the county recorder to show you as the primary lender on the property. If payments are not made, you have the ability to take back the house.

If you choose to finance the sale of your house, it is wise to get a down payment and set up the way payments are to be made. The down payment is the buyers' equity, and that investment of cash makes them less likely to default on the payments. It also gives you built-in equity if the buyer does default.

Here are some points to consider when structuring the transaction.

- **Loan Amount:** Be sure you are not loaning 100 percent of the value of the property. A loan of no more than 80 percent of the value gives you more protection, since buyers who start with a 20 percent investment are less likely to walk away from their equity.
- **Interest Rate:** This rate is usually at least 1 percent higher and often more than two or three percentage points higher than the rates a bank would charge. Check with your state to see if they have a limit on the rate you can charge. A state mandated limit on interest rates is often known as a *usury law. Usury rates* is a term used for illegally high interest rates.
- **Interest-Only Payments Versus a Fully Amortized Loan:** Most sellers who finance property prefer the interest-only version. In this way, they receive a monthly payment, but the amount owed to them never changes. When the buyer refinances or sells the house, the seller gets a full lump sum of the equity they loaned. With a fully amortized loan, a seller receives a little bit of his equity along with the interest each month. Spending the equity instead of saving it for another investment becomes a risk in this scenario. While some sellers will allow for quarterly interest payments, it is best to require monthly payments. In this way, if the buyer does run into financial difficulty, you will learn about it sooner and may be able to take pre-emptive action.
- **Due Date:** Specify the date you want to have the loan paid in full. This will usually range from two to fifteen years. The most common term for seller financing is a five-year term.
- **Due on Sale Clause:** With a due on sale clause, if the buyer sells the house, you get paid in full. It is not wise to allow the buyer to make payments if they no longer own the house, since you will have nothing to keep your loan secure. If you want to continue to

receive interest payments, you can allow your note to be assumed by the next buyer. You would need to qualify any future buyer and be sure that they establish sufficient equity. This is not a guarantee that your note will be assumed, but it may be a good selling point when your buyer becomes a seller.

- **Prepayment Penalty:** If you want a guaranteed amount of interest, you may request a minimum of six months or even a year of interest, even if the buyer sells or refinances quickly. The maximum prepayment penalty is outlined in your state's usury laws.
- **Notification of Delinquent Taxes:** If the buyer doesn't pay his taxes, you want to know. The tax assessor will provide you with this notification.
- **Notification of Delinquent Insurance:** If the buyer doesn't pay his insurance, you want to know. The insurance company gives this notification to you. You should also be named as an additional insured on the buyer's homeowner's insurance. In some cases, you may also require that a buyer purchase a life insurance policy equal to the amount they owe you and naming you as the beneficiary. If the buyer was to pass away, you would be able to collect your equity faster and his heirs would be able to keep the house.
- **Notification of Additional Loans, Liens, or Judgments Against the Property:** You will want to know if the buyer is applying for a second loan against the property. Your loan will still be in primary position, but it is always wise to know what is happening with your investments. Certain liens or judgments may take precedence over your loan. In some cases, IRS debts or child support claims can affect your position.
- **Acceleration Clause:** This clause makes the note due and payable sooner than the original due date. You may want this to occur if the buyer is delinquent for a specified period of time on property taxes, insurance, or the actual loan you are carrying. It is also prudent to have the acceleration clause take effect if you are notified of a judgment or lien that changes your position.

Partial Seller Financing

If you do not own the property free and clear but you do have considerable equity, you may want to consider what is known as *carrying a second*. In this case, the buyer will get a primary loan for the house but may need secondary financing to get a better interest rate or to qualify for the loan.

A bank or financial institution usually makes the primary loan on the house. Then, there is a second mortgage on the house to make up the difference between the primary loan and the sale price. The primary loan, or "first," is the first to be paid off. The second loan is paid next. If you choose to carry a second, you will be in second position behind the primary lender. This information is recorded with the county to guarantee your position.

Let's say you sell your house for $175,000. The buyer can get a loan for $140,000 with a good interest rate but only if the bank lends 80 percent of the purchase price. The buyer has a down payment of only $17,500. There is a $17,500 shortfall. If you have enough equity, you can lend the additional $17,500 to the buyer by not taking the $17,500 in cash but leaving it as equity in the house.

Traditionally, sellers who carry a second can get a good rate of return, even better than the rate they can receive if they carry a first, due to the increased risk. In most states, law limits the maximum interest rate you can charge. Check with your state to find out what is considered usury.

ALERT!

Usury interest rates are rates that are so high that they are illegal. The limit prevents lenders from taking advantage of people by charging an interest rate (such as 50 percent) that makes a loan impossible to pay off.

For example, assume you can charge 10 percent interest. This would give you $1,750.00 per year in income. That is more than you would get if that money was in a savings and loan. If you were planning to put it in savings anyway, why not lend it to the buyer and get a better rate of return?

The advantage to a loan like this is that you can receive a good rate of interest on your money. It is usually a fairly safe investment, since the buyers' equity keeps them from defaulting except in extreme circumstances (such as the buyer's long-term unemployment or a major health issue).

As is the case with any financial investment that has a reward, there is a risk. If the buyer defaults on his first mortgage, there are ways to get your investment back.

1.   When the first mortgage foreclosed, the house would have to sell for enough money in the foreclosure to cover the first mortgage as well as your second mortgage.
2.   Since you are in second position, you would need to pay off the $140,000 first mortgage in order to guarantee your $17,500.
3.   You file a lawsuit to demand payment of your note in full. Once you get a judgment, you will also need to collect. This can be done with a garnishment of wages (if the person is employed) or through a collection agency.

If the buyer were to continue to pay on his first note but stop paying on your note, the options would change a little.

1.   You commence foreclosure proceedings and pay off the first mortgage in order to keep your financial position secure.
2.   You file a lawsuit to demand payment of your note in full.

Carrying a second mortgage is a risk that many people take based on the buyer's credit history, job status, and how the first loan is structured. When faced with extreme circumstances, most people will sell or refinance rather than ruin their credit by allowing their house to go into foreclosure, especially if they have equity.

The majority of lenders require that you carry your note for a minimum of five years. They want the buyer to have time to save the money needed to pay off the second or to have the home's value appreciate enough to allow for a refinance that would pay off the second. If the buyer sells the property, you can request that your second be paid off at sale. This is accomplished with a due on sale clause (see preceding section).

Let's assume your buyers are first-time homebuyers. If they have good credit, pay their student loans on time, and have good jobs, the risk may be worth it. Perhaps your buyer is a person with poor credit. She has lost a house to foreclosure and works in outside sales with an unpredictable income. This may not be worth the risk. There are cases where a person has bad credit, but a legitimate reason for it. This person may still be worth the risk.

Here's an example: A man took some time off from work to care for his wife. She had cancer and was going for daily radiation treatments as well as regular chemotherapy. Luckily, she did recover, but between the huge medical bills and the fact that her husband wasn't working, their credit was less than perfect. They had sold their home during the medical crisis, but with him back at work and she in full remission, they wanted to buy another house. They paid a higher rate on their first loan, and the seller helped them by loaning a second. Within a few years, their credit was restored, and they were able to refinance and pay off the seller.

If you are selling to one of your own children or a family member, your offer to carry a second may be the only way they can get into a house. In that case, your reward can be more than monetary.

FHA, VA, Conventional, and Bridge Loans

The Federal Housing Authority (FHA) guarantees certain loans; they do not make the loans. These guaranteed loans are known as FHA loans. A person receiving an FHA loan must use the house as their primary home.

FHA programs started in the 1940s to help finance military housing and later to finance homes for returning veterans of WWII and their families. These types of loans were later changed to VA loans, and the FHA branched out to guarantee loans for more than just veterans. In the 1950s, 1960s, and 1970s, they began guaranteeing loans for privately owned apartments for the elderly, handicapped, and those with lower incomes. FHA guaranteed loans have continued to change with the economic needs of the country. Today, the FHA's focus is on the first-time homebuyer and the minority buyer.

There are lending limits on an FHA loan, and not all purchases will qualify. Because an FHA loan does not require a substantial down payment, borrowers will need to obtain mortgage insurance as well.

VA loans, sometimes known as the GI Bill, allow for veterans of the armed services to receive up to 100 percent financing on a property they want to purchase. The VA will decide the value of the property based on its appraisal. The maximum loan amount is generally about the national average sales price of a home. If you are selling a home in a higher end market, your buyer may not be able to get a VA loan.

There are two main types of conventional loans: conforming loans and nonconforming loans. A conforming loan has strict guidelines, and loans are given up to a limited dollar amount. These types of loans usually have lower interest rates than the nonconforming loans. Nonconforming loans, sometimes called "subprime" or "B paper," are designed for people with lower credit scores than conventional loans require. There are also nonconforming loans for people with good credit but who are borrowing more than the limit allowed for conforming loans. These loans traditionally have a higher interest rate.

ALERT!

Some of the closing costs and in certain cases all of the closing costs associated with FHA/VA loans cannot be paid by the buyer and must be paid by the seller. This includes but is not limited to the appraisal, any loan fees or points, and any title or escrow fees. A list of costs is outlined in Appendix B.

A buyer will also choose between a fixed rate mortgage and a variable rate mortgage. On a fixed rate loan, the interest rate is fixed, and the monthly payment never changes. On a variable rate loan, the rate can move up or down depending on the specific economic index to which it is tied.

There are numerous loan programs available to help you hold two houses, known as bridge loans. You may want to consider taking a line of credit on your old house before you put it on the market to get the down payment for a new house. From there, a low rate, interest-only loan on the new house will keep your payments down. Once the old house sells, you can pay down the principal on the interest-only loan or refinance to a more conventional loan. Talking to a mortgage broker and learning all the options is a good first step. Remember, you can't refinance your house if it is already on the market; make some of these decisions before placing your house for sale.

Taxes, Escrow, and Utilities

When you are planning your finances, be sure to take into account all the additional costs associated with a sale.

Your property taxes will be prorated as of the date of sale. If you have paid in advance, you will have a refund coming. Usually, the buyer will reimburse this refund to you in escrow, as he assumes the responsibility of the property taxes. If you have not paid the taxes, they will need to be paid at close. Be sure to add this into your calculations.

Escrow costs are outlined in the table in Chapter 1. Due to the customs in different areas or the requirements of your contract, not all of these fees will apply to you. Have your agent give you a breakdown of what you can expect. If you are not working with an agent, check with your attorney or escrow company.

Usually the utilities are transferred as of the close of escrow. The utility company will read the meters on that day, and you will not have any additional fees. If you have oil or propane heat, you may still have fuel in your tank. The amount remaining will be transferred to the buyer at a cost that is outlined in your purchase contract.

FACT

Taking the necessary steps, such as starting a savings account and being sure you have an untapped line of credit, will help you reduce the risk of losing your home in a foreclosure. Selling your home before the financial problems become insurmountable can reduce or even eliminate the risk of having to declare bankruptcy or go into foreclosure. Knowing your true financial picture is your best defense.

Fear of Foreclosure

Financial problems fill many people with such fear that they do nothing. When faced with foreclosure, doing nothing will get you just that—nothing. There are a few things you can do to avoid losing the house or to delay the process long enough to get the house sold.

Steps to Avoid Foreclosure

Your financial situation will help you to avoid a foreclosure. People are usually aware that there is a problem long before the foreclosure process starts. A common mistake is to pretend that the problem does not exist and hope that something will happen to bail you out at the last minute. Confronting the situation can allow you to take the steps necessary to avoid foreclosure.

If you have lost your job, you may not be able to make your mortgage payment. Many people who lose their jobs assume it is only a temporary situation and that they will find another job quickly. This is not always the case. Being prepared for the fact that you could lose your job can help you avoid foreclosure.

QUESTION?

Can a line of credit be used at any time?

Once you have the line of credit, you may discover all sorts of emergencies where you will want to use it. Don't use your line of credit unless you lose your job and need to make mortgage payments. It is a temporary solution and will need to be repaid!

Start a savings plan. Money in the bank will help you avoid, or at least delay, the financial hardships that come with unemployment or a health issue. If you start by saving as little as 5 percent of your paycheck, you will be amazed at how quickly reserves can be built. Once you are used to living on 95 percent, you may be able to increase your savings to 10 percent of the paycheck. By adding your raises to the reserves, you will discover that they grow quickly. It is important not to tap into these reserves. Once you see them grow, you may be tempted to use them for a vacation or for dental work you have been putting off. Keeping this money for the emergency you planned for—not having the ability to make a mortgage payment—is critical.

Secure a line of credit. Do this before you lose your job, especially if you are concerned that a job loss is imminent. If you wait until you are no longer employed, it will be difficult to get a loan. It is best to prepare ahead of time. Remember, you are doing this to secure your home in the event of a financial emergency, not to spend it on new furniture or even on the kids' college education.

A good insurance plan, one that will cover your expenses if you are disabled, is also a wise investment. Check with your insurance carrier to see what type of plan is best for you.

The day you lose your job is the day you should call your mortgage company. Explain the situation to them and ask to speak to someone who can help you through this transition time. Most of the larger mortgage companies have a special division that can temporarily reorganize your payments to keep you from losing your home. You may find a job immediately and not need this service, but calling as soon as the potential arises is important. It may take several months to get the arrangement in place, and if you have not been working for several months before you call, you will be that much further behind.

ALERT!

Mortgage companies are not in the welfare business. They are in the loan business, and they are in that business to make money. Most mortgage companies will work with you on a temporary basis during a real financial crisis. They will not work with you if the crisis becomes permanent or if they discover that it was not a genuine crisis.

If you have a health issue that keeps you from working for a period of time and the expenses of the health issue exceed your budget for them, you can be at risk as well. Most mortgage companies will work with you if you are hospitalized or disabled and not able to work, either temporarily or permanently. Deal with your mortgage company as soon as possible. Don't wait to make the call. If you are unable to work and eligible to apply for disability, you will need to allow time for the overwhelming amount of paperwork involved in applying for disability.

Bankruptcy

If you find yourself in a very difficult financial situation and believe there is no way to avoid the foreclosure, you may decide to declare bankruptcy. Many people who are entitled to bankruptcy will not apply for it out of pride; yet they will allow their home to fall into foreclosure. Bankruptcy, like a foreclosure, will temporarily ruin your credit. Contrary to popular belief, a bankruptcy does not follow you forever. There are many different types of bankruptcies. Some will stay on your credit for up to ten years, but in some cases, your credit worthiness can be restored to a level that will allow you to purchase another home in only two short years. Of course, a foreclosure will affect your credit as well. Why not see what options are available? If you are in a tight financial spot, speak to a bankruptcy attorney. If you have equity, an attorney can often help reorganize your finances to give you reasonable time to sell your house. It may even be possible for you to keep your home, once the reorganization has taken place.

Deed in Lieu

Another solution is called a deed in lieu of foreclosure. If you have little or no equity, you may want to just deed the house to the bank now and avoid the extra costs involved with the foreclosure process. This may also save you some points that would otherwise be deducted from your credit score. A deed in lieu of foreclosure works best if what you owe is approximately equal to what the house is worth.

In some areas, if the bank cannot sufficiently recover all the money that is due to them, they may file a judgment to hold you personally liable for the balance. That judgment will stay on your credit record, along with the deed in lieu or the short sale. Be sure to get all agreements in writing.

Short Sale

In order to make a sale possible, it may be necessary to negotiate with the bank to take less money than is owed on the mortgage. This occurs more often with overencumbered houses or in markets where prices have dropped considerably. It is best to work with your bank on a short sale before they start foreclosure proceedings. If your market value has dropped, a new appraisal can often be enough to show the bank that a short sale may be necessary.

Chapter 7

Selling on Your Own Versus Hiring a Professional

Deciding to sell your house is the first step, and the next step is deciding how to sell it. Generally speaking, you can choose to sell by yourself or with the help of a professional. Under each of these two categories, there are several ways to sell your house, each with its own advantages and disadvantages. This chapter will tell you all the pros and cons of each option and help you get the most bang for your buck.

Available Options

The first possibility is to sell your house completely on your own. This scenario is known as a *for sale by owner* (FSBO). As an FSBO, you are acting as your own agent and will have the responsibilities, duties, and liabilities tied to that job. FSBOs are divided into two main categories:

- **No agent cooperation:** The seller offers no commission to any agent, even if they bring a buyer.
- **Agent cooperation or agent co-op:** The seller offers a commission to any agent who brings a buyer. The commission amount offered is about half of what the seller would normally be expected to pay.

If you do not want to represent yourself, you will need to hire an agent. Hiring an agent is further discussed in Chapter 9, but the two main categories are:

- **Discounted brokerage firm:** When selling through a discounted brokerage firm, the agent has some limited responsibilities, and the seller does a percentage of the work in exchange for paying a lower commission.
- **Full-service brokerage firm:** When selling through a full-service brokerage firm, the agent does virtually everything necessary to sell your home. The agent receives a commission, which is shared with the agent who brings the buyer. This scenario requires the least amount of work on the part of the seller.

For Sale By Owner

Before deciding to sell your house on your own, you need to be aware of the risks and the rewards. Many people think they can save on the commission by selling themselves, thereby saving money. It is true that by selling yourself you may save the commission but you do not always save money. In many cases, the buyer assumes that if you are not paying a commission that it is their savings, and they will offer you a discounted price.

FACT

According to the National Association of Realtors®, the median FSBO (for-sale-by-owner) selling price in 2003 was 20 percent less than the median agent-assisted transaction price. Only 5 percent of buyers in 2003 purchased directly from owners they didn't know in advance of the transaction, down from 11 percent in 2001.

When selling on your own, the biggest risk is the potential liability that comes from doing the considerable paperwork incorrectly and/or not disclosing things that need to be disclosed.

The Mindset

People who purchase FSBOs are usually looking for a bargain. They think that they can save on the price because the seller is not paying a commission. Buyers who look for FSBOs without agents are usually savvy and may take advantage of the uninformed seller.

Here's an example: A woman was working with a real estate agent and also looking at FSBOs. She finally found what she thought was the home of her dreams: a cottage farmhouse at a reasonable price, for sale by owner. The FSBO offered no agent cooperation because he claimed he was selling at such a discount. The woman dropped her real estate agent and made an offer to the FSBO. It was accepted, and she was soon in the throes of a purchase. The FSBO had already had inspections done, and she was able to save money there as well. She was ecstatic and started moving in the day escrow closed.

The woman noticed a bit of a cold coming on and decided it was from the stress of buying a home. Three days later, the cold was worse, and she had developed a rash. She finally went to the doctor only to find that she was violently allergic to mold, which was in her new house! Now, with all her savings tied up in the property, she is trying to find an attorney to take her case for free, or at least a nominal fee. As it turns out, the home inspector was not licensed, and the seller has left the state. The woman can't go back into her house; she is renting and paying a mortgage. She can't sell the house without disclosing the facts about the mold, which means she cannot get a buyer. She can't afford to keep this up and will eventually have to go into foreclosure and lose her down payment or declare bankruptcy!

This story is not meant to terrify and sway you; however, it is a good example to keep in mind. Chances are this woman will be using an agent next time. She'll probably tell everyone she knows to do the same.

Take Steps for Success

Knowing your market conditions and the true value of your house is the first step in selling it yourself. The next step is actually selling it by advertising, getting a yard sign, setting up showings and open houses, flyers, mailers, and all the activities that come with selling the house. Along with your regular job, finding time to do the job of selling your house can be difficult. If you're at work or out of town, you leave the opportunity for selling your house behind.

This does not mean that you cannot sell your house yourself. It just means that you need to have a good plan and all the facts before moving forward. You need to be aware of your home's real value, and you must be ready to perform all the work necessary to get your house sold.

Listing with a Professional Real Estate Agent

As with any professional, enlisting the help of a real estate agent can cost you money. If you do not have the right agent, it could cost you more than just the commission. Without good marketing and good negotiation skills, an agent can cost you time or even the actual sale itself.

On the other hand, a good agent is worth her fee. While you spend time doing your job, she is spending her time marketing and negotiating the sale of your house. She knows all the nuances of the market and the paperwork required for a clean, successful transaction. A good agent can keep you out of court, and even if you do end up in court, a good agent will have Errors and Omission insurance, which can protect you financially. (Errors and Omission insurance is the real estate version of medical malpractice insurance.)

The Mindset

The majority of buyers want representation when purchasing real estate. They believe that sellers who list their homes with a real estate agent are offering them something of value. Since the seller traditionally pays the fees, a buyer can be protected from potential liability for free. Although technically, this protection is part of the sales price they pay. Since the majority of buyers look for property with a real estate agent before looking at FSBO properties, they believe that agent-listed properties are better than FSBO properties.

Finding an Ethical Agent

Real estate agents often get a bad rap. People believe that they are only in it for the commission and don't care about their clients and customers. However, there is good and bad in every profession. If all professionals in one field were purely bad and only out to get your money, that profession would just fade away. The only thing a real estate agent has to sell is his reputation. As in any other profession, a good reputation is what keeps him in business.

Getting referrals from people you know and trust is a great way to find any service provider. You might ask your close friend who just got a great haircut who her stylist is. You might consult a cousin who just got a new car about which dealer he bought from. Referrals can work just as well for real estate.

Start by getting referrals from friends, neighbors, and family members who have had a good experience with a real estate agent (or Realtor®). Ask your hairdresser, butcher, and mechanic—ask everyone. Take those names and put them on a list. Look in the newspaper and glossy real estate magazines, such as *Homes and Land*. Pretend you are a buyer. Which agents have ads that appeal to you? Go on the Internet. What agents appeal to you there? Add these agents to your list as well.

Start calling the agents on your list. You may eliminate some of them just by the way they handle the phone call. Others will impress you. Once you have the list narrowed a bit, set up times to interview them. It's just like hiring an employee. You are looking for someone who fits your needs. Some agents will try to get you to commit to them before you have a chance to talk to anyone else, but try to interview all of the agents on your list before making a decision. You don't want to miss out on a jewel. Even then, sellers will often sign a contract with the last agent they interview. If you can wait, do so. Spend some time that evening considering every agent. Write out the pros and cons of each agent and call back the ones you like best. Be careful to make your best decision. You will be living with that decision for months to come.

ALERT!

Don't choose a real estate agent just because she assigns a higher price for your home than other agents. A competent agent, who gives a realistic price, will likely provide better service over the long haul. By choosing an agent based on the high price she quotes, you are choosing the possibility of being on the market for a long time.

Becoming a real estate agent is easy. Becoming a skilled real estate agent and staying in business is hard. Agents who have been in their community a long time or who have a reason to continue to work and receive referrals will be better at their job than those who are just looking for a few quick sales. Again, the only thing a real estate agent has to sell is her reputation.

The Multiple Listing Service (MLS)

The biggest benefit of the Multiple Listing Service (MLS) is exposure. At the turn of the twentieth century, the only properties agents could sell were those for which they held the listing. So buyers had to go from office to office, looking at what was available. If they missed an office that had a listing on the perfect house, they missed that house. This was a disservice to buyers. Agents began to see that instead of having buyers hunt down listing agents that there would be a great benefit in sharing commissions with other agents who could bring them buyers. Originally, the lists were typed up as follows:

- 123 Main Street $13,500 pays 3 percent
- 456 Second Street $12,600 pays 4 percent
- 789 Banks Way $14,700 pays 2.5 percent

Using this list, agents who had no listings (nothing to sell) could sell the property of other agents. Additionally, agents with lots of homes to sell gained help getting them sold. It became a win-win situation. Now, with the MLS in place, your property has more exposure. Instead of having one agent trying to sell your property, you have hundreds or even thousands trying to do so. The MLS is only available to agents who are also members of the National Association of Realtors® (see Chapter 9 for more information).

Hiring an Agent Who Is a Friend or Family Member

Deciding who you will use as a real estate agent begins with the interview process. If one of your friends or family members is impressive in the interview, he may be the agent that you choose. If you do go with a friend, make sure you lay out the ground rules up front.

FACT

Often your friendship with a real estate agent starts out as a business relationship. One advantage to hiring an agent who is already your friend is that you know how that friend will handle your transaction. Familiarity with this person's strategies, mannerisms, and schedule can help in this case.

Let your friend know that you want to be treated professionally and as well as any other client. Often, family members or friends will take liberties with familiar clients thinking that "Oh, it's just Aunt Lisa. I don't have to worry." The agent would not treat another client that way. Because of your relationship, your friend or family member is likely to work at least as hard for your sale as she would for another client.

Also, you can ask, but don't assume, if you'll receive a break on the commission your agent/friend might be due. If you get her to work for a lower fee, remember you are competing for attention against properties where she did not have to lower her fee.

Working with an Agent

The number one complaint people have about their real estate agent is lack of communication. The agent did not tell them what, if anything, was happening. When you interview agents ask if they give weekly or bimonthly updates. Make sure they know that you expect this type of communication. A good real estate agent will call or e-mail you on a regular basis. She will keep you informed of what the comments were on showings, what marketing she is doing, and what has sold since your house was listed.

If your real estate agent does not call you, call her! Ask her to follow up with the other agents to get feedback from showings. Ask for copies of your flyer and the advertising. Even if there is no news, she should contact you and tell you there is no news. There must be frequent communication.

If there are things about your house that you would like to see on the flyer or in the advertising, let your agent know. If you bought the house because of the creek in the backyard, maybe the next buyer will do the same. Most real estate agents have a good formula for writing ads and flyers. They have been doing it for awhile and know what generates interest, but your ideas can add a fresh perspective and are always welcomed by the professional.

Getting the Most for Your Money

Your real estate agent will counsel you on the correct price for your home, the current market, and how your home fits into it. He will market and show your house, offer advice to prepare it for sale, and bring as much attention to your property as possible. He will do everything you would do yourself, if you had the time and the expertise. All of this is valuable and necessary, but once you receive an offer on your home, that is where the biggest bang for your commission buck is realized.

A good agent will more than make her fee in how she handles the negotiations on the sale and what she does to keep everything on track through the closing. There are many steps in between. From understanding the legal ramifications and filling out the copious paperwork correctly to being sure that the lender's requirements are met and the inspections and repairs are done in a timely manner, an agent completes a lot of work to be sure that your sale runs smoothly. By solving little situations so that they don't become big problems and keeping all parties focused on the end result, she surely earns her fee.

Chapter 8

Do-It-Yourself Homeselling

Becoming an FSBO (For Sale By Owner) can be rewarding and exhausting. You must be able to handle out-of-pocket expenses and commit your time and energy to the process, which is dense with paperwork. You will also be the responsible party in a lawsuit, if the buyer perceives that something has gone wrong. As an FSBO, you will need to distance yourself from the emotional aspects and keep focused on the facts. If this hasn't scared you off, read on for tips to help you sell on your own.

Do You Have a Buyer Waiting?

There are times when someone will knock on the door of a house that is appealing on the outside and ask if the owners are willing to sell it. If you were planning to sell, this can be a great opportunity. More often, this happens when you were not planning to sell, but the knock on the door gets you thinking it might be a good time. If this is the case, be sure to do some research on the market before you accept any offers. While the buyer may be offering you more than you think your house is worth, she is probably well informed about current market values and could be offering less. You, on the other hand, weren't thinking of selling and probably haven't paid attention.

There are other possible ways of having a buyer in the wings. One of the most common is a friend, neighbor, or family member who says, "If you ever want to sell, I'll buy your house." What this usually means is "If you ever want to sell cheap, I have the fantasy of buying your house."

FACT

If the property you plan to sell is a rental, your tenant is a potential buyer. Long-term tenants get comfortable and tend to feel like the house is already their own. While they may be able to afford a different home of their own, buying your house might sound easier than moving.

When you start to think about the selling process, contact all the potential buyers you know and assess their level of interest. Let them know what price you expect. If they are serious enough to make an offer, get it in writing as soon as possible. Take an earnest money deposit that you can have held by the escrow company or a trusted attorney. Sometimes, these types of deals work well and can save you time and frustration.

If you have someone ready to buy your house but the person does not want to pay what you are expecting, discounting a little to sell your house immediately might be worth not going through the showing process. You will need to do a little homework, but you can save the cost of the commission if you were to have an agent or the costs of advertising if you were going the FSBO route. With or without an agent, you will still have other expenses too.

ALERT!

If you have a buyer ready to purchase your home, you still need to put everything in writing. Even if the buyer is a friend or family member, making sure all disclosures and contracts are in order is important. You may never have a problem with that friend, but what will you do if he passes away and you must deal with his heirs? When the buyer goes to sell, any issues that you neglected to disclose may fall back to you.

Now look at the other possibility: You want to do this yourself but do not have a potential buyer yet. Before moving forward, outline everything you plan to do to get your house sold. Your timeline from start to finish may look like this.

- Learn about and understand the market conditions.
- Find out what your home is worth.
- Set a price.
- Determine if you are going to offer agent cooperation or not.
- Purchase a sign for your property.
- Create a flyer, which includes your agent co-op or no agent co-op information.
- Start an advertising campaign.
- Decide when you will be holding open houses and advertise the dates or get flyers to the neighborhood.
- Hold open houses.
- Get copies of the purchase contract used in your area and review it.
- Handle inquiries.
- Qualify any potential buyers.
- Accept an offer if written by a buyer, or write a purchase contract with the buyer that you accept together.
- Coordinate with title, escrow, attorney, inspectors, repair persons, lenders, and others involved in the transaction.

- Be sure all the contingencies are handled in a timely manner.
- Get all releases in writing.
- Schedule necessary repairs.
- Transfer the property.
- Receive a check.

Services and Resources

Real estate agents do many things for which they are not paid. They do these things in the hope of eventually making a sale. There are several things that a real estate agent is willing to do for free. They will often provide a comparative market analysis, also known as a CMA, and give you the statistics in your area. These statistics will help you to see trends so that you can position yourself correctly in the market. Some agents will help with the wording or layout of a flyer. If you receive free services from a real estate agent, you might refer buyers who are not interested in your house to that agent—as a gesture of goodwill.

FACT

Real estate agents do not earn a salary; they are paid when they represent a buyer or a seller (or both, in some cases) in the purchase or sale of a property. They do not get paid until the deal is complete, after the transfer is made, and escrow closes. Once that happens, a portion of the commission is given to their office and a portion to them. From that they pay their expenses and taxes, including self-employment tax.

You should definitely request a CMA, which can help you price your house correctly. There probably isn't an agent out there who is not willing to do one for free. There are several different ways to do a CMA. One is a quick printout from the MLS. This gives you a basic overview of values and is a simple process for an agent to complete. Another, more detailed CMA shows how your property measures up to other properties and is adjusted out by square footage, condition, number of rooms, exterior features, and other factors. This is more time consuming for the real estate agent, but in a market where homes are very dissimilar, it gives a better picture of the true value.

There are also sites on the Internet specifically designed to help FSBOs. Some of these are run by discount brokerage houses that will take a small fee to advertise your home on the Internet. These fees are usually paid up front, although sometimes they are paid upon sale. Some of these sites are just advertising sites, and no brokers are involved. There will still be a charge to pay for the advertising. You will be responsible for handling inquiries, working with buyers, and preparing the contracts. Good sites to check are *www.ForSaleByOwner.com* and *www.HomeSaleDIY.com.* You can also type For Sale By Owner in your search engine and find hundreds of other sites.

For additional guidance, contact your state Division of Real Estate or Real Estate Commission. They will let you know what forms the state law requires for all real estate transactions, whether or not there is a real estate agent involved. Phone numbers for each state board are listed in Appendix A.

Building Your Team

Selling your house is not as simple as placing a sign in the yard. To get maximum results when you are acting as your own real estate agent, you need to do the things that a real estate agent would do. One of those things is to build a team made up of the people who will help you sell your house. Read on to find out who you need on your team.

Title Company

A title company is an insurance company that researches the chain of owners, easements, liens, or other encumbrances on a specific property and then gives the buyer an insurance policy, which promises that they are receiving the property from the true owner with known easements and liens. There are probably several title companies in your community. In order to understand the services of the title company and to see which title company you can work best with, call each of them and set up an appointment to meet with their manager or lead title officer. Find out what additional services they provide, what the title insurance covers, and how much they charge for each type of policy. The title company you like best is the one you can recommend to your buyer. For some buyers, any title company will be fine, but for others, it will be an important issue. It is best to be flexible about which title company you are willing to use. Based on the type of loan the buyer is getting, it may be necessary for the buyer to pick the title company.

Escrow Company

Depending on the area of the country you live in, escrow is handled by either an escrow company or by an attorney. Either way, the job is the same. The escrow company is known as a *disinterested third party*. It is their job to receive all documentation and funds necessary to complete the transaction and distribute everything to the proper parties. They will record all paperwork that must be recorded with the county, such as the deed. They will pay off the existing mortgages and liens and record the reconveyances when they arrive from the lien holders. They will pay all the costs and keep a record of them, noting which costs are the buyer's responsibility and which are the seller's responsibility. They will distribute the proceeds from the sale to the seller and give the buyer the title to the property.

Interviewing an escrow company or escrow attorney and knowing their fees and what jobs they perform will give you comfort. For convenience, some areas of the country place an escrow company and title company under one umbrella. They occupy the same office and have the same managers. This type of situation is convenient, since it gives you just one person to contact throughout the detailed process of both title and escrow.

Attorney

As an FSBO, you want to be sure you have all your bases covered. You do not want to discover too late that you have not completed everything required by your state or by the federal government. Without an agent, there may be things that are overlooked just because of a seller's lack of experience. It is important to bring all your paperwork to a real estate attorney and be assured that everything is done correctly. Some sellers will rely on the escrow company or escrow attorney to assure complete compliance, but they are a disinterested third party and cannot always give you advice. Your own real estate attorney is paid to be on your side and act in your best interest.

Mortgage Lender

Interviewing mortgage lenders will allow you to have one or two available to recommend to the buyer. They can tell you what types of loans are available and give you an idea of the financial qualifications your buyer will need. The buyer may already have a lender, but if not, your recommendations can help speed this part of the transaction along.

Entice Agents to Bring Buyers

Offering a fee to any agent who brings a buyer can increase your pool of available buyers. Most agents who bring you a buyer will want you to sign what is called a one-party listing agreement. This agreement protects the agent. It requires you to pay them a fee if their buyer purchases the property. It also keeps the buyer from going behind the agents back and purchasing directly from you. Most agents will not even let you know about a potential buyer if they are worried they won't get paid. Price your property accordingly and be sure it is the same price for everyone, agent or no agent.

Offering a one-party listing to agents will assure them that they will get paid for bringing you a buyer and they will be more comfortable in doing so. If you plan to cooperate with agents, put that fact on your flyer, along with the fee you are willing to pay.

Create a flyer especially for real estate agents and deliver it to all the offices in your area. On the flyer, include a list of features, some photos, and any incentive you are offering the agents. Be sure to include your contact information as well as instructions for showings. This will notify the agents that your house is available and will expand your pool of potential buyers.

Advertising

Signs and flyers are the easiest and least expensive forms of advertising. Be sure you know the sign ordinance in your community. Some areas restrict the size and type of signs you can use as well as where they can be placed. Have a flyer box adjacent to your sign and keep it full. Keep extras in the house and refill the flyer box regularly.

Your local newspaper is another advertising venue. Real estate buyers use the newspaper the same way that people use a catalog. They go through the pages and circle properties that interest them. If they have an agent, they call that agent and ask about all the properties. If they do not have an agent, they call the individuals who have placed the ads. Display advertising works better than classified advertising. If you can afford a display ad, place one in the real estate section. This will increase your chances of having it seen by the most interested parties. The Internet is also a good place to advertise. It is the number one source for out of town buyers.

While the purpose of advertising is to draw attention to your house, sometimes it can bring too much attention. When you are an FSBO, you will be a target for agents to call, soliciting their services. There is no way to prevent this completely, but you have a few choices on how to handle this. If you advertise with a no solicitation clause, agents will assume you are not offering a fee and you will not have an agent selling your house. If you advertise that you will cooperate with agents (pay them a commission for bringing a buyer), agents will also call to ask for your listing. If you advertise that you will cooperate with agents but also include a no solicitation clause, you will slow down the number of calls. When agents do call, be gracious. They may be looking for the listing today, but they may have a genuine buyer tomorrow. If you treated them poorly, you'll never hear about that buyer.

ALERT!

Open houses give you great exposure, but make sure that an owner of the property holds the open house. Owners are legally allowed to sell their homes, but if you have a friend hold the open house, they could be liable for practicing real estate without a license.

Attracting and Qualifying Buyers

Be sure that your buyer is financially qualified. Has she met with a bank or mortgage broker? Be sure that she will allow you to speak to her loan representative and get information confirming that she is qualified. As a part of the loan process, you also want to be sure that your home will appraise at or above the asking price. Some appraisers will adjust for nonagent sales and the commission savings. They do this in the same way they may adjust for a hardship sale, an estate auction, or any other sale that is out of the ordinary.

If you worked through the team-building process presented earlier, you are already fairly well prepared for an offer. If not, the next step is to get a reputable title company that can research, transfer, and insure the title. If it is customary in your area for attorneys to handle the escrow process, find a good attorney. If it is customary to use an escrow company, it is often easiest (but not required) to use the one in conjunction with your title company. Sometimes title companies and escrow companies are completely separate entities, and sometimes they work together.

After the offer is accepted, the buyer will be doing inspections. Even if your buyers want to save the money and not do any, urge them to do inspections. If they insist on waiving the inspections, get their waiver in writing. Be sure you are protected.

Increase Your Chances for Success

The more prepared you are, the better your chances of success. Don't skip any of the steps; be sure you do everything you can to get your house sold. The following story is one couple's experience.

A couple decided to sell their house themselves. They had an appraisal from refinancing the house recently, and so they knew they were priced right. They wanted to save on the real estate commission, and with the tight budget they had, they thought they could save on advertising costs as well. The woman typed up a list of the home's features and took it to a copy shop. She made 200 bright green copies. Her husband put a sign in the yard with their phone number on it. They placed the flyers in a box at the sign. Although the flyers went quickly, not all of them went to potential buyers. Some green paper could be seen stuck to bushes in their yard and in other yards around them. They could not really afford to make more flyers; once the flyer box was empty, they were left with the sign to attract buyers. Because they both worked during the day, they would come home to several phone calls and several hang ups on the answering machine. Of those who left messages, many were real estate agents hoping for the listing, and others were people who just wanted the price.

The couple also held an open house every weekend. At first, they had a great number of people through, from curious neighbors to passersby. Within a few weeks, the number dwindled to one or two people per weekend. Their weekends were ruined as they waited for a buyer, and they started to get frustrated. With no activity, they finally gave up and listed with a real estate agent. Their agent exposed their house to potential buyers through a broad range of marketing services. They had an offer within a few weeks. The buyer lived in the same community but didn't know their house had been for sale! The couple learned that even if the price is right, no one will buy your house if people can't tell it's for sale.

Changing Your Mind

There are people who are successful at selling their own homes. If you are one of these lucky folks, congratulations! However, there are others who try to sell their own home for awhile and then change their minds. Perhaps they don't have the time to devote to it, or perhaps they just want someone else to handle all the inquiries. If you do decide to list with an agent after being an FSBO, you will recover some free time that had been lost in trying to sell your house yourself.

Be sure to get in touch with every buyer who expressed interest in your property. Let them know you are considering listing with an agent and ask them if they are ready to make a decision to buy now. Sometimes the sense of urgency is enough to get these potential buyers to make a move. If they are not quite ready but could be ready in a few weeks or a month, you can ask to have these buyers excluded from the listing for a period of time. This means that if one of the excluded buyers purchases your home that you handle the transaction yourself and don't pay any commission.

Don't exclude a buyer from the listing agreement for more than thirty days without giving your agent some compensation. From the time you sign the listing agreement, the agent will be working diligently to create marketing materials and generate interest in your property. After thirty days, she has spent considerable effort, time, and money to get your house sold.

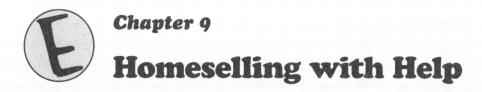

Chapter 9

Homeselling with Help

Finding your dream agent can seem like a daunting task. It may be that you do not know any real estate agents, or it may be that you know too many. You may have friends or relatives in real estate. Many property owners receive regular mailers or phone calls from agents who are looking for business. You will be entrusting what is probably the biggest investment of your life to one person. It is worth making sure you've found the right person.

Different Types of Real Estate Offices

The person you hire to represent you in the sale of your home will not only be giving you his expertise and experience, but also the expertise and experience of the office where he works. There are several different kinds of offices, each with their own style and qualities. The two main types are:

- **Full-service Broker:** This is an office that has agents who take care of everything—for a full commission. The agent is responsible for all advertising, the signs, holding open houses, qualifying buyers, negotiating the sale, handling the paperwork, and being sure that inspections are completed, loans are accomplished, and everything works smoothly through the closing and beyond.
- **Discount Broker:** This is an office that has agents who help the FSBO. They usually charge a flat fee, and they do a percentage of the work. When dealing with a discount broker, the seller is responsible for a percentage of the work as well. In a discount brokerage, the agent will take care of the final paperwork, but it is up to the seller to handle the majority of the advertising, set up showings, hold open houses, qualify buyers, negotiate the sale, coordinate inspections, and other details.

Both full-service and discount brokerages can be divided into four smaller categories: national franchise, local franchise, large nonfranchise, and small nonfranchise.

National Franchise

These are the big names you have heard of on television and radio: Prudential, Coldwell Banker, Century 21, Re-Max, ERA, Red Carpet, and others. These offices are primarily full-service brokerages. One of the largest discount broker franchises is Help-U-Sell. They do just what the name implies: They help you sell your property.

A national franchise often has tools for their agents that allow them to be more efficient in marketing. They often have special training available to their agents on the skills that will help their clients. The national franchises have discovered a formula that works, and they use it in every office. Because they are nationally known and familiar, out of town buyers tend to gravitate toward them. If they had a good experience in their hometown with a national franchise, they may have a good experience in your town as well. Because these offices are franchises and individually owned, there is some personal flavor as well.

Local Franchise

These offices are run in the same manner as the national franchises but have only spread to one or a few regions. Like the national franchises, they provide their agents tools, but they must carve out a place for themselves as a brand. Local franchises have big name recognition in the areas they service and tend to cater to that specific market.

Large Nonfranchise

This type of office has the power of numbers. They usually have a lot of agents, each with their own potential buyers. Offices like this have often been in their town for a long time and have a reputation built on service. They have created their own branding and can be very stylized. Sometimes their physical location in town will attract potential buyers.

Small Nonfranchise

A small nonfranchise office (sometimes known as a *boutique office*) usually has just a few agents; in some cases, there is only one agent in the office. This agent or group of agents will usually find a niche market that they specialize in, a market that some of the larger offices may overlook. They pride themselves in having exceptional customer service. If you are working with an agent in a boutique office, you will often call her on her cellular phone since there are fewer support people in the office. With the overhead of an office and little to no additional help, these agents have to work very hard to keep everything running.

It is important to hire agents who have a working environment that supports their efforts. However, the type of office is less important than the individual agent. It is the agent who you will be working with directly.

Brokers, Agents, and Buyer's Brokers

The sale of your home is a major undertaking and selecting the right person to represent you is essential to a successful experience. Start by getting referrals for an agent from friends who have recently sold their homes. You may have also received mailings from agents who work in your neighborhood. You should contact them as well. Look for more agents in the newspaper and the glossy real estate magazines, such as *Homes and Land*. Collect a list of names and call them to arrange interviews. Three of your choices are brokers, agents, and buyer's brokers.

Brokers are licensed by the state to carry on the business of dealing in real estate. In some states, all agents are also brokers. In other states, a broker has additional education over an agent. A broker either owns or manages an office and has licensed agents working under her broker's license.

Generally, an agent is someone who is representing the interests of someone else. That someone else is usually the buyer or the seller. In the case of real estate agents, it is understood that they have met the education requirements of their state and received a license to sell real estate.

Many agents and brokers specialize in working with buyers. Those agents and/or brokers will contract with their buyers and receive a fee for services, just as a listing agent does with a seller. A buyer's broker will usually credit the buyer for any fees offered through the MLS, but not every property that they find for a buyer will offer compensation. Since a buyer's broker knows they will be paid, even if the seller is not offering compensation, they will also search for non-MLS properties, such as FSBO properties or homes that are not on the market.

REALTORS®

In order to get a real estate license, a person must take a certain number of classes and then take a test according to their state licensing laws. Each state has different laws and different education requirements that real estate agents must abide by and fulfill. Some people stop at the real estate agent level and go no further. These people are allowed to practice real estate according to their state's laws but are not granted access to a pool of properties for sale, called the Multiple Listing Service (MLS). In the case of agents who are working exclusively for a developer and only selling properties that the developer has available, the MLS may not be necessary.

The next level up is known as a Realtor®. They start as real estate agents, licensed by the individual state or states in which they practice. However, not all real estate agents are Realtors®. Real estate agents who are Realtors® subscribe to a national code of ethics that helps to assure the integrity and professionalism of all Realtors®. In addition, they are members of the National Association of Realtors®, a trade organization comprised of real estate professionals from all over the United States.

FACT

Members of the National Association of Realtors® have access to their regional MLS, which is now available nationally through Realtor.com. This is a service where Realtors® pool their available properties for sale, offer to share their commission with other Realtors®, and better serve their clients by having more people available to sell the properties they have listed.

A listing agent has a contract with a seller to sell his property. This agent is working for the seller. A buyer's agent may or may not have an actual contract to find a buyer a piece of property. It may be a verbal understanding or it may be implied, but a buyer's agent is working for the buyer. These different relationships are known as *agency*, and they vary from state to state. In some states, all agents who belong to the MLS work for the seller. They are either the listing agent or a subagent of the listing agent. In these areas, a buyer has no representation unless they pay for it specifically. This practice was the standard in most locations for years, but it has become less and less common. Now, it is more likely that there are representatives for both parties.

A few states have eliminated agency altogether. These agents become facilitators. This means that agents are representing the transaction and not one party or the other.

ALERT!

Some states have another category, called *dual agency*, where an agent represents both parties. If your listing agent finds the buyer, you may be in this situation. It is important that this type of agency, or the possibility of it, be disclosed up front so that no one gives out confidential information about another without consent.

Interviews

Interviewing an agent is just like interviewing a prospective employee. Once you have a list of the agents you want to interview, call each of them and set up an appointment. If you are setting up all the appointments for one day, let them know in advance that you have allowed them a set period of time to tell you their qualifications. One hour is a realistic amount of time to set aside for each agent, although some will go much faster and some may take more time.

The agent will probably bring to you a listing presentation package. A listing presentation package is like a resume with additional information. It explains what the agent will do for you, what his company will do, and statistical information on the marketplace. As you review the listing presentation package together, ask questions to fully understand the process and how the agent will help you with the sale of your home.

Start by giving the agent a tour of your house. As you go through the property, ask him for his opinion. Agents want your business and will usually not say anything to offend you, but you do want to be sure that they notice particular features. Point out things you like about the home and ask if that item will also appeal to the majority of buyers. Welcoming the agent's opinion will gently urge him to tell you what may not appeal to a buyer and suggest any necessary changes.

In order to do her job well, your real estate agent will get to know you personally. She will know about your finances and how neatly you keep your closets. If you connect personally, you will also connect better on a business level. The other questions you may want to pose are:

- How long have you been a real estate agent? With new agents, the office will play a big role in their ability to perform. With experienced agents, the office is of little or no significance, as long as they get the support they need.
- Do you like your office? Why? If he doesn't like his office environment, you may want to consider a different agent.
- Where does your business come from?
- What type of marketing do you do?
- What sets you apart from the competition? Be wary of an agent who says anything negative about the competition. A true professional will tell you what they can do, not what someone else cannot do.
- How many listings do you have?
- How many sales have you made this year?
- Do you have someone to cover your business when you are not around? Do you have an assistant?
- Do you have an attorney or CPA who you can trust to answer questions?

ALERT!

Sellers tend to ask agents about the market and about their house, but it is important to first ask about the agent. This will give you an idea of how she communicates. Agents will often tell you what they think you want to hear about the market—"it's great!"—and about your house— "it's worth a ton!" Don't pick your agent based on the compliments or generalized information she offers.

There are certain questions you might want to ask new agents, in particular: Do you have experience in other fields that translates well to real estate? Do you have a hands-on manager, mentor program, or additional training available through your office? Ask experienced agents: What keeps you in the business? Do you mentor new agents in your office? The answers to these questions will give you an idea of how an agent's experience (or lack thereof) has influenced his outlook and how he handles his clients' needs.

Signing a Listing Contract

When you choose an agent, he will draw up a listing contract. Be sure to read the entire contract. In some areas, these contracts are several pages long and may include addenda as well. The addenda can include an agency disclosure, explaining that your agent is working exclusively for you or that your agent may bring a buyer in the future and will be working for both parties.

FACT

Agents will be writing checks long before a sale is made. They will be paying the out-of-pocket expenses for advertising, signs, mailers, postage, and the other things necessary to sell your house. They will be spending time as well, as they work toward making the sale happen.

Although listing fee percentages are negotiable and not set by law, some offices have a policy that certain percentages are charged for certain types of sales. Most agents become very uncomfortable when asked to negotiate their fee. To understand why they become uncomfortable, you need to understand how an agent gets paid. Most real estate agents are paid on commission. If they do not make a sale, they do not receive any payment. Brokerage companies do not traditionally give an agent draws against potential sales or a salary of any kind.

Chances are good that your buyer will come from another agent. The buyer's agent will be offered a split of the commission, usually one-half of the original fee. After the sale is made, the agent will split the remaining fee with her office. This percentage covers the office's expenses. Expenses include overhead and any services the office provides to make the agent's job easier, such as a receptionist, office manager, copier, and supplies. The agent will give her office as much as 50 percent of what is left after splitting with the buyer's agent. From what remains, the agent must pay regular taxes, as well as self-employment tax, reimburse herself for any expenses, and live on the balance.

Is it wise to ask your agent for a reduced commission fee?
To answer this question, ask yourself another one: If an agent is quick to negotiate away some of her fee, will she be quick to negotiate away some of your money when working on an offer that is presented?

The agent's office may not participate in a negotiation for reduced fees, which means that the agent will be giving her office a percentage of her commission based on the full fee commission that the office expects. This further reduces the net profit to the agent. When faced with ten similar houses, the agent who brings a buyer will show houses that offer a higher commission first. This means that your agent must be competitive with the commission she offers a buyer's agent. If the full commission fee is reduced to begin with, you may have fewer showings, which makes your house less competitive in the marketplace.

This does not mean that an agent will not negotiate his fee. It is always okay to ask. If a seller is doing more than one transaction (for instance, buying and selling with the same agent), agents will often give a discount on the second transaction. If your house is priced competitively and the agent knows he will not have to spend as much on advertising, he may negotiate his fee.

Services You Can Expect

The first and foremost service that a good agent provides is to keep you informed. A good agent will call or e-mail you on a regular basis with updates about your property, feedback on showings, and the market in general. If your agent does not contact you on a regular basis, you need to contact her.

A good agent will also place a sign on your property, with a flyer box (if allowed by ordinance), take photographs of your property, and create flyers with photographs and property information about your home. Additionally, she may hire a company to create a virtual tour. Some agents have the equipment to perform this task on their own. A good agent will also do the following:

- Help you with staging or hire a staging consultant to help you prepare your house for sale.
- Add your property to the Multiple Listing Service (MLS) if he is a Realtor®, which will also connect to *www.Realtor.com*.
- Put your property on the Internet. Many agents have their own personal sites, some use their office Web sites, and some rely on *www. Realtor.com*.
- Send out postcards or letters to potential buyers and other agents about your home.
- Place ads in newspapers and homes-for-sale magazines.
- Hold open houses.
- Qualify buyers.
- Prepare the paperwork.
- Look out for your best interest in the negotiations.
- Schedule inspections.
- Coordinate with the buyer's lender.
- Coordinate with the title company.
- Coordinate with the escrow company or attorney.
- Be sure that any repairs are taken care of in a timely and cost-effective manner.
- Schedule and attend the closing.
- Take care of any follow-up that may be necessary after closing.

If you have a great relationship with an agent, by all means use her! Someone who already understands you and your needs and who works the way you want an agent to work can help relieve your worry in an already stressful time.

Costs You Can Expect

Generally the real estate commission is the only cost of engaging a real estate agent. The commission is not paid until the job is done and the house has sold. If the agent works for one day or one year to sell your house, the fee is the same. There are a few exceptions where additional fees may be charged.

Some offices charge a transaction coordination fee in addition to the commission. This is a set fee, usually about $150, which is paid once a contract is agreed upon. This fee is used in larger offices to fund a transaction coordinator. Transaction coordinators will do some of the services that the agent would usually perform. They take care of all the paperwork that needs to be handled to keep the transaction together. They coordinate inspections and work with the lender, title company, escrow, and attorneys to insure a smooth closing.

FACT

With the copious requirements that are standard today in homeselling, some offices use a transaction coordinator who specializes in the details of a transaction to lower their liability. It also allows their agents to concentrate on taking care of the clients, rather than the details.

Very high-end properties tend to command some unusual marketing requirements. Some luxury homes require advertising that can run into the tens of thousands of dollars. In these cases, the seller may pay some of the advertising fees up front. In many cases, these fees are reimbursed at close of escrow. Though they are rare, these and any other additional fees should be outlined in your listing contract.

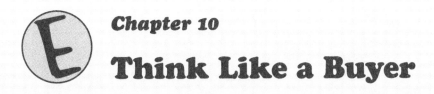

Chapter 10

Think Like a Buyer

In Chapter 1, you learned it is important to know your own motivation for selling. Understanding your buyer's motivation is also an important step in getting your house sold. Of course, most buyers don't come right out and tell you what their reasons are, and so this becomes a guessing game. Luckily, buyers give clues to their motivation, making it an educated guessing game. In this chapter, learn what buyers look for and why.

Features of Your House

To sell the advantages of your home, you must first identify them. Start by making a list of your home's features. Next to each feature, list the benefit of that feature. What is it about this feature that makes it worth having? Buyers look for features, but they buy based on the benefits those features provide. A sample list of your home's features might look like this:

- **Three bedrooms**: room for everyone
- **Two and one-half baths:** no waiting for a bathroom
- **Two-car garage:** extra storage
- **Landscaped half-acre yard:** attractive
- **Living and family rooms:** great for entertaining
- **Just over 2,200 square feet:** big enough but not too big to keep clean
- **Built in 1985:** newer than most homes in town
- **Stucco exterior with tile roof:** low maintenance
- **Floor to ceiling fireplace:** looks expensive
- **Walking distance to schools and shopping:** convenient

After making the list, ask your agent which houses on the market would be similar to yours. If you are not working with an agent, check open houses and the newspaper to find homes that may be similar. Drive by the homes that are a close match to yours. If you have the opportunity to preview them via an open house or by looking with your agent, do that as well. Compare the features and benefits of your house with those of the competition houses. Ask yourself "if I were a buyer, which house would I choose?" Making these comparisons with a critical eye (the eye of a buyer) will help identify adjustments you can make to position your home as the best buy among the competition.

How Buyers Shop for Homes

Buyers looking for a new house in their own community usually know a real estate agent and will likely look for a home with that agent. Based on the buyer's criteria, the agent will research (usually through the MLS) which homes will best fit their needs. When looking at property with the buyers, the agent will take note of their reactions to help adjust and fine-tune the type of property they select to show the buyer.

When buyers look for homes in a new community or when they do not personally know a real estate agent, they often begin their home search on the Internet. This is a great resource for current information and listings, especially if you are not within driving distance of your area of choice. Newspaper real estate sections, homes-for-sale magazines (available for free at most grocery stores), and other publications are also helpful sources for buyers.

FACT

According to the National Association of Realtors® 2004 Profile of Home Buyers and Sellers, 90 percent of buyers used a real estate agent during their search. Fifty-three percent of buyers used the Internet frequently as part of the home search.

Many people find a home by driving around a selected area in search of for sale signs, which are still an important tool for marketing your house. Don't be a secret seller. A sign lets the world know you are selling your home. You never know from where that buyer is coming. A buyer may also find your house by word of mouth. Your neighbor, who is a friend of a buyer, may have seen your sign or received a mailer from your agent.

What Do Buyers Really Want?

Buyers look for a house that will feel like their home. While each buyer has a unique way of determining that feeling, most buyers will justify purchasing a place that feels like "home," even if it is not perfect in other ways.

There are many different needs that a buyer is trying to fulfill when purchasing a home. Not every buyer has the same needs, nor do they satisfy them in the same way. They do not always know how to put these needs into words, but the underlying requirements are there. Buyers looking for prestige may insist on granite countertops, without truly realizing it is the prestige they are after. A buyer looking for privacy may insist on a water view. Having no one in front of him, just a view of water, satisfies his need for privacy. His need could actually be met without the view, but he won't know it unless he sees a private house without a water view.

There are buyers who look for several specific benefits to satisfy their needs. Determining their needs will help you or your agent to point out the benefits of your home for them. The basic needs the average buyer looks to fulfill in his new home can be summed up in this list.

- **Value:** a quality home for a good price
- **Prestige:** prestigious surroundings; a house to impress others
- **Convenience:** easy access to work, school, stores, etc.
- **Security:** a secure house in a safe neighborhood
- **Comfort:** a comfortable, "warm" home
- **Aesthetics:** an attractive home
- **Privacy:** a private location; privacy-conscious architecture and landscaping
- **Entertainment:** easy access to entertainment; the ability to entertain at home
- **Health:** climate and facilities to promote health and well-being
- **Recreation:** easy access to recreational facilities
- **Education:** an exceptional school district or other educational facilities

The previous list is based on a list of basic human needs created by Abraham Maslow, a psychologist who conducted research during the era of Freud and Skinner. He created a pyramid showing the progression of human needs, known as Maslow's Hierarchy of Needs. Maslow's list started with the most basic needs (food, shelter, and warmth) and progressed to more advanced requirements (the need to belong and gain recognition). The preceding list is expanded for its relationship to real estate and addresses the higher human needs, assuming the more basic needs have been met.

As the buyer chooses features to comment on, the agent will begin to discern the benefits and needs to which they are tied. If you are selling on your own, you will not have the firsthand knowledge gained by hearing the buyer's comments at other properties. However, you may want to ask them about other homes they have seen. What did they like or dislike about them? What is it about your home that is better or not as good as the other homes?

Careful listening will help you determine the benefits the buyer seeks to satisfy her needs.

Here is an example of a buyer's requirements: A woman insisted on many safety features, such as an alarm system and no sharp edges on counters or hearths. She had three small children and wanted them to be safe at home. Her agent understood her need for safety, and he showed her several one-story houses, assuming they were safer than houses with stairs. She did not like any of them. After the third one-story house, the agent asked her why a one-story house would not work for her. The woman explained that she was worried someone would climb in a bedroom window and take one of her children. So, a two-story house, with the bedrooms upstairs, was a safety feature the woman wanted.

The key to making your home desirable to buyers is to have as many features as possible that translate into benefits for the buyer—benefits that satisfy one of the basic needs that are important to that specific buyer. Because some features represent different benefits to different buyers and satisfy different needs, it is important to know the needs of your particular buyer.

For each prospective buyer, there will be some needs that are more important than others, and some that will not apply at all. Most buyers will have two or three primary needs from the preceding list that must be satisfied in order for them to purchase a home.

If you get lots of showings and no offers, consider that you may be missing the ability to satisfy a basic need. Since value is one of the basic needs, being sure you are priced correctly is important. If your price is right and you still have no offers, have your agent interview agents who have shown the house to get their buyer's reactions. Your agent may be able to see a trend. If people are looking in your neighborhood because of its close proximity to schools and shopping, you may already be satisfying the "convenience" need. Maybe those buyers are also looking for comfort, and your house is very formal. Maybe they want privacy, and you have neighbors within feet of your side yards. Painting an accent wall in a warm color will add comfort to a formal house. Some special plantings can add privacy to a house with neighbors close by.

ALERT!

Though you may make corrections to meet the needs of one buyer, he may move on to other properties. You will not be able to satisfy the needs of every one, but every little change has the possibility of satisfying a buyer's need. What you are working toward is expanding your potential buyer base.

Although they will not give you as many clues as they would a third party, such as a real estate agent, you can still interview people who have seen the house when you are selling on your own. No one wants to hurt your feelings; they may give vague answers such as "it's not my style." See if you can get more information by asking further about their style. Each little piece will give you something to fill in the puzzle and make modifications to your house for maximum appeal.

Buyers in Search of For Sale By Owner

Sometimes a buyer may look for an FSBO because she has exhausted all other possibilities. She has checked every home available through her agent and wants to see what is available directly from an owner. Since these buyers have seen everything else in their price range, they are pretty sophisticated on market value. If your home is priced competitively, this may be the type of buyer for you.

Usually, a buyer looks at an FSBO expecting a bargain. Because there is no agent involved and the seller is not paying a commission, they believe they can save on the price. Keep in mind that these are often experienced buyers who may know more about the process than you do.

If you feel comfortable with your price, remember it is you who is saving the commission. You may stick to the price but lose the bargain-hunting buyer. Decide what your bottom line is before you get the offer. In this way, you will not be swayed by a smooth-talking bargain hunter and can negotiate to the highest possible amount.

Because buying and selling a home has become more and more complicated over the years, fewer buyers are looking at FSBO properties. Some buyers are actually concerned that they will be taken advantage of if they lack the benefit of an agent's representation. These buyers will tend to steer clear of FSBO properties or, at the very least, request that their agent represent them in the purchase of an FSBO house.

Buyers who have seen everything else have developed a pretty good relationship with their real estate agent and will usually have their agent call to make the appointment. If the buyers do call themselves, they will probably still have their agent write the contract and will expect their agent to be paid a commission.

Buyers Who Use a Real Estate Agent or Realtor®

Most buyers do not have the time to devote to researching available properties and discovering market values. They want to get a good house at a good price, and they don't really know where to start. By having an agent do the research for them, they are free to do their jobs and tend to their families, and they only have to deal with real estate during the days that they are actually looking at homes. Their agent can tell them what similar properties have sold for and whether or not the house they are looking at is well priced. The agent will also tell them about school districts or other facilities in the area, with which they may not be familiar.

Buyers are also concerned about potential liability, and they want someone to represent their interests. Having an agent gives them protection against liability and gives them a representative. Unless the buyer has recently purchased many homes in the area, she will not be aware of all the paperwork that is required. Even if the seller is aware of the paperwork requirements, the buyer may not be comfortable relying on the seller's expertise. The seller is, after all, working for the seller.

In most areas of the country, the majority of homes are listed with a Realtor® and available through the MLS. Because most of the MLS services are also available on the Internet through *www.Realtor.com* and other sites, buyers know that they will need to call an agent to view those properties. Real estate agents and offices do the majority of the advertising that attracts buyers, and even if they are not searching on the Internet, they may be looking at other advertising mediums and find an agent that way.

In communities where real estate is scarce, some buyers hire an agent to find property for them. They contract with that agent and pay them to research homes that are not even on the market. A buyer's broker will knock on doors, make phone calls, send letters, and generally solicit potential sellers who otherwise have not considered selling. Of course, a buyer's broker will also search the listed properties, but in a dominant seller's market, there may not be anything available. Sellers who had not even considered selling or who were not planning to sell for a year or two may be intrigued by the fact that they can have a buyer without going through the process of having their house on the market.

FACT

If the buyer is local, he will usually have a real estate agent who he has worked with in the past or an agent he knows through friends or family members. If the buyer is coming from another community, a real estate agent will likely be his first friend in the area—the person he also calls for a referral to a doctor or a mechanic.

Buyers who are looking for a unit in a particular condominium complex or for a house in a particular neighborhood can often find what they are looking for quickly, rather than waiting for it to arrive on the market months, or even years, after they started their search.

Bargaining Psychology

Most people like to bargain. In fact, many almost expect to bargain on their big purchases, such as cars and houses. Even if a buyer really wants a house, starting out with an offer that they expect the seller to counter is commonplace. Remember, not all buyers fit this profile. The Saturn car company was revolutionary in its "no-hassle, no-haggle sales policy," and it has changed the way some people buy cars. The Saturn is a popular car because not everyone wants to bargain; some just want to get it done. Understanding which kind of buyer you have is the key to getting the most out of any offer that is presented. Do you have a bargaining buyer or a Saturn-style buyer?

Listening to clues will help you decide how to proceed. If you receive an offer and it is presented with the caveat "don't let this die" or "the buyer is flexible," you know that there may be some room for negotiation. If you get an offer like "this is the best they can do" or "there are five other houses just like yours in the neighborhood," you may have a tougher time. Of course, the stated inflexibility may also mean that they are pushing you to take their price. Reading the clues is something your agent will have more experience with, but even the best poker players can get it wrong sometimes. Negotiating is a game of wits; don't expect perfection in this arena.

Go through the offer and determine what is acceptable and what is not. If there are terms that are better than you expect, it may be possible for you to take a lesser price. If the terms are more complicated and difficult, you may want to counter with a higher price and may also clarify the terms.

Don't just bargain for the sake of bargaining. If you have a good offer at the price you were hoping for and terms you find acceptable, take it! Yes, you may be able to squeeze out an extra couple thousand dollars, but you could also lose the sale. There is nothing worse than bargaining away a buyer when you would have accepted his offer.

To determine how much bargaining you are willing to do, think about the ultimate goal. If the ultimate goal is to sell quickly and move to a new location, then sell quickly! If the ultimate goal is to get as much as possible and the time frame doesn't matter, you can play the game. If you don't care about selling, you can be very tough in the bargaining process, and you may lose several buyers before you find one willing to accept your price and terms. However, if you don't care about selling, why is your house on the market?

If you do care about selling, being very tough in the bargaining process can be harmful to your goals. Selling real estate is not a win-lose game. It should be a win-win game, perhaps with a little compromise, where everyone gets what he wants. Getting tough for a matter of principle or because you feel insulted or indignant does not contribute to a sale—just indigestion!

Advice from Your Agent

You will ultimately pay your agent for her service; so take advantage of this valuable resource. Ask your agent what direction you should go in making a counteroffer or accepting an offer as written. Your agent may have some insight about the buyer from meeting with their agent and probably has more experience on buyer psychology than you do.

Practice creates an understanding of buyer psychology. The more buyers you work with, the more developed your skills and intuition regarding buyers will become. This is why your agent can help you determine the best direction. He has probably worked with more buyers than you have, and his experience will help you in making the right decisions.

FACT

Every buyer is a little different, and buyer psychology is not an exact science. Your agent may also know the buyer's agent, who may have a certain psychology as well. The agent's psychology will combine with the buyer's psychology to create something new and filled with its own nuances.

Is the Buyer Serious or "Just Looking"?

Just as each seller has a different motivation to sell, each buyer has a different motivation to buy. A buyer's motivation is one key to his seriousness. Even if buyers are serious about purchasing, they may not be serious about your house. They may have committed to an appointment and feel it is polite to look, but that is all they are doing—looking. The reverse situation can be true as well. Some buyers are just looking and have no intention of purchasing a house for awhile, until a certain house catches their interest and they become serious about purchasing. If your house catches their interest, they could change from lookers to serious buyers in a matter of minutes.

There are times when a seller has to sell and times when a buyer has to buy. Catching a buyer during a "have to buy" time makes him a serious buyer. Maybe a job transfer brought this buyer to your community. If this is the case, he may not appear to be motivated when he is first looking. He is learning about the market and figuring out what is a bargain and what is not. Once he understands the market, he may discover that your home is a good value and return with the intent to buy.

Treat every buyer as if she were a serious buyer; one may be the ultimate buyer of your house. Some do not want the seller to know how they feel and will appear to be disinterested. If your buyer is serious and you treat her as though she is just looking, she may be offended and shy away.

If a buyer has just sold an investment property and is looking at your home as an investment, she may be doing what is known as a 1031 tax deferred exchange. With an exchange, the buyer has a limited amount of time to find a replacement property for the one they are selling or have just sold. If she does not meet this deadline, she may have tax consequences. The short time frame allowed for a 1031 exchange makes her very motivated to make a decision. This may not be information you are privy to, but if you do know about it, you know they have a higher level of motivation than the average buyer.

Inevitably, some buyers are truly just looking. They want to buy, but they don't really know what type of home they want to buy. While each house gets them closer to discovering what they want, their ideas about a home are not yet formed. Eventually, one house will stand out, and they will become ready. It could be your house that changes the buyer's motivation today, or it could be another house, months or years later. Even if you find it annoying, try to be gracious when you discover a less-than-serious buyer is viewing your home. Perhaps this was your situation before you found the house you're selling now. Perhaps the person just appears to be less than serious. If you treat him like a real buyer, he may become one!

Chapter 11

Home Repairs and Improvements

Wear and tear on your home happens over time—so gradually that you may not even notice it. However, potential buyers will notice it! Worn-out areas of your home give it a tired look, but you can liven it up with some simple repairs and improvements. Start by trying to see your home through the eyes of a buyer. Take pictures—of everything. Photograph the interior and exterior, inside cupboards and closets, and do it from several angles. Looking at the photos will give you a fresh perspective.

Spruce Up the Exterior

Even though you're selling your house, the area around your house (including the yard, garage, driveway, and any other features) has the potential to help or hurt you as you try to make a sale. It's worthwhile to freshen things up a bit. Sweep or wash down the driveway, walkways, and steps. Mow the lawn and trim the bushes. Be sure that there are no plants or trees blocking access to the view of your front door. You will be amazed by the difference these simple, no-cost steps can make. Plant some colorful flowers around the front door, in pots if necessary. In the winter months, be sure that the driveway, walkways, and steps are free of snow and ice. If there is a spot that collects ice all the time, keep some ice melt handy and use it regularly. A brightly colored welcome mat is always helpful.

FACT

If an agent or potential buyer is injured by slipping and falling on the ice in front of your home, you may be held liable for her medical expenses. It is wise to place a caution sign near any dangerous spot and always keep all walkways and steps as free of ice as possible.

If you've taken photos of the exterior of your home to get a new perspective, look at them with a critical eye. If the front door looks shabby, paint or restain it. Start by removing any nails, patching the holes, and sanding the door. If there are broken or cracked panes of glass in the front door, replace them. When deciding on a color, pick one that goes well with your house, or go with a traditional red. Don't try to be too artsy and choose a color that doesn't go with anything. A seasonal wreath on the front door can add charm and hide flaws that can't easily be repaired.

It is also important that your front door lock works well. You may know that there is a trick to getting the door open, but not everyone will be able to figure out the trick. If the key sticks even a little or you have to push the door extra hard, you could actually miss a showing when an agent has trouble getting in. Even if he can get the sticky door open, it leaves the potential buyer with a negative first impression. If the front door doesn't work well, a buyer might begin to wonder what else could be wrong with the house. Also, be sure to shine the lock set. A fresh coat of lacquer will keep it from getting tarnished again.

Power washing your house will get rid of cobwebs in the eaves and leaves in the gutters. A good power wash makes the house look fresher, even if you can't afford to paint it. Painting or staining the exterior is the best solution if the house looks worn, but even painting the trim can spruce up the front.

If your driveway is full of cracks and looks worn, a fresh coat of sealer will make it look new again. It is not always necessary to replace the entire driveway; sometimes filling the cracks and resealing is enough. Additionally, if you have exposed trash cans, building a lattice fence around them can hide their unsightly appearance. If you have storage items in your yard such as tires or old pieces of equipment, now is the time to get rid of them.

Play equipment that is broken, old, shabby-looking, or outgrown can detract from the look of the yard. It can also be a liability. Unless the play equipment is in good condition and still in use, remove it and take it to the dump. Be sure to spruce up the landscaping where the play equipment has been. Some fresh sod or mulch where feet were dragging under the swings will brighten up that spot again.

Be sure that your swimming pool is clean and serviced. Repair any broken tiles and paint the edges if necessary. Fill any cracks in the cement in and around the pool, and be sure the area is free of debris. Trim shrubbery away from the pool. A caution sign on the door to the pool and/or one on the diving board will also reduce your liability if someone was to fall in.

Any exterior steps should be tightly fastened. Loose steps and deck boards are a sign of poor maintenance. Make sure handrails are secure, sanded smooth, and painted. There should be no chances of getting a splinter from the railings.

Once you have finished the outside, take "after" pictures. Is there anything else that you notice about the exterior that you missed the first time through? If so, address those items.

Showcase the Interior

Check the pictures you took of the interior of your house and identify what looks shabby. As a general rule, clean things first. If a good cleaning job doesn't greatly improve the appearance, paint, seal, or polish.

To make your interior look neat and clean, the first thing to do is get rid of clutter, junk, and damaged or broken items. If you see an item and ask yourself "why is this on my shelf when I wouldn't pay 10 cents for it at a garage sale," it's time to part with it. Getting rid of things is one of the hardest jobs, but you will find it easier to start now than when it is time to pack. Use logic. If you have user manuals to products you don't even own anymore, get rid of them. If you've been hanging on to socks without mates, now is the time to toss them. Throw away all broken or otherwise useless items. Making those crucial decisions about what to keep and what to toss will be easier if you recruit a friend to help.

FACT

It's undisputable: Clutter will detract from the appearance of your home. You may really love to cover every available surface with knick-knacks, but potential buyers want to see your home—not your belongings. Keep a few picture frames, books, and other colorful or interesting items on display, but make sure items look organized and neat.

Once you've gotten rid of unwanted junk, the next way to brighten up your home is to do a thorough cleaning. Clean all the windows, inside and out. Take down drapes and blinds for a thorough cleaning of them as well. Scrub the hard surface floors and the baseboards. Vacuum the carpeted areas. If the carpet has not been cleaned recently, have it professionally cleaned or rent a steam cleaner and do it yourself. Wash all the cabinet faces and clean all the mirrors. Finally, don't forget about the ceilings! Few visitors look up at the ceilings in a home, but buyers might. Clear away all cobwebs and give ceilings a good wipe-down with a damp cloth. This will brighten up a dingy room.

Cleaning the Kitchen

The kitchen is one of the most important rooms in the house. It is the room that can make or break a sale and the one into which you will need to put the most effort. The majority of buyers want to see the inside of cabinets, the oven, and even the dishwasher. They want to see if their dishes and appliances will fit in your kitchen. They also want to see if it is easy to clean. If your cabinets are organized, they will appear spacious and able to accommodate the buyer's things. If the kitchen is clean, it will appear easy to clean.

Start by cleaning out your cabinets and drawers. Doing one or two cabinets at a time will make the job less intimidating. Remove everything from one cabinet or drawer and put it on a table. (If you don't have a table in your kitchen, a card table will do.) This is easier than using the counters and will also keep them clear so you can continue to use the kitchen while you are in the process of getting it ready. Once you have removed everything, wash the interior of the cabinet or drawer and add new shelf paper. Return to the cabinet or drawer only those items you actually need. Box up items you want to keep but do not immediately need. Set the boxes aside for storage and give away or throw away the rest.

Check the dates on your food items. If you have a large pantry with areas that are hard to reach, you may have food in there that is past its expiration date. Throw it out. If there is food that you will not eat and it has not expired, consider donating it to a local charity, such as a homeless shelter, church, or food bank. This isn't something the buyer will notice, but it will empty out the pantry and make it look bigger.

Clean the interior of the oven, the stovetop, and the sink. If you haven't done so already, wash down the fronts of the cabinets and the fronts of the dishwasher, oven, and trash compactor. Clean out the refrigerator and wash the shelves. You should also clean off the front of the refrigerator. It is acceptable to have one or two items under magnets on the front of the refrigerator but avoid having the whole thing covered with kids' artwork and pizza delivery phone numbers.

Remove as many items from the counters as possible. Even decorative canisters should be placed in a cabinet. Having clear counters makes the kitchen look bigger. Carefully caulk the tile around the sink and along the back, where it meets the splash. Remove rugs from the kitchen floor. A rug breaks up the room and makes it look smaller. If you must have rugs in the kitchen, be sure that they are the nonslip type. You do not want someone falling on the kitchen floor.

Keep the trash emptied. Some buyers have a keen nose, and the smell of garbage is a turnoff. It is also best to hide the trash bin in a cabinet, such as the one under the sink. If you do not have room to do this, be sure to have a trash bin with a lid.

QUESTION?

How do you dress up a kitchen table?
If you have a kitchen table, spruce it up with a tablecloth and place settings or a bowl of fruit. If you use real fruit, pay attention to the bottom of the bowl. In most climates, it only takes a few days for the fruit at the bottom to start rotting. Fake fruit might be easier, especially during busy weeks packed with showings.

Take another picture of the kitchen once you have cleaned it. Does it still look shabby? If so, there are a few additional things you can do. If you have wood cabinet faces, wash them with Liquid Gold. If they are painted, a fresh coat of paint may be necessary. New knobs can also dress up your cabinets and make them look fresh again.

Check the light fixture. Are there bugs in it? Clean them out. Be sure to use the brightest bulbs your fixture allows. A bright kitchen is appealing to most people. If the fixture has dark tinted glass, replace it with white frosted glass to make it brighter. If you have fluorescent lights in the kitchen, replace the standard bulbs with full spectrum light bulbs. They give a more natural appearance and quality of light than the harsh glare of the usual fluorescents. If your fluorescent lights are housed in a dropped ceiling or light box, be sure that the plastic covers are not cracked or yellowed. Replace them with the brightest white you can find to allow for maximum light in the room.

Neatening Bedrooms and Closets

Take a moment and evaluate the state of your bedrooms and closets. Chances are these areas contain the most clutter. Is there exercise equipment with clothing hung on it? If so, remove the equipment and store it in the garage. A bedroom should house a bed, dressers, end tables, and lamps. It should not be home to stacks of papers, unused exercise equipment, or an ironing board. Anything that does not belong in the bedrooms should be boxed up and stored. Be sure that the tops of dressers and end tables are empty, except for a lamp, a clock, and maybe the book you are currently reading. Without clutter, the bedroom will look bigger. Be sure that doors can be opened all the way. If there is furniture behind the door, move it or remove it from the room. There should be a path around the bed that can be walked without turning sideways.

Remove everything from your closet and put it on the bed. Create three piles: one to keep, one to give away, and one to throw away. If you are not ready to part with some of the clothing, make two separate piles of things to keep. One pile is for clothing that you wear now, and one is for clothing that you hope to wear again. Pack up the hope-to-wear pile and put it in storage.

If the rod in your closet is sagging, replace it immediately. A sagging closet rod makes it look like there isn't room for clothing. Put back into the closet the clothes that you actually wear. Grouping your clothes according to type (shirts, slacks, skirts, and dresses) will also make the closet look neater and more spacious. Keep the floor of the closet as clear as possible. It is okay to have shoes on the floor in neat rows, but no more stacks of junk.

Tidying Bathrooms

As in the kitchen, clean out the interiors of the cabinets first. Set up a card table and put everything from inside the cabinets and under the sink onto the table. Throw away expired medicines and anything you have not used recently. Wash the interior of the medicine cabinet and wash down the cabinet under the sink and add shelf paper. Replace only those items you actually use; throw everything else away. Keep the counters completely clear, if you can. Leave your toothbrush, toothpaste, and a few toiletries on the counter only if you must. Get rid of any dusty decorative items, such as soaps, potpourri, and flower arrangements.

ALERT!

Clear the shower/tub of all extraneous shampoos and soaps. Keep only those you use. Be sure to remove any mildew with a solution of one part bleach and nine parts water. Wash the glass of the shower enclosure and use something to remove soap scum such as X-19 or Scrubbing Bubbles. Be sure to clean the tracks as well.

Wipe up all the hair with a wet cloth. Be sure the drains run clear and easily; many people will turn on the faucets. If you have stickers in the tub to keep from slipping, be sure that they are not torn or damaged. Remove them with Goo Gone or replace them with stickers that fit over the original torn ones.

Adding Value

Cleaning and getting rid of clutter not only helps you prepare to move, but it also helps your house sell. You can take things a step further by replacing appliances, fixtures, floor tiles, and so on. These replacements will add value to your home. Adding value is just part of what happens when you fix up a house. The other part is creating the appeal that makes your house sell faster. The faster your house sells, the fewer mortgage payments you continue to make. In other words, time is money. There are some bigger improvements you can make that will add value and, depending on the area of the country you are in, are worth the time, effort, and money.

The Kitchen

When selling a house, the room that can make or break it for you is the kitchen. Even people who don't cook find the kitchen to be important. If your kitchen is dated, it can be a turnoff to many buyers, even if it is clean and in working order. They will calculate the cost of updating the kitchen, and if they do make an offer, they will lower it by the cost of a new kitchen. If you are competing against newer homes, an updated kitchen is even more important.

Take a close look at your appliances. Are they gold or green? Is the stove a different color than the dishwasher? How do your cabinets look? Are they worn? Do the doors and drawers open and close properly? If your kitchen looks tired, mismatched, or dated, a renovation can be the difference between a sale and no sale. In many cases, you will get back the money you put into the renovation, and you may even make a profit.

If your kitchen needs attention, make a list of all the appliances you have (don't forget the range hood) and do some comparison shopping. Home improvement stores such as Home Depot, Lowes, and Sears have good bargains on appliances, but you may have a locally owned shop near you that can do as well. If you select all the appliances in the same color and, if possible, the same brand, your kitchen will have continuity. Don't go with the color of the day, stick to timeless white or stainless steel.

Find out if the company you purchase the appliances from will install the new ones and remove the old ones. Unless you are very handy at this sort of thing, you can save the headache of finding someone to do this work, and the appliance company will guarantee it is done correctly.

Most houses sell without the refrigerator, but it is the largest appliance in the kitchen and makes an impression when seen with the others. It will look best if it matches. Though your washer and dryer are also normally excluded from the sale, if they are in the kitchen, be sure they match as well.

Replacing cabinets can be very expensive, but there are ways to keep the costs down. Start with the dimensions of your kitchen and, if possible, a drawing showing their placement. You could go to a cabinet shop and have new cabinets made, but because you want to sell your house, you probably don't want to go through the expense and time involved in getting custom cabinets. Take the drawing and dimensions to the kitchen center of your local home improvement store. They will set up your kitchen in a computer program that can determine which standard cabinets you can use. They may even have some in stock, but if you have to order them, standard cabinets come fairly quickly. Unless you are handy or know a reputable contractor, the home improvement store can coordinate installation. Usually, the simpler the style, the lower the cost. Don't go for lots of specialty features; remember, you are selling your house.

ALERT!

Refacing cabinets may be an acceptable alternative to replacement. Refacing companies put a veneer on the old cabinets, change doors when necessary, and fix up the old cabinets instead of replacing them completely. You can scrub and oil older wood cabinets to freshen them. If you have painted cabinets and don't want to pay the extra money for refacing, a fresh coat of paint and new knobs can make a difference.

When replacing cabinets, the countertops and the kitchen sink will often need to be replaced as well. Once again the rule is to keep it simple. If laminate (such as Formica) is popular in your area, by all means use it. If granite is popular and slab granite is out of the budget, large granite tiles are less expensive and should be acceptable. (A good size would be 12" x 12" or even 18" x 18".) Check with your agent or check out some open houses to see what is the best choice in countertops.

The kitchen sink should match either the appliances or the countertop. The designer who helps you with the kitchen in the home improvement store will be able to give you a good idea of what works with your other choices. With a new sink, you will need a faucet and a garbage disposal as well.

With all this work, you will be without a kitchen for a few weeks. You may want to consider moving a refrigerator, microwave, coffeemaker, and hot plate into the dining room or family room so that you don't have to live on take-out food. You can also barbeque, use a toaster oven, or invite yourself to visit friends and relatives for a few meals.

Check with your local building department to see if you need a permit to upgrade. If it is required, get one. Any nonpermitted work needs to be disclosed. Buyers will be concerned that nonpermitted work was not done to current building codes. This can increase your liability if something was to go wrong after close of escrow (such as an electrical fire).

Bathrooms

The same rules apply for bathrooms as for kitchens. Mauve or turquoise porcelain and frosted swans on the shower door can turn off potential buyers. If your bathrooms look tired, mismatched, or dated, a renovation can be the difference between a sale and no sale. If you have more than one bathroom, renovating a bathroom can be less inconvenient than doing a kitchen. Doing one bathroom at a time will give you the option of using another while there is work in progress.

Start with the master bath. After the kitchen, it is the next most important room for selling a house. Just as you did for the kitchen, create a plan and head back to your home improvement store. This time, rather than appliances, you will make a list of fixtures. Measure the cabinet(s) you have now. Also measure from the edge of the wall to the centerline of the sink or to the centerline of each sink, if you have more than one. The home improvement store will need this information when determining which standard cabinets work for you. As with the kitchen, keep it simple and keep the colors neutral.

Landscaping

Although they may make your home sell faster, landscaping features do not usually bring you more money. However, crabgrass lawns and muddy areas can be transformed to give your house curb appeal. Begin by creating a plan for the landscaping. Because you want to get your house on the market as soon as possible, it is best to lay sod instead of using grass seed. Plant large trees instead of seedlings and plant blooming flowers instead of using seeds. Find out if the nursery or home improvement store you use has a return policy. If larger trees and shrubs die within the first thirty days, you want to be able to return them for healthier plants.

Additions and Windows

Adding on to the house when you are planning to sell may seem like a daunting task, but there are a few items that can be worth the effort. In the front, adding or expanding a deck can give your house fresh curb appeal. In the back, it can give better access to the yard and create a space for entertaining. If you live in an area where it snows and you don't have a garage, adding a garage can actually pay for itself in many cases.

QUESTION?

What if I like my house after doing all this work and decide not to sell?
After preparing their house for sale, some sellers discover that it isn't such a bad house after all. If you don't have to sell, you may decide to keep the house or just to enjoy it for one more year. Re-evaluate your initial reasons for selling and decide if they are still valid.

If you have single pane windows, changing to dual pane windows can attract a buyer who would not otherwise look at your house. With energy costs going up every year, many buyers are concerned about energy-efficient homes and will not even consider a home that does not have dual pane windows. Call at least two different glass companies to get quotes for replacement to dual pane. If you decide that the expense is beyond your budget, you can at least share these quotes with potential buyers.

Chapter 12

Staging Your House for Sale

Think of each room of your house as a stage for the buyer to view. In order to set the stage, review the pictures you took while reading Chapter 11. As you do, go through your house one room at a time. Do the doors open and close easily? Do you have to squeeze past anything to get into or around the room? Are the countertops clear? Is it perilous to open the closets for fear something may fall on you? Take note of all problems and take action to fix them.

Storage Areas

Good storage is one of the most important features of a home to many buyers. Buying in bulk, saving family heirlooms, keeping the children's furniture and toys for the next child, sports equipment, and all the paraphernalia of the modern lifestyle make ample storage a necessity. If your storage areas are full, a buyer's perception will be that there is not room for his things. You may not have everything organized. After years in a house, people seldom do. It is possible that you have not even moved some of the boxes in these storage areas since you moved into your house. You may have empty boxes from things that you purchased, such as a microwave or stereo. You may even be saving empty boxes from items you no longer own. The point is you probably have more storage room than a buyer can see. Rationally, a buyer knows that he does not have to fit into the house with you there. But subconsciously, he cannot imagine where things will go.

FACT

If there is a lot of stuff in your storage areas, buyers will worry that it will be impossible for you to move. They picture you dragging everything up the stairs from the basement or down from the attic, and they worry that you will not be up to the task. They may not want to inconvenience you by making an offer.

It is time to get rid of stuff. The easiest way to do this is locate an open area near the storage area into which you can empty the stored contents. This will allow you to completely empty the storage area and get it ready for a buyer's viewing.

If some of the areas you need to clean out are large areas with lots of stored items, start with a small closet. Take everything out of the closet and put it in the middle of the room or on a table or bed. It is easier work in an open space than to sort items directly from a closet. One item at a time, sort through the things to create five different categories.

- **Keep for immediate use:** Those things that you need on a daily basis.
- **Pack for the new house:** Holiday decorations, photo albums, and things you want to keep but do not need immediately.
- **Pack for storage:** Financial records, sentimental items, such as the kids' school work or gifts from special people, and other things you want to keep but at which you rarely look.
- **Give away:** Outdated or ill-fitting clothing and things in good condition that you don't need anymore.
- **Throw away:** Broken appliances, games with missing parts, and other things you can't figure out why you own.

Once you have sorted everything, it is time to box up or bag up what you are not using immediately. Bag up the give-away and throw-away piles and get them out of the house immediately. Don't wait for a full carload before you go to the thrift store or a full truckload before you go to the dump. You can make more than one trip; if you have lived in your house a long time, you will probably make several trips. By getting rid of things a little bit at a time, you will keep the job from seeming like it will go on forever.

If you discover that your throw-away pile is going to be larger than expected, consider ordering a dumpster. In this way, you can fill the dumpster and avoid multiple trips to the dump. This is a good idea for those who have done multiple construction projects around the house. Chances are you have kept scraps of wood and other items that you will not need again.

It is hard to get rid of things that seem to have some value. A scrap of wood or a bit of pipe that might be useful in a future project may seem like a treasure to you, but it is just junk to the next person. Unless you have use for it immediately, get rid of it.

Make a small stack of boxes in the corner of the room that are packed for the new house or for storage. These boxes will be moved later; don't make them too heavy. Label each box to show what it contains. It is helpful if the boxes are all about the same size. This makes stacking easier, and they will look more organized. Paint or at least wash down the interior of the closet and neatly replace the things you will need immediately.

Once you have tackled the closets, move on to the basement or attic. In bigger spaces like this, it is easier to move things a little at a time. Create a staging area where you can make your piles. By moving things to one side or the other, you can set up a table to sort smaller items. If this is not possible, you may want to bring things out of the basement or attic, one armload at a time, and create a sorting space in a larger room such as the living room or family room. Make the same categories you used for the closet and start sorting. When you have created some space, rearrange and continue sorting. Paint or wash down the empty areas as you go. Once you have a decent amount of free space, you can start putting back into place those things you will use immediately.

The last thing to tackle is the garage. It would be nice to show the buyer that there is room for a car. Move everything out of the garage and onto the driveway. Sort by category, as you did in the other areas of the house, and stack boxes for the new house and the boxes for storage in one of the corners. Go back to your temporary storage areas and bring the boxes for the new house and for storage, adding them to the garage as well. Now you have everything in one place, organized and ready to move. By using the garage as the main storage area, you will have an easier time of packing the moving van. More importantly, the buyer can see what type of storage they have available.

Make It Their House—Not Yours

Once you put your house on the market, it is no longer your home—it is just a house. It needs to be viewed as a product for sale. Any other person who views the house should have the ability to see himself living there. To make it look less like your personal home, put away or pack up as many personal things as possible. With a critical buyer's eye, look around the house to see what makes it personal.

Photographs are among the most personal items you may have on display. The top of a piano, built-in bookcases, walls of a hallway, and walls bordering a staircase are notorious places for swarms of personal photos. If you have a lot of photographs of family and friends, pack some up. If you remove hanging items, be sure to patch and paint the walls.

ALERT!

Many families have portraits of ancestors in their homes. Although these portraits may connect you to the past, they might make other people uncomfortable. Unfamiliar, stern faces peering down from the wall could scare a buyer off. Think of it as an excuse to get a head start on your packing and put these items in storage while you're showing.

If this depersonalization proves overwhelming, don't remove all photos. A little personalization will help you through this stressful time and may even allow the buyer to relate to you in some way: "My granddaughter was a pumpkin for Halloween, too" or "We went there on vacation last year." Just don't get carried away. No one is exactly like you, and relating is easier with only one or two photos than with a wall full of photos. You want to let the buyer visualize himself in your home.

Once you pack up your personal things, your home may seem empty. It may not even seem like your home. That is good! It isn't your home anymore. This allows buyers to fill up the spaces with their own personal things and visualize themselves there. Give them the ability to truly make it their home and you will have a sale.

An Extra Touch

When it comes to selling your house, the little things really can make a big difference. Having the table set, as mentioned in Chapter 11, gives the impression that a buyer is in a model home. Once you have cleared off the bedside tables completely, a book and a pair of reading glasses will add a special touch. Light a fire in the fireplace with a few pieces of wood and some kindling or large pinecones. A vase of flowers on an empty coffee table or a stack of oversized coffee table books will add a homey touch to the living room.

FACT

Everyone knows that items like toothpaste, soap, and cotton swabs belong in a bathroom, but that doesn't mean potential buyers necessarily want to see these things in your house when they view it. Hide all personal hygiene items, but replace them with attractive accent pieces like bud vases, candles, or nice bottles of perfumed hand lotion.

More than staging, a clean, uncluttered environment creates the biggest impact. Cluttered table displays and sprawling collections of figurines may give you pleasure, but to a buyer, it is just one more thing blocking the image of the house as his future home.

Pets and Other Distractions

Pets are just one of the distractions that a buyer may encounter when looking at your home. As discussed in Chapter 3, having your pets out of the house is the best way to prevent that distraction. Believe it or not, having you out of the house is as important as having the pets out of the house. To a buyer, your mere presence reinforces the fact that this house is your home and not his. You may be lounging comfortably in your slippers, or you may be working away in your home office. But either way, your house stays your home in the mind of the buyer.

ESSENTIAL

It's important not to have any visits from friends, family, or service providers interrupt a showing of your house. These interruptions will distract and discomfort the buyer. To avoid this, be sure to keep your schedule clear of visitors, and ask friends and family not to drop by without a phone call during this time.

Children are also a distraction. There are times when you cannot be away from home but as an adult you understand how to stay out of the way of the buyer and their agent. Children have a more difficult time with this. It may be hard for them to sell their home, or they may be proud of it and want to show the buyers. This behavior is cute, but it may make the buyers feel like this is not a house in which they can picture themselves. Talk with the children and find something for them to do when buyers are viewing your house. As strange as it sounds to parents, there are actually people who don't like children or are uncomfortable around them.

Dealing with Smells and Stains

Getting rid of nasty smells and stains may sound obvious, but you might be surprised. Some stains have been there for so long that you don't even see them. If it is possible to remove them, do so. If not, you may want to cover them with a throw rug or a plant. Smells are not as detectable as you think. Most people are immune to the scent of their own home and are not always aware that it might offend other people.

FACT

A scent many people cannot tolerate is the smell of mothballs. If you use mothballs, it may be time to switch to cedar shavings. Cedar is a natural moth repellent and has a much more natural, refreshing scent than mothballs.

One big offender is cigarette smoke. Smoke penetrates the drapes, carpet, and furniture. Over the years, it can even penetrate the woodwork and leave a film of odor on walls. Remove and clean all the ashtrays and evidence of smoking. If you still want to smoke, try to do it outside. If you cannot smoke outside due to the weather, smoke at an open window or door. This will not be ideal since smoke will travel back into the house, but it will be an improvement. Have the drapes and carpet professionally cleaned. Use a product like Febreze on your upholstery. Wash down the walls and woodwork with Pine-Sol or Lysol. Even if you smoke only in one area of the house, the smell of smoke will permeate every room. Wash windows and open them. Try to keep the house as aired out as possible. Do not use cover-up scents; they usually make the smoke smell stronger.

If you do all of these things and still have a problem, check an industrial cleaning supply house for odor-neutralizing "bombs." They have formulations designed specifically for smoke odors that work in the same manner as pest control bombs. You close up the house, set them off, and leave the premises for a couple of hours while the gas penetrates and does its work.

Old cooking odors can also be a distraction. Wash down the walls of the kitchen to be sure they are free of grease. Keep the fan running while you cook and be sure to keep the garbage can emptied. Last night's fish really does smell like last night's fish!

QUESTION?

I cleaned and painted, and now my house smells like cleaners and paint! What should I do?

These smells do dissipate fairly quickly, but keep doors and windows open for a faster recovery. Be sure that cleaning supplies and paint cans are covered securely and stored away. Remember, the smell of paint and cleaning products is better than the smell of dirt and neglect.

The smell of mold is a certain turnoff to buyers, but it can also mean that there may be a problem. Don't leave damp towels in the bathroom. Rather than reusing them, you may have to wash towels more often, because the smell of damp towels can mimic that of mold. Be sure to wash down all wet areas with a solution of one part bleach to nine parts water to keep mold from forming.

As mentioned earlier, most people are immune to the scent of their own home and are not aware that it may have an odor that could offend other people. It's very important to be aware of this when selling the home of an elderly person. When an older person has lived in their home for a long time, often with declining health and vitality, the home can fall into disrepair. Along with this unintentional neglect, a home can develop stagnant odors that elicit thoughts of aging and even death in the buyer's mind. If this is your dad's house, you may be used to the scent and therefore unaware of it. You'd be wise to ask a friend to come over and do a "smell check." To treat this odor problem, use the methods previously outlined for cigarette smoke.

Older people may not have the energy to do general cleaning as often as they once did. Being sure that sheets are changed regularly, towels are washed frequently, and laundry is done daily will keep the house smelling fresh. If it is your home and you don't have the energy to do this anymore, have your kids help you or hire a service while your house is on the market.

Staging an Empty House

If you have already moved, you will still need to stage your house to make it feel inviting. In many areas of the country, a furnished house sells better than an unfurnished one. If you are not living there, you may have to sell your house without the benefit of furniture for showings. Some buyers are not able to visualize how furniture can be placed in a room; this is where your photographs can come in handy. Set them on the kitchen counter so the buyer can get an idea of how the house would look furnished.

When selling an empty house, it is very important that it is extremely clean. If it looks like someone just moved out, it looks tired, and it also looks like a bargain. After moving out, you will notice that a fresh coat of paint is probably needed. Don't leave wires dangling where the speakers were. Don't leave nails and picture hangers on the wall; remove them, patch, and paint. There should not be any trash in or around the house. Set the stage as if the house was brand-new. Make it look as though no one has ever lived there. Clean the carpets and put down some plastic runners. Clean windows, kitchen, and baths will make the house more appealing.

The minimum requirements for an empty house are toilet paper in every bathroom, working utilities, and heat or air-conditioning (depending on the season) to keep the house comfortable when being viewed. Also, keep the landscaping maintained in the summer and the ice and snow cleared away in the winter.

If you are in an area where a furnished house sells better, you may wish to leave some furniture until the house sells. A well-placed table and chairs with a tablecloth and a setting of dishes can be enough to fill the whole dining room. In the master bedroom, a bed and a bedside table can be enough. You don't have to leave your own bed; a nicely dressed air mattress will do the trick. By adding a lamp and a book to the bedside table, the sense that someone could live there is maintained. Towels in the bathroom and a little dish of decorative soaps, a wreath on the front door, and a bowl of fruit on the kitchen counter will all give the illusion that the house can be a home.

If necessary, additional staging can be done by a professional. These professionals are usually trained in decorating or other staging arts, such as Feng Shui. If, after you think the house is ready, you see that more should be done but are not sure what to do, you may want to hire a staging expert. These professionals can rearrange things, add things, and take things away to make your house more appealing to the majority of buyers.

Chapter 13

Pricing Your House to Sell

Pricing your house is one of the most important steps you will take to get it sold. If your house is priced right, it will sell. You have already read about how to maximize that price by making the necessary modifications to the condition. Now you need to discover exactly what that price is. The right price is the highest price that a buyer will pay for your property within the time frame desired for selling your house.

A Certified Appraisal

To get a certified appraisal, it is necessary to hire a professional real estate appraiser. Most states require a real estate appraiser to learn the trade by taking specific classes and apprenticing under a licensed appraiser for a set period of time. The appraiser becomes licensed after the state requirements are met. An appraiser ought to be a disinterested third party who has no connection in the real estate transaction. He should not be related to the buyer, the seller, or either of their real estate companies. The appraiser may be an independent contractor or work for the bank. The lender may hire an independent contractor to appraise properties requiring a loan. If there is no loan involved, the buyer might still request an appraisal to be comfortable with the value of the house.

Lenders use the results of a real estate appraisal to determine their exposure when lending on a piece of property. When the appraisal shows that the property is worth at least what the buyer has offered, the lender can be more confident about making a loan on the property. Based on the appraisal and the down payment, the lender can establish the buyer's initial equity in the property. If the buyer has sufficient equity, the lender can be assured that the buyer will probably not default on the loan. If the lender does receive the property back through a foreclosure or other proceeding, an adequate appraisal amount insures that they will be able to sell the property quickly for an amount sufficient to cover or exceed the original loan amount.

FACT

An appraisal is one of the ways a buyer, seller, or lender can determine the value of the property. Buyers and sellers rely on the appraisal to be sure the property is priced correctly, but it is of primary concern to a lender.

Types of Appraisals

There are three basic types of appraisals: Sales Comparison Approach, Cost Approach, and Income Capitalization Approach. It is also possible for an appraiser to combine two or more of these types for a more detailed appraisal. Some lenders require a blended appraisal to be sure that the value is the same using different approaches. If one approach shows a considerably higher value than another, it is cause for concern.

Sales Comparison Approach

This is the most common type of appraisal for residential properties. The appraiser uses the sold prices of recently sold properties (called comparables) to determine the value of the subject property. The appraiser usually chooses between three and five similar properties to compare to the subject property. None of these will be an exact match since every property has its own unique features.

When locating comparable properties, everything counts. Even in a condominium complex, where every unit is alike, there are minor differences that affect value. The location of the unit, the direction it faces, the view, the interior condition, and upgrades make it necessary to adjust for each comparable property, even if it is only slightly.

The appraiser will make adjustments for each comparable property to create a list of properties that are as equal as possible to each other. For example, a house with a fireplace could be compared to a house without a fireplace after an adjustment is made for the value of the fireplace. This adjustment may be greater in the colder areas of the country where a fireplace is expected and may be lesser in the warmer areas of the country where a fireplace is used more for decoration.

An appraiser photographs the subject property and each of the comparable properties and also provides a map showing the location of each property. The appraiser also creates a side-by-side comparison table listing the properties with their features. The table shows the adjustments for each line item and the total adjustments on the appraisal.

When using comparable properties, most of the adjustments will be relatively small. The amount of an adjustment varies from region to region and among different appraisers. When an appraiser needs to make large adjustments to verify a price, it can be a red flag to the lender that there is something wrong with the price of the property.

Cost Approach

This type of appraisal is determined by calculating what it would cost to replace the house as it sits on the property today. The appraiser takes into account the land value and the cost of the improvements separately. Improvements include the house and any other structures, such as out buildings, a guesthouse, or a detached garage. He then places a depreciation value on the improvements to come up with a final value. Depreciation is traditionally not calculated on the value of the land; it is only calculated on the value of the improvements.

FACT

Many appraisers will combine the Sales Comparison Approach with the Cost Approach, especially in markets where there are very few comparable properties or where many of the properties are newer.

Depreciation is a lessening of the value of the improvements based on wear and tear, obsolescence of certain features, and age of the improvements. If the house was built before the out buildings, guesthouse, or garage, the depreciation may be factored differently for the different structures.

Income Capitalization Approach

This approach is rarely used for single-family homes. It is used more often for rental properties. If your home is in an area made up primarily of rentals, the income capitalization approach may be used or it may be used in conjunction with one or more of the other approaches. This calculation usually takes longer since the appraiser needs to determine what the average capitalization rate (CAP rate) is in your area before determining your value. They do this by taking the sale prices of similar homes that are also rentals and dividing them by the annual net rental income. This gives the appraiser the CAP rate.

For example: Assuming rents of $1,650 per month, less expenses of $150 per month, gives a total rental income of $1,500 per month (or $18,000 per year).

If the sales price of a comparable property is $240,000, that amount is divided by the $18,000 annual rental income to determine the CAP rate of 7.5 percent.

To determine the value of your property, an appraiser would divide your annual net rents by 7.5 percent.

For example: Assuming rents of $1,800 per month, less expenses of $135 per month, your total rental income is $1,665 per month (or $19,980 per year).

Taking the $19,980 and dividing it by the 7.5 percent CAP rate gives you a value of $266,400.

ALERT!

If a buyer is purchasing your home as an investment and has signed a lease with a tenant to commence at close of escrow or is taking over an existing lease, some lenders will count the rental income as part of the buyer's income. If this is the case, the lender may require the Income Capitalization Approach to be used as a part of the appraisal.

Who Provides and Pays for an Appraisal?

In general, the bank or another lender will provide an appraisal since this information is most valuable to them. In the case of an estate sale, where an appraisal is needed to determine value at the time of death, the estate or the heirs will purchase an appraisal. Except in rare cases, the bank will not use this appraisal. The bank will want its own appraisal with the most current comparable sales. If a seller has recently refinanced, he may show prospective buyers his appraisal to prove the house is priced competitively. However, the bank cannot use that appraisal either. Some FSBO sellers will also purchase a certified appraisal to show prospective buyers that the property is priced competitively. While appraisals have their place, most buyers and sellers rely on the real estate agent's comparative market analysis (CMA), described later in this chapter.

Although the bank usually hires the appraiser, the buyer typically pays for the cost of the appraisal. The cost is commonly in the $300 to $400 range. For larger homes or more complicated properties, it can be considerably higher. With some loan programs, such as VA loans, it may be necessary for the seller to pay the cost of the appraisal. In the purchase contract, be sure to clarify who is responsible for paying for the appraisal.

Why and When to Get an Appraisal

A certified appraisal will give you a good picture of what a bank believes your house is worth. If you are hoping to price aggressively, it can also help by allowing you to state "priced below recent appraisal" in your advertising. If you do this, you can give a copy of the appraisal to any potential buyers. A certified appraisal will include the dimensions of the house and its square footage, which allows you to post an accurate square footage in the MLS or on your flyer.

When lenders require a certified appraisal, they usually make the necessary arrangements. However, there are situations when it is wise to contract for an appraisal yourself. If you are selling a property you inherit (see Chapter 21), you will want to get an appraisal as of the date of death of the person from whom you inherited. If you are selling the home as a result of divorce or other splitting of the parties who own the property, an appraisal can help determine value. This is especially helpful if one party is buying out the other party. With a divorce or the dissolution of a partnership that owns a house together, each party may elect to get his own appraisal. They will then choose a disinterested third party (often the judge in a divorce case) to come up with a determination of value based on these appraisals.

A Comparative Market Analysis (CMA)

While it can also help you to determine value, a CMA is not an appraisal. It will usually include things that an appraisal rarely includes, but it does not adhere to all the guidelines a licensed appraiser must follow.

While most appraisals are based on sales prices, a CMA takes the competition into account as well. In other words, the asking price of comparable homes is also used to determine value. If prices were based on sale prices alone, homes would never increase in value. Therefore, a CMA takes the supply and demand factor into account. If there are very few properties available that can compete with yours, your value will go up.

The CMA also uses the prices of comparable properties that did not sell, known in real estate jargon as *expireds*. If there are a lot of expired properties, it means that the market is tough on a seller. Your value may actually be lower than the recent sales.

Some people are more comfortable with a CMA because it factors in the growth or decline of a market. Lenders do not use CMAs because an interested party to the transaction initially performs them.

There are times when an appraisal needs to be verified by another party. In this case, the lender may ask a nonparticipating agent for a CMA (called a Broker's Price Opinion or BPO). This CMA will either prove or disprove what the appraisal has stated. If it is dramatically different, the lender may require a new appraisal or may turn down the loan.

Who Provides and Pays for a CMA?

A CMA is generally provided either by your real estate agent or the agent for the buyer. When planning to sell your house, your agent will determine the value through a CMA. A buyer's agent may also provide a CMA to show her buyer what your house is worth. Because comparable properties are never an exact match, values produced in CMAs can vary within a range. Your agent's CMA may be in the higher range, while the buyer's agent may provide a CMA to justify a lower offering price.

FACT

In general, a real estate agent will provide a CMA as a free service. They often use it as a marketing tool to solicit your business, and they do not expect to be paid. Your agent may do several CMAs during the time your house is on the market as changes in the market occur. This will allow you to be sure your home is priced correctly.

Some real estate agents will inflate the value of your house in order to get your business. They want to please you and will try to prove a value based on the value that you desire, rather than a more realistic value. They may use comparable properties that are not truly comparable, or they may not make adjustments when they should. This is known as *buying the listing*. Agents do this for a number of reasons.

- They may want to please you and hope you will hire them based on the value they assign the property, rather than their qualifications as an agent.
- Even if the property is overpriced, they may want the advertising opportunity that listing your home would provide in order to get buyers to call them.
- They may know they are pricing too high initially and are hoping they will be able to convince you to reduce your price once they have you under a listing contract.
- They may honestly believe that if they work hard enough that the property will sell for the escalated price. This belief is usually borne of inexperience, either in real estate in general or in the area or type of home you have.

When you interview agents, note the different values they place on your property. If one value is considerably higher than the others, consider that this is wishful thinking on the part of the real estate agent or you. To prevent this as much as possible, it is wise to allow the agent to determine the value without telling them your hopes for the asking price. If an agent asks you what price you think the property should be marketed at, ask them to come up with a value first. After all, they are the professionals.

Why and When to Get a CMA

A good CMA can give you an authentic determination of value and show what the market is doing at the time you place your home for sale. For example, if homes are not selling and dropping off the market after a period of time, you can adjust your price to keep from being one of them. If homes are selling quickly and there is no competition for the type of home you have, you can take advantage of the market and get a higher price than the prices of properties that have already sold. It is a rare thing to get so much value in something that has no cost attached to it.

Get a CMA as soon as you decide to sell your house. You may even want to get two. Ask for a CMA as soon as you decide to place your home on the market and have another done after making any improvements to prepare your home for sale. Don't be dismayed if the value doesn't change after making improvements. Even if they don't increase the actual value, they will make the home sell faster. Having a sale now, instead of six months from now, has a value of six months' holding costs. This is known as the *time value of money*. A lot can happen in six months. National or local changes in the economic climate could adversely affect the value of your property. The future holds the unknown, which makes a quicker sale a better sale.

The Importance of Proper Pricing

Pricing the home correctly is the most important thing a seller can do. Price is a primary factor for most homebuyers, and they often will not even inquire about properties beyond their range. To ensure that the most potential buyers see your home, it's important that your price is in line with the competition. An overpriced home will not sell, and worse, it will get stale. Because buyers are concerned about how long a house has been on the market, a stale house will not usually sell, even after reducing it to the correct price.

Here's an example: A couple had their house on the market for more than three years. When they first put it up for sale, they told their agent they would not sell for less than $250,000, due to the custom features they had added to the house. Although their value was about $175,000, the agent agreed to price it at $250,000. After six months, the house had not sold, and they decided their agent wasn't doing a good job. They switched agents and dropped the price to $225,000. As time marched on, the couple changed real estate agents and dropped the price every six months.

After three years, values in the area increased, and their value increased as well. The house was now worth about $180,000, but the couple was only asking $170,000. They were sick of being on the market. They had left the area and wanted the house sold right now. The problem was that they were very stale. Every buyer who went through the house wanted to know why it had been on the market so long. Every buyer was afraid that if they needed to sell in the future that it would take three years. The couple finally received an offer of $150,000. They countered at $160,000 and settled for $155,000. If they had priced their house at $175,000 to start with, they would have saved three years and $20,000!

Often a seller will want a particular price for his house. This price is not based on the price of similar sold properties or on the competition. It is based on what the seller needs or wants to move forward into another piece of property. The market does not care what a seller needs or wants; it only cares what the value is. If you are pricing based on expectations rather than realities, you can wait a long time for a buyer.

ALERT!

Some sellers price their homes based on a false perception of the market. They will not believe that homes like theirs are not selling for the price they want, even if it is proved to them with an appraisal or a CMA. They believe that their homes are unique and special, and that a buyer will come along who is willing to pay their price.

There are also sellers who put a price tag on nostalgia. Whether they are aware of it or not, they believe that their memories have a value and that their home needs to be priced to take those memories into account.

Another type of seller believes that "a sucker is born every minute." They hold that some person, uneducated in the area's market values, will fall in love with their house and pay what they are asking, without regard for the true value of the property. While it is doubtful this would actually happen, if it did happen, that buyer may get a reality check when the lender's appraiser cannot prove the value.

By pricing your house too high, you are secretly sabotaging the sale. If you are not ready to price your house correctly, you are probably not really ready to sell. You may be in a position where you have to sell but you may not want to sell. If you are not really ready, it may be best to wait. The couple in the earlier example had their house on the market for three years before they were really ready. They wound up having to dump their house, which is much worse than just waiting and not placing your house on the market at all.

Chapter 14

Marketing Your House

There are many avenues available to market your house. If you have an agent, she has discovered what works best for her and will use that knowledge to your benefit. If you are an FSBO, you will be engaging in some trial and error. Choosing the best advertising methods for your property may feel like a guessing game, but understanding how each method works will help you make the right marketing decisions.

Print Advertising

Print advertising is a primary component of your marketing plan, and there are many local, regional, and national publications available for real estate print ads. Some publications are specific to the real estate market; others are more general. All of them can be useful depending on your situation.

Local Newspaper

For more than one hundred years, the most popular form of advertising has been the local newspaper. Although it has lost some of its appeal as newer forms of advertising become available, there is still a need for newspaper advertising. The cost is relatively inexpensive in a regional newspaper, such as those geared toward smaller towns or specific suburbs of a large city.

Many local papers have a real estate section with articles and ads related specifically to real estate. This section of the paper is not printed every day; it usually comes out a few times a week or, at the least, on Sunday. Those who want to advertise in the paper can purchase a display ad or a classified ad that specifically targets homebuyers. Many potential buyers check the real estate section to see if any new properties have come on the market, so this should be a part of your marketing plan. Many real estate offices purchase a full page to advertise their listings. There is usually a section for individual display ads, as well as a classified section.

FACT

Believe it or not, a newspaper ad must be viewed by someone eight times to be remembered. This does not mean it will not be noticed the first time, but don't be surprised if your ad runs for awhile before you see a measurable response.

As an FSBO, you will probably want to use the classified section. Be sure your property is listed in the subsection of the area where you live so that it does not end up in general real estate. This will give you the best chance of having it read by your potential buyer.

Display ads are usually larger, more prominent, and more expensive than classified ads. A display ad is what real estate agents use to get the phone to ring. Agents' display ads are usually designed to sell more than one piece of property, even if only one piece of property is featured in the ad. The property they feature may not be your property, but it gets buyers interested enough to call.

Some buyers also use the newspaper like a catalog and call their agent when a new property appears in a display ad, even if it is listed with another office. For this reason, even if your agent is not sure he can sell your property by advertising in the paper, he will place an ad in case it is seen by another agent's buyer.

Depending on the cost of ads, some agents will group a number of properties together in the classified section under the heading of their office. By doing this, they only mention the office once and have more room to advertise as many houses as possible.

Big City Newspaper

Advertising in the classified section of a big city newspaper can be very expensive. Unless your ad stands out, you could be lost in the sea of classifieds that they provide. Placing an ad in a big city paper can work well if you have a very special property, but it is usually not effective for the average home.

A special property is usually a home designed by a well-known architect, such as Frank Lloyd Wright, or one that is on the National Historical Registry. Other examples of a special property include large estates or homes that were once owned by famous people. Your "special house" may not qualify under these criteria.

National newspapers such as *The Wall Street Journal* and *USA Today* can be classified as big city newspapers. They can attract buyers to your property but at a cost that may not make it worth the expense. There are regional editions of national newspapers. For example, you could advertise in the

West Coast section only, which may give you a more affordable option if you want to go this route.

Classified-Ad-Only-Newspaper

Some classified-ad-only newspapers are great for selling cars and furniture, but they don't capture the real estate market. The ad prices are reasonable, but they don't always have an extensive real estate category. Check your local classified-only paper to see how many real estate ads they have. If there are several, this might be a good publication. If you don't find any real estate ads, you may want to skip it.

Local Real Estate Magazine

Glossy magazines such as *Homes and Land* and *The Real Estate Guide* are known nationally, but editions are produced regionally. They do not usually allow FSBO advertising out of courtesy to their real estate customers, who typically pay for the magazine. If she has found it effective in your marketplace, your agent will place an ad in this type of publication. If these ads are unreasonably expensive in your area, the agent may know of other homebuyers' guides that will work for you.

Nationwide Glossy Magazine

These magazines, such as *Distinctive Homes,* show properties from all over the country. They look like coffee table books. Most of the homes in them are very expensive, and so is the cost of advertising in them. If you have an expensive property, you may want to have your agent check into these publications.

FACT

Your agent probably has a budget for advertising and uses those funds in the area she finds to be most effective. If you want to advertise in a medium that she wouldn't normally use and that exceeds her budget, you may want to pay for it yourself. You can also negotiate to pay a portion of it and be reimbursed, up to a certain amount, upon the sale of your property.

Some offices will purchase a page or two in a glossy publication and divide up the page to feature about eight houses. Each agent has the opportunity to place a house in the ad on a prorated basis. If your agent's office does this, you can get additional exposure, even if you have a budget property.

Flyers and Signs

If you are working with a real estate agent, she will probably elect to create a professional flyer for you. This is the best choice since she knows which features of your house should be emphasized and also the type of information potential buyers expect from a flyer. If you are selling yourself and need to create the flyer, check flyer boxes at other homes for sale to see what the competition is doing. A flyer will always have at least one picture of your property (more pictures if your property is photogenic), the asking price, a list of some or all of the features of your home, and the contact information for your agent. If you are an FSBO, be sure to include contact information for yourself with day and evening phone numbers or a cellular phone number. With all the computer programs available, digital photos, and quality photo paper, it is easier than ever to create professional-looking flyers.

FACT

Driving around looking for signs used to be the way most buyers started their search. While they often begin on the Internet now, many buyers still do the driving around as well. Adding a flyer box to your for sale sign post will allow buyers to learn a little more about the house before calling you, your agent, or the agent with which they are working.

Your agent will know if there is a sign ordinance in your county. If you are an FSBO, you may want to check with the local government authorities. Some sign ordinances limit the size of a real estate sign, its location on the property, and/or the color scheme. Be sure that you have the maximum size sign allowed by ordinance. If you can, get a two-sided sign so it can be seen driving up or down the street. If you live in a condominium or other property with a homeowner's association, check their rules and regulations. Some associations do not allow any signs at all, and some allow small window signs only.

The MLS and the Internet

The MLS is the most valuable tool a real estate agent has available. They use it to search for properties for a prospective buyer and to determine the value of the properties they find. As soon as a new property is listed with an agent who belongs to the MLS, it is entered into the system. At that point, every member of the MLS has access to the information on that property. If your agent does not belong to the MLS, you are losing out on the ability to draw other agents to your home. FSBOs cannot post their properties in the MLS, but a full-service office and certain discount offices can.

Be sure your agent posts as many pictures of your home as possible on the MLS. This will help trigger the memory of the other agents and will also transfer to the Internet sites more effectively.

If your home is in the MLS, chances are it is automatically on the Internet as well. Check with your agent to see if this is the case with the MLS to which they belong. According to the National Association of Realtors®, more than 90 percent of all home buyers start their search on the Internet, which makes it an important part of your marketing plan.

Posting the maximum number of photos allowed by the Internet site plus a virtual tour will help sell your house. A virtual tour is a 360 degree view of several key rooms in your house. If your house is not presentable from all 360 degrees, a slide show can be just as effective. Most potential buyers will actually skip over houses without a photo or with only one photograph, especially in an area where there are a lot of homes for sale.

As an FSBO, there are Internet sites where you can post your property for sale. Some of these sites are advertising sites only, and some are run by what would be considered very discounted brokerages. (See Chapter 9 for more on discount brokerages.) There is an up-front cost to post on these sites. There may also be a time commitment where you are expected to pay for the advertising for several months or more. Consider this as you plan your advertising budget.

Many agents have their own personal Web sites, Web sites for their offices, and Web sites for their franchise, if they belong to one. Your home will be advertised on these sites as well as *www.Realtor.com* for MLS properties. They may have your home advertised on a newspaper's Internet site, as well as on the Internet site for the pertinent glossy magazines. The more places your home is located on the Internet, the better chance it has of being found.

If you are an FSBO, you may want to consider creating your own Web page or having a service design one for you. Most services have a template site, where they can just fill in the blanks. Once you sell your house, be sure to remove it from all the Internet sites where you advertise. Some Internet sites will not remove your ad automatically, and you could be out there for years to come.

ALERT!

The very discounted brokerages can get you posted into *www.Realtor. com*, but it may not be worth the expense. These companies may place you on an MLS that is not in your region; thus, you pay for advertising with no chance of results. Be sure to spend some time on their sites, researching as if you were a buyer, before you spend money for a posting.

If your agent is a Realtor®, he will be able to have all his MLS listings posted to *www.Realtor.com*. The largest site that homebuyers use when searching the Internet for a home is *www.Realtor.com*. With more than 1 million members of the National Association of Realtors®, Realtor.com is well managed and offers additional benefits to members. Some Realtors® will get homes advertised on a featured page, which comes up first when searching in a region. They can also have flyers and other advertising formatted through Realtor.com so that it all works together.

Open House

Getting people into your house is the first step in getting it sold, but not all open houses actually sell your house. There are two kinds of open houses, one for agents and one for the general public. It is best to have your agent hold an open house for other agents in the community. Chances are that they coordinate these types of open houses regularly. There is usually one day, every week or two, when agents tour new properties for sale. If you know that there will be several other homes on the tour that day, you may want to offer an incentive to agents who show up. This can be a simple thing, such as offering some snacks or a drawing for lunch at a popular restaurant. The tour for agents is the most productive open house you will have. Agents will remember your house better and think of it when they have a potential buyer if they have seen it in person rather than in a print-out from the MLS.

FACT

The general public open house is less likely to produce a buyer. You can expect the neighbors, especially those you don't know, because they are curious about your home. You may have a few people who are just looking, and you will have your share of folks who go to every open house just for fun. The open house can also produce leads for your agent but not necessarily buyers for your house.

If you are an FSBO and holding open houses on your own, there are a few safety tips to consider. Be sure that several of your friends know you are holding an open house. (Agents who hold open houses let their office know that they are holding one.) Have your friends check in on you, by stopping by or calling. Don't hold the open house too late in the day; you want to be closed up at least one hour before dark. Ask everyone who views the house to sign your guest book, giving their name and phone number. Let them know you are selling on your own and will not be calling them for multiple houses, but you do want to keep a list of everyone who has been by to see the house. If they are not willing to sign the guest book, be cautious. You may even consider letting them know that you do not want to show your home to anyone who does not sign in. Sometimes they are not willing to sign because they don't want further solicitations, but it is always best to err on the side of safety.

Direct Mail, Television, and Word of Mouth

You have probably received a "Just Listed in Your Neighborhood" card in the mail. Direct mail and hand delivery of flyer campaigns let your neighbors know that your house is for sale. Your neighbors may have friends that they would like to see move into the neighborhood. If they know your home is available, they can tell those friends. This type of advertising is hit-and-miss and may or may not work. Agents who are consistent about sending this type of mailer will get responses, but a one shot deal may head straight to the trash can. You do have a better chance of getting your information read if it is on a postcard. Most people do not open all the mail they receive, especially if it appears to be a bulk mailing or some other type of junk mail. A postcard can be read without opening it.

Direct mail can work well for condominium owners or owners of cooperative properties. Owners in these complexes usually have a friend who has said, "Let me know if anything ever comes up for sale in your building." Most people are not reading the classifieds unless they are actively looking for something, and a postcard about your property may be the only way other owners in your complex will know your place is for sale.

Depending on your market place, you may have the opportunity to put your house on television. There are a number of real estate shows that showcase different houses each week. Most of these shows are sponsored by a real estate company and do not showcase FSBO properties, but if you are listed with an agent, this infomercial-style show can provide some good exposure.

Be sure you can provide several good interior and exterior photos of your house for television. Usually your agent can take these photos. A high-resolution digital photograph works fine. Most of the television programs use a slide show, but if they use a virtual tour, your agent can have one done for you.

Word of mouth is another great form of advertising for your home. A good agent will be calling every potential buyer they have worked with to see if one of them would be interested in your house or knows of someone who would be. They will also be in touch with other real estate agents, asking if they know of a potential buyer. Whether you have an agent or not, just talking to people about your house for sale could be the way a buyer is found. In conversations at parties, at the kids' ball games, or anywhere that you have the opportunity to talk about your house, you have the chance of meeting a potential buyer or meeting someone who knows of one. If you are working with an agent, hand out his card with your address on the back. If you are an FSBO, hand out your own card. If you don't have a business card, get one! You can have 1,000 business cards printed up for under $100. Put your name, phone number, and description of your house on the card. The more people who know your house is for sale, the better.

FACT

Repetition is the best way to advertise. This does not mean that you can't catch someone on the first mention; it just means that repetition is the best way to advertise. Don't give up if you run an ad once with no results. Repetition is the best way to advertise. See?

Of course, your own campaign does not include the personal promotion that many agents also do. This personal promotion gets people to call them, people who may end up being interested in your house. From a huge billboard to a tiny grocery cart sign, each of the advertising mediums has worked at one time or another. While none of them work every time, they are all important to consider.

Principles of Effective Advertising

Real estate agents find that the best advertisements are catchy and get the phone to ring. An ad that gives too much information is less likely to appeal to a potential buyer than a simple one.

"Custom built and secluded. Lovely three-bedroom home with state-of-the-art kitchen. Call for details. $350,000" is more likely to create interest than "Custom built by Smith and Jones Construction. Four miles up Canyon Road in a quiet setting, this three-bedroom home with two and one-half baths has a two-car garage, kitchen with stainless steel appliances and maple cabinets, family room, formal dining room, and fully landscaped yard. $350,000." A buyer may immediately dismiss this ad thinking, "I heard Smith and Jones were not great contractors," or "I want a three-car garage," or "four miles up Canyon Road is too far," or "I hate stainless steel," or "I don't need a formal dining room."

If they had a chance to see the house before eliminating it, they may have found that Smith and Jones do beautiful work, a two-car garage was enough, four miles wasn't that far, that stainless looks great with maple, or that formal dining room would make a great office. The less said, the better.

Budgeting for Marketing Expenses

Advertising can be very expensive. If you do not decide up front how much you will spend and divide it fairly over the expected market time, you will probably spend too much.

Expenses: FSBO

As an FSBO, you will have certain expenses that would otherwise be covered by your real estate agent. One of them is advertising. Your FSBO status also limits the type of advertising you can do, and you will have to compensate in other ways. Since many of the mainstream advertising outlets specific to real estate do not allow FSBOs to advertise, flyers, signs, and newspapers will be your best advertising avenues.

You will need to purchase a for sale sign with a flyer box for the property. You will also need a flyer. Color flyers may cost about $1 each; black and white copies cost considerably less. Think about the image you want to portray and think about your budget. You may want to use the black and white flyers for the flyer box and save the color flyers for potential buyers. You will also have the cost of any mass mailings you decide to do. There are many advertising opportunities at different sites on the Internet. Costs will vary according to the type of site. The number one site for buyers to check is *www.Realtor.com*, but only a Realtor® can advertise on that site.

The next expense is needed to keep you out of court. Having an attorney you can check with about how contracts are written and having all the correct forms is critical for the FSBO. Unless you have sold your house a dozen times *recently* (and you would not be reading this book if you had), you may miss something that is required and create a huge liability for yourself.

ALERT!

One expense that an FSBO needs to consider is the potential of having to cut your price because a buyer wants to save the commission. Keep this in mind when negotiating with potential buyers.

Probably the biggest expense that an FSBO will have is the value of their time. If you are doing all the things necessary to sell your house, you may be neglecting other things in your life. You may be on the phone with a potential buyer as your boss walks by. You may have to cancel weekend trips or vacations to keep from missing a potential buyer. The value of your time should also be taken into consideration as you determine the costs of being an FSBO.

Expenses: Using a Professional Agent

The biggest expense you will have by using a professional agent is the commission. Although they do not receive any commission until your house sells and closes escrow, they will be spending money and assuming (or hoping) that the commission will eventually come. They will cover the costs of advertising and marketing your property. The signs, flyers, mailers, newspaper advertising, glossy magazine advertising, and Internet advertising will all come out of their pocket.

There are some exceptions to what an agent pays for.

- If you want to use an expensive advertising medium that the agent feels is out of the norm, you can negotiate to share the cost with the agent or absorb it on your own.
- If your home is priced in multiple millions of dollars, the cost of advertising is often shared.

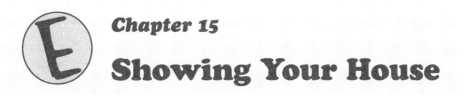

Chapter 15

Showing Your House

R eal estate agents and buyers need to see your house; if no one ever sees the house, it will never sell. Unfortunately, showings will sometimes feel very inconvenient, even invasive. This is a tough part of home-selling, but it's the only way for potential buyers to really gain interest in your house. The key to minimizing the stress is to keep your home in showing condition at all times, make appointments with the agents who call, and realize that it won't always happen as planned.

First Things First

The more people who have the opportunity to see your house, the more chances you have of making a sale. Homes that are difficult to view get a bad reputation among real estate agents and are not shown, even if agents feel they are the right homes for their clients. If you are not accommodating about showing your house, agents and buyers assume you are not motivated to sell. If the seller misses a showing, it is unlikely they will ever get a second chance with that buyer. The motivated buyer will have already bought elsewhere.

FACT

As an FSBO, you will need to be especially accommodating of potential buyers and their agents. This is because many buyers are skittish about FSBOs. If you don't make it easy on them, they will make it easy on themselves and visit a house listed with an agent instead.

Before your listing agent leaves your house the day you sign the listing contract, she will also have to settle the question of a sign. Some sellers object to a real estate office's sign on their front lawn because they worry that people will show up unannounced. The truth is people may show up unannounced anyway, and a sign will be helpful to your sale. More often than you think, a neighbor two blocks away will see that sign on the way to work and tell a coworker about the new house for sale near him. Also, that sign will help an agent locate your property without scanning each doorway and mailbox for numbers. Signs are a no-cost way to attract attention, and you need attention. (See Chapter 14 for more information about marketing and signs.)

Giving Access to Your Property

Every real estate community has its traditions for access to property. The most common one, when listed with a real estate agent who is also a Realtor®, is to have a lockbox on your house. Sometimes called a key lockbox, the lockbox symbolizes your commitment to open your house to strangers. This allows all the agents who belong to the local Board or Association of Realtors® access to your property, even if you are not home. The agents call you to set up a time to show your home. If they get your answering machine, they leave a message as to when they are showing and use the lockbox.

With a lockbox, there is the remote possibility you will be caught in the shower or sleeping and won't hear the doorbell. If you are concerned that an agent will drop in without prior notice, write a note that says "Do Not Disturb" and cover the lockbox with your note. Don't forget to remove the note when you are ready for showings again or before you go out.

Modern lockboxes can be programmed to let your agent know the names of agents who have entered the home and what time they were there. The listing agent gets a printout of that information so they can follow up. This system also provides more supervision for lockbox visits. Each agent has her own special access key to the lockbox, which holds your house key within. Access keys are often programmed with a PIN (personal identification number) for additional security so that no one can use the access key except the agent who owns it.

Once your listing agent snaps a lockbox on your front door, entry to your house is available to virtually every member of the local Board of Realtors®. Most listing sheets and flyers ask that the agent call the owner for advance permission to enter. On the very rare occasion that an agent shows up unannounced, he will usually leave his business card on a kitchen counter so you know the house has been shown. Having a guest book and requesting agents to sign in will also help in case the agent forgot to bring a card. If you have a modern lockbox, the information is recorded there as well. Lockboxes are the most convenient way to get the maximum number of showings, and the recording device within makes them more secure than handing out keys. A lockbox enables agents on an active board to show your house without depending on the listing agent to open it and without requiring you to stay home while your house is for sale.

FACT

It's already been mentioned that a real estate agent's career is built on his reputation. However, in the discussion of house showings, this statement warrants repeating. An agent's reputation is a commodity that most won't want to compromise by showing up unannounced or by violating your wishes for how and when the house is shown.

If you object to a lockbox, you can ask the listing agent to note that there is no lockbox on the house and to indicate on the listing form "Shown by Appointment Only." Appointment-only homes get fewer showings because it is less convenient. You can also leave a key at your agent's office for other agents to use. This works fairly well if the listing office is located close to your property. Few agents will drive miles out of their way to get a key, drive back to the property, show it, and then drive back to the listing office to return the key. They will simply recommend other houses that are easier to show. Even a key with a code number can get lost, and the risk of having keys out all over town is often greater than the risk of a lockbox.

You can request that your listing agent be responsible for every showing and meet selling agents from other offices at the property in order to open it, answer any questions, and lock it up. But again, this could be viewed as an inconvenience and decrease the number of showings.

ESSENTIAL

The fewer restrictions you place on showing the house, the better. For religious reasons you may request no showings on the Sabbath or on other holy days. This is something that you need to feel comfortable with, but from a real estate point of view, it may decrease the number of showings.

If your home is FSBO, you will not have access to the modern lockboxes, but you can purchase a simple combination lockbox. This presents a security risk because you cannot track who has entered your property. Giving a few trusted agents the code to your lockbox may be okay, but giving out the combination to the general public is dangerous. If you do use a combination lockbox, it is a good idea to change the combination on a regular basis. If you are selling your home without an agent and choose not to use a combination lockbox, you will have to be home to show your house. This also means no showings if you are at work, at the store, at a family gathering, or out of town. You may miss showings, but you will not be at risk as you would be with the combination lockbox.

As an FSBO, be careful about allowing a nonlicensed person who is also not the owner to show your property. It could be considered practicing real estate without a license, and both you and your friend could be held liable according to the laws of your state.

Appointments Versus Drop-ins

Be available to show your home on short notice. If you have company, let them know your house is on the market and that there may be showings. Don't quit showing the house just because your cousins are in town. If the house doesn't look as perfect as you'd like, it is still important to show it. Make your apologies and clean up as much as you can before anyone arrives.

If you have a tenant, you may be required to show according to the tenants' rights. Many leases have a twenty-four-hour notice clause built into them. Some tenants are happy to allow the house to be shown, but often, a little motivation helps. A discount on the rent for every showing or a bonus once the house sells can put the tenant on your side. Tenants will often tell prospective buyers everything that is wrong with the house. They will often not keep the house in showing condition, even if they usually live neatly. Why? They are afraid that if the house sells they will have to move. Anything you can do to make the transition easier on your tenants will earn you an advocate in selling the property.

Appointments by Phone

Once your listing is out on the MLS, agents will call you to make appointments, ask questions, change or cancel appointments, and sometimes do some preliminary negotiating or testing for the firmness of your price. Check your voice mail often and answer your call waiting. If you don't have either of those services, even if it means a temporary change in lifestyle, try to keep your personal phone conversations short. Most agents are diligent in trying to reach homeowners for an appointment. If busy signals are constant, they may appear at your door without advance notice, or worse, they may never appear at all, choosing instead a house that was easier to see.

Unexpected Showings

Many sellers are annoyed by agents who stop in without an appointment and have customers in tow. In some instances, their irritation is justified. The house is a wreck, someone is ill or sleeping, or you are simply not ready for a showing at that moment. You can tell the agent it is not a convenient time but you would be happy to make an appointment for later in the day or for another day. Unannounced arrivals are unlikely, but they do happen. You should be prepared to deal with them.

Sometimes drop-in customers are actually very strong potential buyers. Here is a common situation: Your house is not among those selected by the agent for showing that day because it is a little over the dollar limit the buyers had set. But, as the agent drives down your street to another house, one member of the couple spots the sign on your lawn. "Oh, I love that one!" she says. "Could you drive by it once more?" her husband chimes in. The second time around, the agent stops in front of the house. The couple agrees that your house is "Beautiful. Exactly what we want," and they ask the agent the price. When she tells them, the wife says, "Well, maybe we could go that high for something that looks perfect. Do you think we could go in and see it?"

As the seller, you know nothing of this conversation when the agent comes to the door, and you must make your decision based on the state of your world. Consider this: Most people drawn in by a sign on impulse have a strong, positive attitude toward the property before they begin their inspection.

While drop-ins still happen, the growing popularity of cell phones has contributed to a significant decrease in the number of these occurrences. If an agent has a cell phone as she drives by your house, she will likely give you a quick call before bringing the buyers up to your door.

The No Show

Every bit as irksome as the agent who arrives without an appointment is the agent who makes a firm appointment and then doesn't show up or shows up two hours late. Unfortunately, this is a common occurrence in the real estate business and one that you must also try to take in stride. It happens because people are unpredictable.

Here's an example: When a buyer's agent calls you at 10:00 A.M. to make an appointment for 3:00 P.M., she is most likely scheduling a series of five or six house visits along a planned route. Let's say your house is number five. Her clients arrive at her office at 12:30 P.M. They enter house number one at 1:00 P.M. The agent allowed fifteen minutes on her schedule, but they have no interest, spend fewer than five minutes, and leave. They arrive at house number two at 1:20 P.M. They are early. Their appointment was scheduled for 1:45 P.M.

They love it. They walk through every room at least twice. They walk around and around the outside of the house. They send the agent back inside for the survey map the sellers left on the dining room table. They walk the boundaries of the property. They go back inside, linger in every room, and mentally begin to place their furniture. They flush some toilets, poke some beams, and finally sit down in the living room to ask questions about the neighborhood and the schools. They have spent more than an hour at the house, but the agent does not rush them because she can sense an impending sale.

ALERT!

Not everyone who makes an appointment will show up at the correct time. If an agent is showing buyers through several properties, it can be difficult to pinpoint exactly when they will arrive at your house, even if it is within a one- or two-hour window. Some people will not show up at all. Don't let this discourage you!

Finally, they decide to look at the other houses on the schedule. They arrive at house number three late and go through it quickly. They continue to house number four and walk through but scarcely look at it. As soon as they are back in the car, they tell the agent that they want to go back to house number two.

Now yours is house number five, and you know that your house is nicer than number two and more fairly priced. Perhaps the agent even thought that your house and number six were the best she had to show and intentionally scheduled them at the end of the day. Will that agent then try to persuade her customers to see the last two houses on her schedule? Never. Not if she has had even a half hour of experience or training.

When customers want to drop everything and return to a house, they are ready to buy. Few agents will complicate matters by trying to show other properties. As house number five, you will be left with a "no show." If the agent is courteous, she will call to apologize and explain later in the day, or she will have her office call you to cancel. Try to grin and bear it.

In all likelihood, you will play the role of house number one, three, and four several times before you are the lucky number two. Customers may walk through your house uninterested. Some will be more courteous than others; they will make appreciative remarks, ask a few questions, and walk around the yard. Others will be in a hurry. Sometimes they won't look at the yard or even the upstairs bedrooms. It will be a whirlwind, five-minute showing. Then they are gone, and you end up thinking "I washed the kitchen floor for *that*?"

This is yet another reason to be away from the house during showings. You may never be aware of this reaction if you're off running your errands. The benefit you gain by not knowing is preservation of your balanced emotions and positive thoughts. You had another showing! Every showing brings you closer to the sale.

If an agent schedules a repeat showing to a very interested party, it is imperative that you leave the property, even more so than on a first visit. Repeat showings usually precede an offer, but they can take a long time. Would-be buyers often tour round and round the house several times, re-entering rooms and imagining the placement of their furniture. Sometimes they even measure windows, climb into attics, test plumbing, and poke into the corners of closets and basements. They can spend an hour or more talking with the agent. All of this can be disquieting to a seller, but don't worry about being around to answer questions. If there are any, the agent will call you later.

Try not to be upset with the agent whose buyers want to cancel their appointment to see your house. These situations are just a natural part of the homeselling process. Real estate agents are a little like matchmakers. They can bring a buyer and a house together, but they can't make them love each other.

The Showing Process

If you are an FSBO, you will be home when the property is shown and may need to play the role of agent. However, if a real estate agent is present (the buyer's or your own) do not try to point out the special features and attractions of your house. Let the agents do their work. They know their customers; they know what will appeal to them. If you happen to be home when buyers arrive with their agent, grab your kids and your dog and take a walk.

If you must be at home when an agent and clients arrive for a showing, cordial silence on your part is the stronger hand. Smile through the introductions, and then gather all the family members in one room and remain there throughout the showing. The living room or family room is usually best, especially in winter when you can have a roaring fire and pleasant music on the stereo. Try to stay out of the kitchen; people like to feel roominess there and look closely at appliances.

Arranging to be out of the house will be relatively easy if the agent has made an appointment with you, but sometimes you'll have a showing on short notice.

Quick Cleanup

Showing your home on short notice can be difficult, but you can prepare your home in as little as fifteen minutes. If you have a family, divvy up the tasks among the members to use time even more effectively. Here are some basic steps to follow.

1. Turn on all the lights.
2. Make all the beds.

3. Close closet doors.
4. Put laundry into baskets in the laundry room.
5. Load the dishwasher.
6. Straighten the rugs and fluff up throw pillows.
7. Clear surfaces of food products and clutter.
8. Contain all pets.
9. Briefly run the vacuum over rugs and floors.
10. Head out to run errands.

This can be done easily if, showing or no showing, the house is kept in good order every day. A simple maintenance routine will shorten prep time and limit effort.

Some days will be more difficult than others. Perhaps you oversleep. You don't make the bed when you get out of it, last night's dishes are in the sink, and you feel like your house is a disaster. You get the call that someone is in the driveway and wants to see the house. Make your apologies and show it anyway! It is better to be a little embarrassed than to miss having a potential buyer see the house. Don't make it a regular habit to show the house in disaster condition, but once in awhile, it's better than not showing at all.

Adding an Extra Touch

The smell of fresh cookies or bread always makes a house more inviting, but don't worry about doing it every time. Sprinkle a little cinnamon on a cookie sheet and place it in the oven on warm if you don't want to bake that day. You can also use the slice and bake cookies and just make them one or two at a time. Baking cookies for an open house is a good idea; everyone can eat the cookies as they tour your home. In the winter, your homemade stew or spaghetti sauce left all day in a Crock-Pot is an inviting smell. Avoid garlic if you can since it has a stronger odor that does not please everyone.

Holding an Open House

Holding an open house is a great way to get lots of potential buyers into your home in one day. In this way, you only have to clean up and prepare your house once. There are two kinds of open houses: an open house designed for agents on tour and a public open house. You will have to be away from home for both of them.

The Agents' Open House

Agents' open houses are an effective tool that you should use. They are always held on a weekday, soon after a listing comes out. The open house is announced in the MLS bulletin with the date and specific hours. While you are out, your agent will play host as agents from the surrounding area arrive to view your property. The listing agent will point out any special features and answer any questions.

Some agents' open houses are very successful, with anywhere from twenty-five to fifty or more agents making preinspection visits. If you have good attendance, that's excellent. The more agents who see your house, the more potential customers you will have.

The Public Open House

Sunday afternoon is the most popular time for a public open house; although in some markets, it is Saturday afternoon. The date and hours are usually advertised in the weekend edition real estate section of the newspaper. Your listing agent will arrive early and set out open house signs, a large one on your front lawn near the street and sometimes several directional arrows at cross streets nearby.

While attendance at public open houses can be unpredictable, you never know how or when your buyer will appear. If your listing agent wants to hold an open house, it is probably worth the effort to try it a few times. You may have a lot of people, or you may have only one or two. You will have some people who are just curious. Houses can sell as the result of an open house, and it is a good idea to see if yours is among them. Some houses don't sell that way, and the open house becomes a way for the agent to meet buyers for other houses or just catch up on some reading.

Most real estate agents are careful and honorable and so are most homebuyers. However, any pre-emptive action you can take will help prevent unnecessary loss. Put your valuables away. Your agent will appreciate the effort. If the response to your open house is good, he may not be able to personally accompany the droves that are interested in buying your property.

The people who walk through your house will be strangers to the agent, and she may not be able to supervise their inspection as closely as desired, especially if two or more groups come in at the same time. Do put away favorite or precious objects and things that can be easily knocked over or broken. All valuables and personal items should be out of sight before having your property shown. This includes children's toys. Some buyers will allow and even encourage their children to play in your child's room while they inspect the rest of the house. Broken toys will only make the whole process harder on your kids.

Controlling Your Pets, Your Kids, and Yourself

You may not realize it because you are so used to their company, but pets and children can be a big distraction to potential buyers who are trying to check out your house. Furthermore, you will have to keep *yourself* in check during showings. Talking too much, being pushy, or otherwise nagging buyers can drive them right out of your house!

Your Pets

Animal encounters are the most common perpetrators of "war stories" told by real estate agents. Yet, few homesellers have any concept of the intimidation buyers and agents feel when faced with a German shepherd barking, snarling, jumping, and clawing at the door. Seeing the dog, some people will not even get out of the car. If they are convinced the dog is secured, most will go through the house—but there is a constant sense of anxiety that is in direct proportion to the size of the dog and the frequency and ferocity of the barking.

While a house is being shown, the best place for a dog is a fenced enclosure at the back line of the property. In this way, buyers and agents will be less pressured by the barking and regard the dog as unthreatening. You may not want to build an outdoor pen just for the time your house is on the market. In that case, consider purchasing a dog crate.

Pet crates, suitable for every breed, are available at most pet shops. Their price is small in comparison to the security they provide. You will also find a pet crate useful during your move, for traveling, housebreaking future puppies, and introducing a new pet to the household.

Cats are less of a problem than dogs, except when young children accompany their parents while house hunting. Toddlers tend to pounce on sleeping animals and chase moving ones. Almost invariably the child gets scratched. Also, some people are highly allergic to them. It is safer to confine cats in pet crates or in one room with a note on the door reading "Cats inside—do not let out." If you confine your cats to a room this way, people may be reluctant to open the door at all. So, choose the room thoughtfully. You don't want your buyer to miss the master suite. If you would rather give your cats the run of the house, a sign at each door that warns people not to let the cat outside is a wise decision, especially if you live in an area with predators such as coyotes.

It is also a good idea to indicate on your listing form exactly what animals are on the property and where they are kept. This is particularly applicable if you happen to have a python, iguana, or other exotic friend. (See Chapter 3 for more about handling pets.)

Any pets you have are going to be somewhat disturbed by the changes in your house, your lifestyle, the comings and goings of agents and customers, and the increased emotional tension in your family. Sometimes a docile dog will snap, or a stay-at-home cat will disappear for several days. But the stress and confusion the animals demonstrate is only a small part of what your children will be working through while your house is for sale.

Your Kids

Teenagers and school-age children are always curious about what's happening. They may want to know the asking price, what the agents said, what the customers said, and how the negotiating is progressing. Depending on your family's style, you may have some difficulty discussing some of these points. You certainly shouldn't go beyond what you consider the prerogatives of adult privacy. However, it is important to talk about the selling experience with your children. They may have fears and uncertainties about selling, about family finances, and about the impending move. Their questions are far better answered by you than by their imaginations or the conclusions of their friends. Sharing the process with your children gives you an opportunity to teach them about selling a home. They will likely face this in adulthood, and it's an experience for which there is little training or education available.

Preschoolers are different and perhaps more difficult. They respond emotionally to the tension. They need to keep their toys picked up and tolerate strangers walking about their rooms. Often their response is fear, and it is most important that you talk with them about what is happening. Explain that you are selling this house and will soon have a new house. Talk about the child's new room, explain about the sign on the front lawn, and tell a little about what a real estate agent does and why the child is not allowed to answer the phone during the selling time.

ALERT!

You must walk a fine line between overburdening a young child with facts and helping him feel comfortable with the changes that selling your house has caused. Above all, try to answer questions honestly and clearly. Also understand that children need time to grieve, but they are also very resilient.

Most of all, try to help the child understand that you and the real estate agents are trying to find the "right" family for your house. This is important because some children do not understand why the people who come through the house do not buy it. They might even feel personally rejected.

You may have a social child who wants to help the potential buyers. They may want to show their room and may even pull someone along by the arm. Let your kids know in advance that this is not acceptable. Once again, being out of the house during showings will prevent this from being a problem.

You

This advice sounds simpler than it actually is. You may find yourself confronting your own unanswered questions and fears more often than you'd like to admit. You may find that your responses are sometimes both emotional and irrational. This is especially true if your house does not sell within the time frame you allowed. You will be mad at every agent who doesn't show, shows late, or shows without an appointment. As mentioned previously, realizing why this can occur and knowing that it is all part of the process will help to subdue that anger.

Having your house on the market can be stressful. It can be exhausting and sometimes confusing. To add to the complexity, it is also an experience filled with emotion. Be ready for the feelings and recognize them for what they are: normal reactions to the stress and demands of your situation. Let your feelings run their course but don't act out of emotion. Being rational is one of the strongest assets a player can have in this game. A big part of being rational is recognizing when you are not and waiting until you are.

Chapter 16

Preparing for the Offer

Being presented with an offer begins a new cycle of questions, answers, and challenges. The offer you receive may be lower than you had hoped for, or it may have other terms that you find unacceptable. You may have to wait quite awhile, with growing impatience, for the right offer. A buyer may have been back several times, leaving you to assume an offer is forthcoming, but it never shows up. You could also get the right offer sooner than you expect, perhaps before you are really ready to move.

Closing the Buyer

You know the buyer likes the house but he needs that little push. He is still raising objections that you or your agent must overcome. When a buyer is close to making a decision, she will outline the pros and cons, either on paper or in her head. She will voice some of the negatives, and it is your job or the job of your agent to overcome them. The conversation may go something like this:

Buyer: "I am not sure I can get insurance for the shake roof."
Agent: "I checked with an insurance company that will cover it for the same fee as any other roof. Here is their quote. Are you ready to write an offer?"
Buyer: "I still think the living room is too small."
Agent: "Remember the seller has three couches. You only have two. Let's write an offer and see how it goes."

Once the buyer runs out of the objections on her pros and cons list, she will be ready to write an offer.

Keep the following in mind: Indignant sellers don't usually get what they want. To illustrate this fact, here's an example: An offer came in on one property, a bit lower than the seller had hoped. The seller's agent prepared a counteroffer, which the seller signed, and presented it back to the buyer's agent. The buyer's agent was excited. He had told the buyer to expect this exact counter and felt it would be accepted. Then the twist came. The buyer said he would accept the counter, but he wanted the seller to throw in the collector car that the buyer had admired in the seller's garage. The seller was enraged! How could the buyer demand such an item? He became angry and hurt. The seller said no, and the buyer angrily gave up.

It wasn't until later that the seller realized he could find the collector car on eBay® and take that amount off the price of the house. He did not have to sell his personal car; he could just give the buyer a better price so the buyer could get a similar car. He could have even done the eBay® negotiations for the buyer. It was too late for this buyer because he did not want to deal with such an angry seller; but for the seller, it was a lesson learned.

ALERT!

FSBOs often find it harder to control their emotions since they are frequently face-to-face with the buyer. Without an agent as the go-between in a transaction, a seller may lose his temper unintentionally. Be careful with your emotions or you could lose a sale that would have otherwise gone through.

Buyers do not waste time writing an offer just to insult you. That is not their intention. They do intend to get your house for the best possible price. They don't want to make you mad; they want to make you sell! Often a buyer will wonder, "How low can I go without making the seller mad?" Because they have much less emotional attachment than you do, their dollar amount may be much lower than the dollar amount you would consider.

Negotiating Skills

Though it may be on a smaller economic scale, you have probably already had some experience with negotiating. If you have purchased anything at a garage sale, tag sale, or flea market, you likely did some "haggling." If you have purchased a car, you surely did some "bargaining." These are the same skills you will use when selling your house. The only difference is that the stakes are higher, and you can think of it as "negotiating."

FACT

Rarely do sellers receive the perfect offer of full price with no loan requirement and the best possible close of escrow date. Buyers are hoping that their offer will be accepted without changes, but they also know that a deal may require some give and take.

It is not possible to give you specific suggestions for handling yourself in your own particular negotiating sessions. Each situation is as different as each buyer and seller and their particular temperaments. Choosing the "right" negotiating move is often as much a matter of art as it is of science.

Customs vary from region to region as to how an offer is presented to the seller. In some locations, the buyer's agent presents the offer to the seller's agent, who then presents the offer to the seller. In other areas, the buyer's agent presents the offer directly to the seller. If the buyer's agent presents the offer directly to you, it is important to have your agent present as well.

Listen carefully to everything that the buyer's agent has to say. They will probably give you some background on the buyer as well as the reasons they think the offer is worth accepting. Taking notes during this time will help you remember the details you want to revisit later. Having the job of taking notes also keeps you from getting emotionally involved. It is best to keep your comments to a minimum, but asking questions to further clarify the offer and the buyer's situation is okay.

QUESTION?

If I am selling my house myself, how can I be sure I don't tip my hand?
If you are an FSBO who is receiving an offer directly from a buyer, it is easy to get emotionally involved. Don't let it show. Put on your best poker face and listen to what the buyer has to say. If you need to, you can rant and rave after she leaves.

It is at this point that many sellers fail in their negotiations. They may tell the buyer's agent their bottom line, even if they are planning to make a counteroffer for more than that amount. They may get angry at the offer and reject it without thinking about it. They may be offended with the presentation style of the buyer's agent. Perhaps she only speaks to one of the parties and not the other. Taking that offense to heart can make it impossible to hear if the offer is good or not. These actions can be fuel for the buyer's agent. If they know you will take less money, they may convey that to the buyer. If they think the offer has been rejected, even if you decide later to counter the offer, they may take that information to the buyer as well. The buyer may get emotionally involved, too, (this is not just reserved for sellers) and decide not to accept your counteroffer on principle, since they had originally been told the offer was rejected. They may have even moved on to another property when they thought you had rejected them.

ALERT!

Take a tip from the flea market concessionaire and the car dealer. If they receive a low offer, they always make a counteroffer. It is not a waste of time. There is a chance that the counteroffer will be accepted. By making a counteroffer, you keep the door open and give the buyer the opportunity to respond.

Rather than making any decisions while the buyer's agent is present, it is best to spend some time reviewing the offer and talking about it with any co-owner(s) and with your agent. If the buyer's agent insists on an answer right away, you will still want some time to discuss the offer without the buyer's agent present. You may want to excuse yourselves for awhile or ask the agent to return later.

Why Some Negotiations Fail

Now that you have an offer, make some notes about the buyer and why the offer was made the way it was made. To get the perspective you need to perform your negotiations and get the most from your deal, it is important to understand why some negotiations fail. Here are some common causes.

- **The buyer cannot afford the house:** This may not always be the fault of the buyer. Perhaps the buyer told the agent he could afford a certain price, and the agent pushed his budget, hoping he could actually go higher. Hence, the buyer falls in love with a house he can't afford but makes an offer at the price he can afford, with the hope that the seller will take it.
- **The house is overpriced:** If a number of offers come in on the property at a price lower than you expect, perhaps the offered prices are more realistic than the asking price. Countering each of these offers may be just what the buyer needs to re-evaluate her offer and

realize she would be paying too much if she gave you your price. Have your agent give you an updated market analysis, and be sure you are priced correctly.

- **The sellers are not ready to sell:** Sellers may think they are ready to sell, but when an offer comes in, they are shocked by the fact that they have to move. Once the reality hits them, they may find that they are not as motivated as they once thought.

- **The buyers are not ready to buy:** Buyers can get caught up in the moment. They start out getting a feel for the market, not expecting to find something, just expecting an education. They make an offer and then start having second thoughts, known as *buyer's remorse*. Perhaps their motivating factor is a job transfer that hasn't gone through yet. Perhaps they meant to wait until their last kid graduates from high school. Regardless, if the buyer isn't ready, you can't do anything about it.

- **Someone is given an ultimatum:** By countering an offer with the word "firm" after the price, you are closing the door on negotiations. Even if the buyer was willing to pay that price, the word "firm" makes him believe you are going to be hard to work with as the sale progresses, and he won't be willing to move forward. Usually, an ultimatum will make the other party dig in his heels and refuse to budge.

- **One party is offended during negotiations:** If one party insults another, even if it is unintentional, it is hard to get past the insult and back to the table. Calling the buyer Kathy instead of Kathryn, as she prefers, can be enough to set her off. A sarcastic remark has no place in real estate negotiations, even if it is meant as a joke. Be careful of what you say and how you say it. Also, be thick-skinned in case the other party is not so careful.

- **Racial, cultural, or social prejudice:** It is unfortunate, but personal prejudice still exists. If it comes up in your negotiations, defuse, ignore, or otherwise set aside any social bias you or the buyer may carry. Just focus on the outcome. If the bias is removed, will the negotiations fail? Probably not, unless there are other factors as outlined previously.

- **Outside influence:** In a divorce situation, one person may want the other to suffer, even if she has to suffer in the process. She may demand more than she was demanding when she put the house on the market. Another outside influence can be the experience of knowing someone who had a difficult time selling their house and imparted that bias to you. You may also have family members or friends trying to help you make the right decisions but burdening you in the process.

- **Ignorance of the buyer's hot buttons:** With some buyers, price is the only thing that matters. With others, you can sweeten the pot without a high cost to you. Agreeing to additional repairs or the replacement of something (such as an older dishwasher) can make a buyer more comfortable with a purchase.

Sometimes you can do things for a buyer that have no real cost to you. Perhaps you are leaving snow country for the desert, throw in your snow blower for free. If you are moving to a condominium, give them the lawn mower. Fancy drapes with a matching spread, the hutch that works in the dining room but won't fit in your new home, anything that could be considered valuable to a buyer may keep the doors open.

Paying points or carrying a second, paying for an inspection, a home warranty, HOA dues for a period of time, closing costs, any of these things can make a buyer feel like he is getting a "deal." Be sure any fees you pay are okay with the lender.

When both parties have reached the maximum level of compromise and there is still no deal, negotiations can fail. Often both the buyer and the seller will have made compromises on the offer and the counteroffers, as they move forward to put the deal together. They have usually compromised more than they planned to when they first started the negotiation process. They are at their maximum breaking point, and any small item can push them into backing out of the deal. When the buyer does this, it is often looked at as buyer's remorse, but it just means that the buyer has had enough and it isn't worth going through with the purchase.

If you are willing to budge, say so. Go back to your agent and ask him to approach the buyers. Outline your revised terms and let them know you want to make it work. Maybe your gesture will soothe the sting of buyer's remorse.

What You Need to Know about the Buyer

Some people like to know everything about the person who is buying their property. Is he nice? Is he planning to live in the house, or is he buying it as an investment? Does he have kids? By asking yourself these questions, what you're really asking is, "Is the buyer just like me?" Truthfully, these things don't matter, and in some cases, these questions can't even be asked due to the potential of discrimination. What matters is this: Is the buyer financially qualified to buy the house? Is she willing to pay a price that you can accept, with accompanying terms and conditions that you can accept?

The details you need to know about the buyer are:

- How much of a down payment can she make?
- Has she been prequalified or preapproved for a mortgage?
- What size mortgage can she afford to carry?
- Does the prospective buyer have a house to sell?
- How soon does she want to close and move in?

It is acceptable to have contingencies for a loan, inspections, review of homeowner's documents, title documents, and virtually anything else that may be important to the buyer. These *due diligence* items will protect you, too.

If you don't have any contingencies, you are setting yourself up for a disaster. You want to be totally sure that the buyer is satisfied with the purchase before completing the sale. You don't want the buyers to discover something after the sale that is so disappointing to them that they decide to sue you.

Some sellers will be insulted by the fact that the buyer wants to have an inspection. They are proud of their property and do not believe that there is anything wrong. Keep the following in mind: If there is nothing wrong, then you have no cause for concern in an inspection process. If there was something wrong, a proud seller would want to know about it so he could make any necessary repairs.

Multiple Offers

Multiple offers have become common. As a matter of a fact, homes are deliberately priced below market values in some areas to urge multiple offers. The presence of multiple offers will often take the house above market value. The lower price can create a frenzy. If the home was priced at market value, there may not be multiple offers.

In a multiple offer situation, many buyers will submit resumes, waive all contingencies, and either pay cash or have a loan ready to fund. If you are expecting multiple offers, it is wise to hire a home inspector and a pest inspector before placing your home on the market. Give all prospective buyers these inspections to ensure they will have no surprises after close of escrow. Even if a buyer comes in without contingencies, you can still be liable for undisclosed or unknown defects after the sale.

There are several ways to handle a multiple offer situation.

- Reject all offers, request that everyone submit his best offer, and open all offers at a specified time.
- Reject some offers and counter one or several other offers.
- Counter all offers.

There are also a couple of ways to present the counteroffers. For one, you can give the counteroffers back to the respective agents or buyers at the same time and create a race. Whoever responds first receives the house. On the other hand, you can let each buyer know that you are sending counteroffers to more than one prospective purchaser. Let them know that it is not a race and that you will select the buyer from among the counteroffers that are returned by a certain time. The buyers can counter higher if they'd like, they can accept your counter, or they can counter at a lower price. If more than one buyer accepts the counteroffer as presented by you, you still have the right to choose one, as long as it comes in before your specified deadline. All other counteroffers become void.

An offer consists not only of a purchase price, but also of other terms and conditions. Price may be the primary factor in determining whether or not a contract is acceptable, but there are other things that are important when you are selling your house. Timing may be a factor. If you knew you could get $250,000 for your house this month or get $255,000 in a year, would it be worth waiting the year for the other $5,000? For some people, getting the $250,000 today is the best deal. For someone else, it may be worth waiting for the extra $5,000.

FACT

Being able to select a strong buyer, who will likely see the sale through, is another factor to consider. A buyer who is already qualified for a loan may be stronger than one who is hoping for 100 percent financing. Some offers are contingent on the sale of another property. While this is common, it is a weak position for the buyer. However, if the buyer's other property is already in escrow, it makes them stronger than if the property is not yet on the market.

Another factor in selling your house is how the contingencies are structured. If one buyer is asking for a large amount of money toward potential repairs and the other buyer is asking for very little, it may be worth considering the buyer who expects less in repairs.

Sometimes convenience is a factor. Perhaps there is a buyer who will allow you time to move with a free or low cost rent back. A buyer may want to purchase some of your furniture. You were planning to sell it anyway, and so this situation becomes convenient. Consider price but weigh all the factors when determining which offer will suit you in the long run.

A Single Offer

More common than multiple offers is a single offer, presented in a reasonable time from the date you placed your home on the market. This offer may or may not be exactly what you are looking for but it is a good gauge as to what the market is doing. If you were expecting to sell within thirty days and the offer comes within thirty days, you are right on track!

If you receive a full price offer, you and your agent did a great job of pricing the house. Do not think, as many sellers do, that you left money on the table and that you should have asked for more if you got an offer this quickly. If you were undervalued, you would have received multiple offers.

If the single offer is not acceptable as written, it is still important to make a counteroffer. Do not feel like it is a waste of time. The buyer is hoping for you to accept what he has written, but many buyers do expect a counteroffer. If the offer is acceptable as written, then by all means, accept it. It is said that your first offer is generally your best offer, so don't try to squeeze a few extra dollars out of the buyers if you are happy with what you are getting.

Legalizing the Paperwork

This is part of what your agent (and your attorney in certain parts of the country) is doing for you. If you are an FSBO, you will probably need additional help in this area. Contact an attorney to review your contract and to be sure that you comply with everything required by your state and the federal government. If you live in an area of the country where attorneys handle the closing, be sure to employ a different attorney for this purpose. You should not rely on the closing attorney, who is a *disinterested third party* by definition. You want someone with your best interests at heart, not the transaction attorney.

If you've received an offer, you've come a long way. The following chapters delve deeper into the subjects of accepting an offer and dealing with paperwork. If you haven't received an offer yet, don't worry. The next chapter is especially for you.

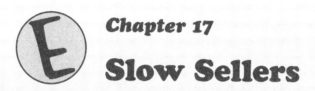

Chapter 17

Slow Sellers

Unfortunately, not all houses sell the first time around. The good news is that all houses will sell at the right price. If your house isn't selling, you need to figure out what is keeping it from selling. Is the price too high? Is the condition less desirable than the condition of other properties? Are there things that need to be fixed, updated, or changed? Price and condition are the two biggest factors to address. This chapter will help you do a reality check when and if you hit a home-selling slump.

Remove the Rose-colored Glasses

You've seen that older couple. They hold hands and look at each other with stars in their eyes. They have been married for a half a century and are still in love. She doesn't notice the hair growing out of his oversized ears; he doesn't notice that she sports a few more chins than she had on their wedding day. Looking through the eyes of love, each sees the other as beautiful.

Many sellers see their homes this way. They don't notice the peeling paint on the trim outside; they don't realize that the closets are really small by today's standards. All they see is the house they love, and they assume others will see it the same way.

Don't try to sell around a negative comment. If the buyers do not like the burnt orange tile on the kitchen counters, don't try to convince them that burnt orange is back in style. Instead, find out the cost to change the kitchen counters to a more neutral color and have them replaced.

As a seller, it is hard to hear negative comments from a buyer about your house. Instead of taking these comments as a personal attack, take them as a guide to an easier sale with the next buyer. It may be hard to grasp, but there are things about your house that a buyer will not like. There may even be things that you find acceptable that a buyer will find distasteful. Think of these comments as the road map to selling your property. The more you can get into the mind of the buyer, the easier it will be to get your house sold.

You will not hear anything negative or positive if you do not ask questions. If you're selling your house without an agent, you will need to confront the buyers directly. Try asking, "What is it about this house that has made you decide not to purchase it?" Most buyers will not want to hurt your feelings and will make general comments like "it isn't for us" or "it didn't feel right." If you have the opportunity, ask a more in-depth question like "What is it about the house that isn't for you? Is there something I could do to make it more appealing?" Notice that you are saying "the house" instead of "my home." By depersonalizing your property, you give the buyer a chance to be more direct in her answers. If you find that the buyer dodges your questions, try asking them in a different way. For example: "I know the house isn't for you, but is there something I could do to make it work for the next buyer?"

If you have an agent working for you, you should be able to get a more detailed response from most buyers. While some buyers' agents will not pass on negative comments and instead say things like "it wasn't their style," more often than not, you will get a detailed and honest answer. Because the buyer's agent may someday need comments from your agent on a showing of one of their listings, they are more likely to help out when asked for feedback from your agent. When talking with their own agents, buyers will usually explain all the negatives about your property. Acting as a buffer zone, their agent can inform your agent without worrying about hurting your feelings. The buyer's agent relies on your agent to filter out anything you may find offensive. If you have a good relationship with your agent, he will not do any filtering.

If it is not your agent's custom to call the other agents for feedback, you may choose to do this yourself. To monitor buyer response, save all the business cards of agents who show your house and mark each with the date of the showing. When you have a collection of cards, gather them together, sit down at the phone with pencil and paper, and call each agent. Introduce yourself, mention that you are the owner of the property for sale on Harmony Avenue, and ask the agent if they remember showing your home on June 2. Then say something like "Do you remember how your clients responded to this property or any particular comments that they made about it?" Most agents will be happy to take a few minutes to talk to you about their buyers' responses. Although, because they are talking to you directly, they may not be as frank as they would be with your agent. Because many agents have a secret hope of picking up listings that expire, they are extra nice to sellers.

ALERT!

Comments like "too small," "too close to a major road," "don't want to live in that town," and "not enough trees on the property" indicate that the house was not quite right for those specific buyers and/or the price was not sweet enough. You can't do anything about a busy street, but many buyers seem to notice it less at a lower price.

Watch for patterns of repetition in the responses you receive. Is there something you have not noticed about the house about which all the buyers are commenting? Do most of their comments touch upon condition, decorating, location, or price? If buyers are mentioning condition, you may want to spend some time and money on paint and redecorating. But you must listen carefully to what is being said. Very few people will actually say that the house is too dirty. You are more likely to hear "Well, it needs more work than my clients wanted to do." Make an effort to get some specifics. "Did they mention anything in particular? We were all down with the flu the week before you came through, and the house really wasn't looking its best." That gives an agent the opportunity to pick up on your necessary neglect and explain further if she chooses.

A Realistic Asking Price

People in retail know that everything will sell at the right price. If something doesn't sell, it needs to be discounted. If it still doesn't sell then, it needs to be discounted again. To get people in the door looking, retailers can place a full-page ad in the newspaper, have great Internet exposure, and commercials on television, but they know it is the price of their products that makes customers buy.

Reducing the price can be very painful, but sitting on the market for months and months can be worse. Losing money on a real estate investment is never satisfying, but you may have to sacrifice your equity in order to make a necessary move. Remember that recovery can come from the next investment. It usually does.

Marketing lets people know your house is on the market, but it is the price that will ultimately sell your house. It doesn't matter what you want or what you think the house is worth; it only matters what a buyer thinks the house is worth.

If the comments you hear from potential buyers indicate that your house is priced too high, then it is. Have your agent do a new comparative market analysis for you. Find out where your house should be priced and reduce the price to that amount.

If all the answers you get in your investigation of buyer responses sound like variations of "too much money," and you absolutely cannot reduce the price without paying money out of your pocket to close the sale, and you must sell, there is a shot in the dark you might try. You can wait for the listing to expire and then advertise the house again as For Sale By Owner, with a price reduction reflecting your savings in the amount of the commission. This is a big gamble. If your house does not sell at this price and you need help from an agent again, you will be placing your home on the market with a real estate agent at the new reduced price and perhaps spending money from savings to pay the commission.

FACT

Sometimes taking a ride with your agent to see "the competition" can help you see what a buyer is seeing. This will help you be more realistic about what your house is really worth. Another way to see what a buyer sees is to go to open houses. For the most revealing comparison, select homes that are in your price range and see how they measure up to yours.

What if you try all this and there are still no buyers? What do you do then? Remember, many people have been in your position. It's very hard to be patient when you need to sell, but *every* house is eventually sold if the seller wants to sell. Either the price of the house is reduced until it meets with the market or the market expands to meet the price of the house. Keep your home as clean and well maintained as you can, and bide your time.

Renting Your House

If you need to sell and it isn't happening at your price and in your time frame, you may want to think about renting your house and waiting for a better market. True, there are horror stories about having a rental. Owners are afraid that tenants will destroy their house, the rent won't be paid, and it will be impossible to remove the tenants from the property. Don't let such scenarios scare you. There are lots of people who actually make money through rentals; so it can't always be a nightmare.

FACT

According to the U.S. Census Bureau, there are 33.1 million renters in the United States and 73.8 million homeowners. Renters represent approximately 33 percent of the population. With this many people renting, it is likely that you will find a good tenant during your time as a landlord.

Hiring a reputable property manager helps, especially if you are moving to another area. At the worst, you will have some fix-up costs when your tenant vacates. An adequate security deposit will help along those lines. A good rule of thumb is a deposit amount equal to one month or one-and-one-half months rent. Just be sure it is enough to cover the repair and replacement costs of items that are easily damaged. At best and more often than the worst case, the market will improve, and you will be able to sell quickly once your tenants move out.

Lease Option

The other possibility for a home you must leave but can't sell is a lease option, which combines a rental and a sale. In a lease option, the buyer gives you some option money to allow them to buy at a future date at an agreed upon price. That option money goes toward the purchase price and is nonrefundable. During the established time frame (usually one year), the buyer pays fair market rent plus an additional sum. That additional sum also goes toward the purchase price. At the predetermined date, the buyer obtains a loan and purchases the house. If they cannot perform, you keep the money you have received to date and put the house back on the market.

This is often touted as a good way to find a buyer for your house. At the very least, you gain a tenant with a vested interest in taking good care of your property. This option is very popular among buyers, particularly those who can afford a monthly mortgage payment but have not been able to put together the amount of a typical down payment.

In a three-part lease option contract, the tenant agrees:

- To pay you a specified rent each month for an agreed upon length of time.
- To have a portion of that rent (usually an amount over and above fair market rent) applied toward a down payment, if he wants to exercise the option part of the contract.
- To pay you a small, up-front, nonrefundable deposit of 3 percent to 5 percent of the purchase price.

At the end of an agreed-on time, the tenant can exercise the option to buy or cancel the plan, thereby losing the rental credits.

If the sale price of houses in your area has risen during that time and the buyer wants to go ahead with the sale, then the buyer wins, and you lose what might have been a greater profit on the sale. Remember though, you did receive several thousand dollars in rent during that year or so.

ALERT!

In a lease option situation, if the sale price of houses in your area has dropped and the buyer says no thanks, he can walk away without any penalty, and you have to start selling (or leasing) again. That is, unless you want to renegotiate the sale price with your exiting tenants to bring it in line with the current market.

Lease option, also known as lease purchase or "rent to own," can be set up on virtually any terms to which you and a tenant-buyer agree. These include length of the lease, amount of rent, and amount of down payment to be paid up front. This can work for you, or it can be a pain in the neck. Some real estate agents will handle a sale like this, waiting for their commission to come in when the sale eventually closes escrow. They usually take a small fee for handling the rental, which is a good thing to take advantage of if you have moved out of the area. Be sure your tenant is preapproved for a mortgage. What is the point of offering a buying option if he will not qualify for a home loan in a year or eighteen months? You want someone who will be able to come up with the remainder of the down payment, after subtracting your rent credits from the total amount needed.

FACT

Most lenders do not allow all of the rent to be credited toward the purchase price. They will expect that you received fair market rent during the term of the lease and that anything over and above fair market rent is credited toward the purchase price.

On the plus side: Tenants in a lease option plan seem to take better care of the rental property. This is probably because they are going to buy and consider themselves homeowners. On the down side: Your house is off the market during this time with the outcome (a sale for you) assumed, but not 100 percent certain. Whether you view it as positive or negative, you become a landlord and assume the management responsibilities that go along with that role.

Rent with Right of First Refusal

Another variation that might work better for you is to rent to someone who voices interest in buying, and offering your tenant *right of first refusal* when you put the house on the market again. This is not a rent-to-own plan, and the tenant does not receive any credits toward a down payment. In a year or whenever the market in your area has improved, you can offer to sell the property to your tenant at current market value. If the tenant is not interested, there will likely be a pool of interested buyers by then.

If the majority of prospective buyers looking at your house cannot obtain financing, offering seller financing may be a good option. If you have sufficient equity in the property and/or you own it free and clear, financing all or part of the sale can actually net you a higher amount than a straight purchase. You would receive interest on the equity that you leave in the property, and eventually your equity would be paid to you in full.

Incentives for a Quick Sale

Perhaps you are in a market where there are lots of homes for sale. Your home may be priced right, but you still want to stand out from the crowd. To get a quicker sale, there are some things you can offer as an incentive.

You can create an incentive for agents to show and sell your house. If you have not had an open house for agents, have your agent hold one. If you have had an open house for agents, hold another. Serve some snacks and create a party atmosphere. If you have a great sunset view, hold the open house at sunset. If you have the perfect morning house, serve a brunch. Enter everyone who comes to the open house in a drawing to win a basket of goodies, a gift certificate to a restaurant, or a bottle of wine. By creating an atmosphere of good times, your house will more likely stick in the agents' minds. That means your house will be one they are more likely to show.

FACT

Holding weekly or monthly drawings for everyone who views the house will boost interest. The award does not have to be extravagant. Movie tickets make a great prize. Agents may also respond well to a commission bonus, if they bring a buyer who actually buys the house. Not all agents will respond favorably to this, since they must disclose what they are being paid and the buyer might like to receive that bonus as a discount on the house.

Incentives for buyers can also be a part of your plan to stand out. Offering to pay for a weekend trip or to pay the cost of moving expenses can be a good incentive for a buyer. However, the best incentive for the buyer is a reduced price. If there are twenty homes in your subdivision, all similar in age and condition, but yours is the least expensive, which one do you think the most buyers will see?

Double-check Your Marketing Plan

There are times when proper marketing is lacking, and no one is aware that your house is for sale. Marketing does not sell your house (price and condition sell your house), but it does get the word out that your home is available. Find out what types of marketing work best in your area. When you interviewed agents, what did they say was working best?

If you find that your home is being marketed by the same methods as other homes in the area that are selling, the marketing may be just right. If you feel you need more visibility, investigate the options by paying close attention to the real estate advertising you encounter. Do most of your neighbors read the classifieds? Do you receive mass mailers from real estate agents advertising their properties? If so, these may be another form of marketing that works in your area. Do you have a sign in the yard? Is your property advertised on the Internet? When considering your marketing options, be sure to research their potential effectiveness by checking which marketing methods were used on properties in your area that sold.

It is easy to blame the agents and their marketing when your house has not sold. Many sellers give up on their first agent and may use two or three agents before their house sells. Sometimes it is the agent and their marketing that keeps a house from selling, but often, it is just the price. By the time a seller has worked with three or four agents, he is tired of having his house on the market and more willing to reduce the price. If the house sells without a price reduction, it is likely the market has risen to meet the price the seller expected—a price that was too high with the first agent those many months ago.

Chapter 18

Paperwork

We live in a litigious society. Because of this, the amount of paperwork needed to sell a home is overwhelming. Most of the paperwork contains language that is necessary to protect the seller or the buyer if something goes wrong. However, if you did not have to be concerned with misunderstandings, a contract could be as simple as this: "Mary Jones agrees to buy John Smith's house at 123 Main Street, Anytown, USA for the amount of $250,000." This chapter explains all the intricacies of homeselling paperwork.

What Is a Sales Contract?

The sales contract, often called the purchase agreement, is the written version of the conversation that a buyer and a seller have when negotiating a sale. First, a buyer submits a purchase agreement to a seller. This agreement outlines what the buyer is willing to pay for the property, the terms of the sale, and any contingencies the buyer may want. The sellers may accept this contract as written, they may reject the contract completely, or they may make a counteroffer to the buyer.

In the counteroffer, the sellers outline the changes they desire from the original offer. They may change the price but not the terms; they may change the price and terms but not the contingencies. They may clarify certain things in the original offer that appear to be vague.

QUESTION?

Do you have to make a counteroffer?
It is always a good idea to keep the lines of communication open. Even if you find most of the offer objectionable, making a counteroffer lets the buyer know what price and terms you are willing to take, and they may respond favorably.

The buyer may accept, reject, or counter back to the seller. This process can continue for several counteroffers until one party or the other either accepts or gives up. If they do give up, this action is shown by a rejection of the final counteroffer. Rejection of the offer or the subsequent counteroffer means that the house did not sell. Acceptance of an offer or a subsequent counteroffer means the house did sell, and the escrow process begins.

Parts of a Sales Contract

There are certain details that should be in every sales contract, starting with the offering price. The offering price should be broken down into several sections, including the earnest money deposit, down payment, loan amount, amount of any secondary loan, unusual compensation, and total offering price.

Earnest Money Deposit

Along with the contract, the buyer submits a deposit, known as an *earnest money deposit.* The escrow company or the attorney handling the transaction holds the earnest money deposit in their trust account. In some states, they are held in the real estate agent's trust account, but this is less common. The earnest money deposit is not as large as the down payment. Depending on the area of the country you are in, it can be as little as a few hundred dollars and as much as 10 percent of the offering price. These funds are considered good faith on the part of the buyer to show their intention to follow through with the sale. If the buyer cancels the contract due to the inability to satisfy themselves on the contingencies, this money is refunded to them, less any costs they have incurred (such as inspections).

Down Payment

Since most buyers need to obtain financing to purchase and since available financing for 100 percent of the purchase price is rare, this is the amount of cash that a buyer is willing to put toward the purchase of the house. If the buyer is obtaining 100 percent financing (an option available with VA loans and certain FHA financing), the down payment may be nonexistent. In cases such as these, it is a good idea to be sure the buyer is qualified for the loan fairly quickly.

ALERT!

If a buyer is paying all cash, be sure to get a letter from her bank, CPA, or other financial consultant assuring that she has adequate funds to purchase the property. You don't want a buyer to promise you cash and secretly go for a loan that doesn't get approved.

The most common down payment and the amount required for the majority of financing is 20 percent. With a down payment of at least 20 percent, the buyer will be able to qualify for the best rates and terms. Loan programs vary widely, and there are several programs available with down payments of 0 percent, 3 percent, 5 percent, 10 percent, and 15 percent.

Virtually any down payment has a loan to match it, but with down payments of less than 20 percent, the guidelines are tougher. If the buyer is putting down an amount larger than 20 percent of the purchase price, financing is usually easier to obtain. There are loan programs that will not verify income or assets but instead just look at a buyer's credit and down payment. A buyer may give a larger down payment to show you that it will be easy for them to qualify for a loan.

Loan Amount

This is the amount of money the buyer is financing for the purchase of your house. Many forms have a time frame in which the loan must be approved and a maximum interest rate that the buyer is willing to pay along with the loan terms. The time frame is a contingency of the offer, and the maximum interest rate and loan terms are also contingencies. Even if the buyer has full loan approval, if interest rates go up above the rate the buyer indicated on the offer, the buyer is not obligated to buy. Be sure that the buyer is removing the contingency on rates and terms when they remove the contingency on loan approval.

Amount of Any Secondary Loan

Sometimes it is necessary for a buyer to obtain two separate loans on the property. The secondary loan will also need to be approved, usually in conjunction with the primary loan. Be sure that the loan contingency on this loan is removed along with the primary loan contingency. If the buyer is asking you to grant them a secondary loan and you are willing to give one, you will want to get his financial information and have time to approve his qualifications.

Unusual Compensation

It is possible that a buyer may offer some unusual compensation and assign it a dollar value. One item of compensation that has become more common is a time-share. The value of the time-share would go toward the purchase price. Cars, boats, and jewelry can also be considered for a portion of the purchase price. Anything that is acceptable to the seller as a trade item can be considered. A promissory note, money owed to the buyer, can be transferred to the seller as a portion of the purchase price.

Some buyers may offer another residence as a portion of their purchase price. If you like the property, this may be an option for you. An independent appraisal and a CMA will help you determine value. Be sure you are comfortable with the value of the property they are offering before you accept a contract like this. You will also need a purchase agreement for the property they offer in trade. In essence, they are the seller on one property and you are the buyer, while you are the seller on the other property and they are the buyer. You will be inspecting the other property and going for a loan if necessary. If something happens to keep you from purchasing their property, you will also lose the sale on your property. However, if everything goes smoothly, this can be a beneficial solution.

Here's an example: A couple was trying to sell their house. Their kids were grown, and they were planning to scale down to a condominium and spend more time traveling. A man had looked at the couple's house three times. He really liked it, but he had a condominium to sell and no offers yet. Luckily, the couple's agent called the man's agent to find out why he had not made an offer after three showings. When it was discovered that he had a condominium to sell, the couple's agent took them to see the man's condominium. The couple liked the condominium and made an offer with their house as compensation. The deal came together, and the two parties traded homes.

Total Offering Price

Be sure that this amount is the total of the earnest money deposit, balance of the down payment, and loans all added together. If they don't add up correctly, you will need to clarify the total offering price in a counteroffer.

Contingencies and Time Frames

The next set of details will take into account the contingencies and the time frames related to them. All contingencies need to be released within a specified period of time, preferably before close of escrow and not on the day of close. If the contingencies are not released before close of escrow, you may end up moving without total assurance that the buyers are going to proceed.

When the contingencies are not met, you receive no compensation if the buyers do not go through with the purchase. Contingencies outlined should include loan approval or proof of funds for a cash transaction; inspections, evaluations, and disclosures; sale of another residence; and time frame to respond to the offer. Time frame to respond to the offer is usually a period of several days, after which any offers that have not been responded to will expire. Read on for explanations of the other contingencies.

Loan Approval or Proof of Funds for a Cash Transaction

Proof of funds for a cash transaction can occur in a matter of five days or less. Loan approval takes more time. The buyer must fill out a loan application and submit it to the lender. The lender will order an appraisal and will have to work with the appraiser's time frame. An appraisal can take three weeks or more to schedule and perform. Once the lender receives the loan application, they will need to verify everything on the application. They will send notices to the buyer's bank or other financial institutions, asking for average balances and balances to date. They will get verifications of employment and proof of other incomes. They will need a preliminary title report and any documentation relating to a homeowner's association, if one exists. They will run a credit report and obtain a credit score for the buyer. This gathering process takes about thirty days.

Once they have gathered all the necessary information, the lender packages the loan and sends it to underwriting for approval. The underwriter may request additional information, such as bank statements for the past two years or an explanation of a credit glitch. Once the underwriter is satisfied, they approve the loan, and it goes to the next department for the drawing of the loan documents. Loan documents are then sent to the escrow company or attorney or to the main lender's office for the buyer to sign. Once signed, the loan documents are then sent back to the lender and reviewed to be sure they were completed properly. When the final review is complete, they are sent to the funding department. From there, the loan is funded. This is usually accomplished by wire transfer to the escrow company or attorney handling the transaction, and the property is ready to close escrow. There are subcategorized dates for the loan contingency, such as the date to complete the loan application and the date that the lender will review the credit report and submit a prequalification letter.

Although there are buyers who pay cash, the majority of buyers are looking to obtain financing. It is important to know, as soon as possible, if the buyer is qualified. By having her complete a loan application and a credit report in the first few days and having the lender review it, you can receive what is commonly known as a prequalification letter. This letter basically says: The buyer's credit is good, and as long as everything on the application checks out, the house appraises at an acceptable value, and there are no surprises on the title, the loan will be approved.

Inspections, Evaluations, and Disclosures

Inspections are the next most common contingency, after the loan. A buyer wants to be sure he is purchasing a home that is in good repair. He does not want to discover any hidden defects after purchasing the home, especially defects that are expensive to fix. Having this knowledge up front allows the buyer peace of mind that he is making a purchase with no later hidden costs. There is a time frame for ordering the inspections, a time frame for receiving the inspections, and a time frame for getting a cost on the repairs outlined in the inspections. The final time frame is approval of the inspections and the cost of the repairs relating to it. This is usually expected to be accomplished within fifteen to twenty-one days. The contract will outline who pays for the repairs. There is usually a maximum dollar amount for which the seller is responsible. If the costs exceed that amount, there are three things that can occur.

- The buyer can decide to pay the balance of the costs not covered by the seller.
- The buyer and seller can negotiate who will pay the balance of the costs.
- The buyer may cancel the contract.

There are homes that look great on the surface but have underlying problems that are in need of repair. It is possible that the seller is not even aware of these items since they may have deteriorated slowly over time and gone unnoticed. Having an inspection will remove the potential of surprises later.

There are a number of different kinds of inspections. The primary ones are a general physical inspection and a pest inspection. Usually, a professional home inspector or a licensed contractor will perform the general home inspection, and a licensed pest control operator will perform the pest inspection. Once a physical inspection is obtained, there may be questions on certain items that are outside the scope of the inspector's expertise. The inspector may recommend that further investigation be done on one or several of the components of the house. Further inspection may be necessary by another type of inspector. These may include:

- Appraisal
- Fireplace or wood burning stove and chimney
- Heater
- Air conditioning
- Humidifier
- Roof
- Hazardous materials (radon, asbestos, lead paint)
- Mold
- Underground storage tank
- Sewer, septic, and/or leach field
- Well
- Spa, swimming pool
- Engineering report
- As-built survey
- Building department or other regulatory agency
- Seller's disclosure statement (required by most states)

Sale of Another Residence

This contingency is usually expected to be removed within a few days of the close of escrow on the property a buyer is purchasing. Subcategorized dates include a time when the property is to be listed for sale and a time when it must be in escrow.

The majority of buyers cannot purchase one house without selling another. The contingency on the sale of another house is common. When this contingency exists, it is important for the seller to learn about the other house. The other house should be on the market for sale. If it is not for sale, you will have a contingency that will tie your house up with no chance of getting it sold.

If the other property does not sell within the specified time frame, you may either cancel the contract or give the buyers an extension, allowing them more time to sell. An extension may be in order, if the buyer's house is in escrow and subject to only a small delay. Why put your house back on the market if you are close to having a completed transaction? However, when a contract is subject to the sale of another house, it is wise to solicit backup offers. If the buyers cannot perform on the sale of the other residence, you'll have a ready opportunity to sell your house to someone else. If you receive another offer, you give the current buyers a time frame in which to remove the contingency on the sale of their house, usually 72 hours. (This needs to be outlined in your original offer.) You may wish to have the buyers increase their earnest money deposit when they remove this contingency. If they cannot remove the contingency of the sale of their house, you can move on to the new buyers.

ALERT!

You will have a smaller pool of buyers once your house is in escrow contingent on the sale of another residence. Most buyers don't want to look at a house and get excited about it if they think they have little to no chance of getting it.

Meeting Deadlines

Every contract has deadlines that must be met. Inspections need to be ordered by a certain date and approved by a certain date. Loans must be approved on time. The house the buyer is selling must be in escrow and close by a certain date, and money must be deposited by a certain date. If these deadlines are not met, the party not meeting the deadlines is considered *out of contract*. This means that you no longer have a deal. If your agent does not provide you with a calendar of events, create one. Put every clause of the contract that has a date in it on the calendar, with a notation as to who is responsible for the action. By keeping track of these events, you can be sure that important dates are not missed.

ALERT!

The more offers and counteroffers there are, the more opportunity for misunderstanding. Some agents like to condense the offers and counteroffers into one new and final offer that is agreed upon by both parties. Be sure to read it carefully; it is possible for some of the changes to be missed in the consolidation offer.

Legal Issues with a Sales Contract

Once a purchase agreement and subsequent counteroffers are signed, the sales contract is in place. Throughout the escrow period, addenda can also be made to modify the contract. As a seller, you cannot break the contract. It is up to the buyer to perform. If the buyer does not perform, the contract is void, unless modifications are agreed upon between the parties. There is also a section of the contract that will address what happens if something goes wrong. What happens if a contingency date isn't met? What happens if the buyer defaults? What happens if the seller changes his mind and refuses to sell?

There are rare occasions when the seller also has a contingency to meet. Perhaps a seller will not sell unless he finds another place to purchase, for example, within ten days of acceptance of the contract. If this is the case and the seller cannot perform, the contract becomes void.

It is said that every time there is a lawsuit another paragraph is added to a contract. In some states, the purchase contracts with all the required disclosures can be as many as fifty pages!

A Binder: An Offer to Purchase

When first submitting an offer to purchase, a buyer will sometimes not submit a complete offer. She may submit a binder instead. With a binder, the buyer submits her offering price and an earnest money deposit. The binder is contingent on an actual contract being written by the seller's attorney and approved by the buyer's attorney. A clause such as this should be present in a binder: "This agreement is subject to contracts being drawn by a reputable attorney and executed by all parties concerned within ___ days." Usually five days is sufficient to accomplish this task.

In some areas of the country, the binder is known as a *letter of intent*. A letter of intent also outlines the price and terms a buyer is willing to offer, but it does not always have an accompanying earnest money deposit. It is also contingent on the buyer and the seller executing a purchase contract, where the earnest money deposit is outlined and submitted.

Paperwork by an FSBO

Each state has different requirements for sales contracts and disclosures. As an FSBO, knowing what paperwork you need can be the difference between a smooth transaction and one fraught with problems and potential lawsuits.

In some states, you may use a generic sales contract; in others, you must use one approved by the state. Some states have forms that are required for certain disclosures but none for the actual purchase agreement. To be sure you are using the proper documentation, check with your state's Division of Real Estate. The phone numbers for each state are listed in Appendix A.

ALERT!

The federal government requires a lead paint disclosure for any home built before 1978. It also requires that the seller give the buyer the pamphlet titled *Protect Your Family From Lead in Your Home.* Information about this law, the pamphlet, and the required form can be found on the Internet at *www.pueblo.gsa.gov* or *www.epa.gov.*

Most local Realtor® boards have specific forms that they use, even if there isn't a standard form required by the state. As an FSBO, you will not have access to these forms. However, unless specific forms are required by your state, you can technically use any form you like. To be sure that you do not miss any of the points of a purchase contract, you may want to find some generic forms on the Internet at *www.uslegalforms.com.* It is also important to consult with an attorney.

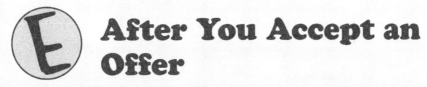

Chapter 19

After You Accept an Offer

Once you accept an offer, the real work begins. Accepting an offer is just the first in a long list of items that need to be accomplished before your property can change hands. Because the majority of these items need to be accomplished by the buyer, the seller spends many days waiting. Creating a list of what needs to be accomplished and when will make the waiting easier. This chapter will tell you all you need to know to get things done correctly.

Creating a Timeline

If you are working with an agent, she should create a timeline for you. If this is not normally done for sellers in your area, you will want to create one for yourself. If you are an FSBO, you will want to create one timeline for yourself and one for the buyer. Knowing what items need to be completed and the dates by which they need to be completed will help to keep everything running smoothly.

ALERT!

Be sure you have the buyer's permission to check on loan status. If not, the lender may not be able to give you any information. When checking on status, ask if the appraisal has been completed, if there are verifications of the buyer's employment and bank deposits, and if the loan has been sent to underwriting for final approval.

Every contingency in the contract needs to be removed by a certain date and before close of escrow. For example, if you have a forty-five day escrow, the buyer may have thirty-five days in which to obtain a loan. Marking a calendar with the day that the loan needs to be approved will allow you to keep track of it. For a loan that must be approved within thirty-five days, you should mark your calendar to check the loan status at the fifteen day and the twenty-five day marks. If you are working with an agent, be sure he checks on the loan status for you. Checking the loan status throughout the process will give you a heads-up on any issues that need to be handled and keep those issues from becoming last minute problems.

Disclosures: What to Tell Before You Sell

There are a number of different disclosures that you may be required to complete. Each state and region has different regulations. Your agent will know what disclosures are required in your area. If you are not working with an agent, check with the governing body in your state that regulates the real estate industry. It is often called the Division of Real Estate or the

CHAPTER 19: AFTER YOU ACCEPT AN OFFER

Department of Business and Industry Real Estate Division. (The phone numbers for all state real estate regulatory bodies are listed in Appendix A.)

Seller's Disclosure Statements

Most states require a seller's disclosure statement. This is usually a form, provided by the state, which a seller must complete. In this form, the seller states everything they know to be true about the components of the home. Many sellers do not want to tell the buyer anything negative about the house for fear that they will scare the buyer away. Properly filling out a seller's disclosure statement will protect you from future liabilities; so filling it out correctly is necessary, even if there are negative features to share.

Most sellers' disclosure forms have a list of the components of the house to remind the seller of everything he needs to disclose. An average disclosure may look something like this.

Are you aware of any problems with the following? If so, please explain.

- Electrical system
- Range/oven/hood/cook top/trash compactor/warming drawers/ microwave
- Built-in refrigerator/wine refrigerator/icemaker
- Plumbing system
- Water heater
- Water softener/purification system
- Dishwasher/garbage disposal
- Sinks, showers, toilets, bathtubs
- Sewer system and sewer line
- Septic system and leach field
- Water system and water line
- Well and pump
- Heater/air conditioner/humidifier
- Fireplace/wood burning stove
- Alarm system/interior fire sprinkler system/smoke detectors
- Sauna/hot tub/swimming pool

- Yard sprinkler system/fountains/French drains
- Central vacuum
- Intercom
- Satellite dish/cable/data communication
- Foundation
- Water infiltration/high water table/settling
- Structural defects
- Unpermitted work
- Roof
- Mold
- Pest infestation
- Environmental hazards (such as lead paint, radon, fuel tanks, asbestos)
- Other

Lead-based Paint

Any home built before 1978 is subject to a Lead-based Paint Disclosure. This is a federal law, and the penalties for not complying can run into multiple thousands of dollars. Not only is the disclosure required, it is also necessary to give your buyer a pamphlet created by the U.S. Environmental Protection Agency (EPA). This pamphlet is titled *Protect Your Family From Lead in Your Home.* Your agent can provide the pamphlet for you. As an FSBO, it can be obtained through the EPA. If you have records regarding the use of lead paint in your house, those records must be submitted to the buyer as well.

Lead paint can be very dangerous, especially to children. There is a concern that young children may ingest lead paint chips, but older children can also be at risk. For example, lead paint dust can transfer to a stuffed animal left leaning on a painted wall. This dust can be harmful as the child may inhale it when playing or sleeping with the toy. Depending on the level of exposure, it is also possible for lead to create health concerns for adults. Effects can be as minimal as headaches or as sinister as damage to the brain and nervous system. Lead exposure can create problems with pregnancy or slowed growth in children, as well as problems with the digestive system, high blood pressure, and muscle or joint pain.

FACT

In most areas, a buyer's walk-through is not considered a contingency, but it is a necessary part of the selling process. This walk-through is usually performed within a few days of the close of escrow. The buyer uses the walk-through to ascertain that all the repairs agreed to were completed and that the property is vacant, clean, and ready for them to occupy.

The buyer is given a time frame to assess the lead paint situation at the property. If there is an issue, a lead paint abatement may need to be accomplished. A contractor who specializes in this type of work can remove or seal the paint to prevent future problems. If this was accomplished when you purchased the home, these records must be given to the buyer.

Mold

Some types of mold are benign, but some can be very dangerous. Mold has received a considerable amount of press in the last few years because certain molds are now known to be a high allergen. This means that many people are allergic to these molds and can have very strong reactions if exposed. A toxic black mold, called *Stachybotrys chartarum*, has been known to cause rashes, breathing problems, and brain malfunction. Because of the fear of this type of mold, buyers may be wary of the more benign molds as well.

ALERT!

There may be mold in places you cannot see such as inside the walls, behind siding, and under the house. Unchecked leaks and water seepage are the biggest causes of this unseen mold. Even a pinhole-size leak can cause mold to grow.

Molds are everywhere, both inside and outside the home. When exposed to moisture, microscopic spores will eventually grow to a proportion that is visible to the naked eye.

If you keep your home free of mold or mildew by washing areas with a solution of one part bleach to nine parts water, you can eliminate some, if not all, of the problems with mold.

If you have had a problem with mold, it is important to disclose this to a prospective buyer. Some buyers will not be concerned. Other buyers, especially someone with a high allergic reaction to mold, may decide to cancel the contract. It is better to know now that a buyer is concerned about mold than to have that buyer sue after the sale because of their reaction to the mold.

FACT

Most states do not require a mold expert to have a special license. Many so-called experts have started working in the field to cash in on potential profits. Some mold experts will give a false report and recommend a remediation company that pays the expert a fee for falsely finding "dangerous" mold. Be sure to get referrals from reputable sources.

If a buyer has concerns about mold, he may require a mold expert to test the home. These experts take air samples and actual samples in several areas of the house, inside as well as outside. They determine if the air inside the home has similar readings to the air outside. If the mold count on the interior of the home is too high or of a dangerous nature, a remediation expert must be called in. This person will eliminate the mold and prepare the home for another test. Then, the mold expert comes back to give the home a clean bill of health.

Radon

Radon is an odorless, colorless, and tasteless radioactive gas that is known to cause certain kinds of lung cancer. It is a naturally occurring phenomenon. In enclosed spaces, such as your basement, it can be very dangerous. If you know you have radon, it is important to disclose that fact.

A buyer may also have a test for radon performed at your house. They may use a passive testing device. This device is usually a charcoal-filled canister that is left in the home for a specified period of time. A passive device cannot be moved while it is recording data. If the buyer has a huge concern about radon, they may use an active device. The active device requires power to function and is a more expensive and more reliable option than a passive device. Active devices have meters that continuously measure and record radon in the air. These devices can be moved to record radon in different areas of the house.

Asbestos

Asbestos is a mineral fiber that can be identified with a special microscope. The inhalation of asbestos has been known to increase the risk of lung cancer. Asbestos is a fire retardant material that was commonly used in building products until the mid-1970s, when the health risks became known. Asbestos can be found in textured paint and patching compounds, which are common in the acoustical ceilings of older homes. It can also be found in the insulation of houses built between about 1930 and 1950. Asbestos was also used in vinyl floor tiles, gaskets for oil or coal furnaces, walls and floors around wood burning stoves, hot water pipe insulation (in older homes), and other areas where there may be a danger of fire. As long as asbestos is left in good condition and the fibers are not released into the air, it is not considered dangerous. For more information on asbestos, you can go to *www.epa.gov/asbestos* on the Internet.

Environmental Concerns

There are environmental concerns that do not fall under the radon, lead paint, and asbestos categories. Many of these are regional concerns. If there was a factory that deposited toxic waste into the water or soil, even if that factory is no longer producing, this must be disclosed. It is also important to disclose if any environmental agencies that dictate building regulations or how a property can be used have jurisdiction over the property.

You may be located in an avalanche area, on a flood plain, or in an area of crumbling coastline. If you do not know if your location is environmentally hazardous, check with your agent. It is their job to know what disclosures you need. If you are an FSBO, you can get information from the U.S. Geological Survey (*www.usgs.gov*), the Army Corp of Engineers (*www.usace.army.mil*), or the U.S. Bureau of Reclamation (*www.usbr.gov*).

Planned Developments

There are several types of properties that have association regulations and fees. Planned unit developments may look like freestanding homes, but they have common facilities, and they have an association. Condominiums, townhomes, and cooperatives also have association regulations and fees. It is important to disclose to a potential buyer what those fees are and how the fees are used. Some states have regulations regarding what is disclosed, and some states have even created forms to help you remember what needs to be disclosed. Some states do not have requirements about this type of disclosure, but even if your state does not have regulations for disclosure, it is wise to give your buyer the following information.

- CC&Rs (Covenants, Conditions, and Restrictions)
- Bylaws
- Any additional rules and regulations
- Amounts for monthly dues and any additional assessments
- Budget, financial statement, balance sheet, and reserves
- Any pending legal action against the homeowner's association or by the homeowner's association against another entity or person (such as a contractor)
- Minutes of the last several meetings of the board of directors, plus the annual meeting
- Common facilities and their use

Financing Arrangements

If the buyer is obtaining a loan, there will be several deadlines that need to be met. The first deadline is submitting a loan application. This should be done quickly, usually within five to ten days from acceptance of the offer. There are also deadlines for the appraisal, loan approval, removing the loan contingency, signing the loan, and funding of the loan.

Banks and other financial institutions want to be sure that they are lending on a property that has a value of the purchase price or better. To be sure of this, they hire a licensed appraiser to determine the value. How an appraiser determines the value is outlined in Chapter 13.

Once the bank hires the appraiser, the appraiser will call for access to the property. There are rare occasions when the appraiser does not need access, but most of the time, an appraiser will need to get inside the house. They will measure the house and take photographs to use as they compare your house to similar homes that have sold. It is important to allow the appraiser access as soon as possible. After the appraiser visits your home, she will still need to find comparables, take photos of them, and prepare the report. If the appraiser is delayed in seeing your house, it can hold up the entire loan process.

Title Review Contingency

The buyer will have the opportunity to review a preliminary title report. This report will show the amount you owe on the property. That amount will be paid off at sale. It also shows any easements, mineral rights, and other items associated with the property. A buyer will look at several things. If you owe more on the property than they are paying, they will want to be sure that you have the cash to close the transaction. If you have refinanced and the original loan has not yet been removed from the title (reconveyed), it may look like you owe more than you actually do. The title company will be able to clear up these types of discrepancies.

FACT

In some areas, the escrow company or attorney will draw up instructions detailing the items in the contract. These instructions must be approved by both parties within a specified time frame.

Most of the easements will be standard easements for access by power companies or road maintenance. There may be an easement for a neighbor to cross a portion of your driveway to get to his driveway. A buyer will review everything to assure himself that he can be comfortable with any easement that remains with the property. Once in awhile, there will be something that a buyer finds objectionable. If this is the case, he may request that you have it eliminated from the title. If you can have the objectionable item eliminated, he will proceed. If it is not possible, the contract may be canceled, and you will be putting your home back on the market.

Home Inspections

The buyer may order several different types of home inspections depending on the customs of your area, the types of things they want to learn about, and the age of your property. The two most common home inspections are pest inspection and physical inspection.

Pest Inspection

Check for existing pest infestations, the potential for infestation of pests, and damage from previous infestations. The most common pests are termites, carpenter ants, and wood-destroying fungi. Rodents, woodpeckers, and other creatures that cause damage to property can also be included in the report. A pest report will also take into account areas of the home that have the potential for problems. If there is debris under the house that makes a good breeding ground for pests, it will be noted. This debris is often called cellulose debris. A pest inspector will also note if there is any earth to wood contact. If portions of the siding or structural posts are touching earthen terrain or if firewood is stacked against the house, wood destroying pests have easy access into the house.

Physical Inspection

Physical inspections are very common. A professional home inspector visits the property and looks it over to see that there are no obvious defects in the structure or systems. In most states, the home inspectors are licensed. Some states do not have licensing laws for home inspectors, but in these areas, an inspector may be a contractor or retired building department official. The American Society of Home Inspectors (ASHI) is an organization of home inspectors who complete specialized education programs and subscribe to a code of ethics. If your state does not require licensing, an ASHI inspector may be your best choice. For further information, you can check their Web site *www.ashi.com.*

Most physical inspectors will give an overview of the property. If a buyer is concerned about the roof or the fireplace, they may ask for those inspections as well. The inspector may suggest certain inspections that are out of their area of expertise, such as an electrical or alarm system inspection.

There are times when the physical inspection will point to things that may need further investigation. If this is the case, additional inspections may be performed. These may include:

- Roof
- Engineering
- Foundation
- Chimney/fireplace/woodstove
- Underground storage tank, such as one for fuel oil
- Mold
- Hazardous materials
- Lead paint
- Survey
- Septic system
- Well
- Heating/cooling system
- Verification of acreage of the land or square footage of the house

The buyer's approval of these inspections is one of the contingencies on the sale of your house. Depending on the number of inspections and average time frame for getting them completed in your area, removal of this contingency can take anywhere from a few weeks to thirty days or more. Sometimes, a buyer will remove the contingencies on the inspections subject to certain repairs being performed by the seller. In your contract there should have been a dollar limit placed on those potential repairs. As long as the requested repairs come within the dollar limit, you can complete the repairs, and the buyer can remove that contingency. If the repairs exceed the dollar limit, you have several choices.

- You can complete the requested repairs, even though you will be spending more than expected.
- You can ask the buyer to complete the balance of the repairs.
- You can come to a mutually agreeable amount for each of you to complete.

If you ask the buyer to complete repairs that are over and above the dollar limit, he has the right to say no. If this happens, you may be placing your home back on the market.

QUESTION?

Should you order inspections yourself?
If you are in a seller's market and expecting multiple offers, having the inspections done in advance will eliminate surprises and allow potential buyers to come in without that contingency. If you are not in a seller's market, most buyers expect to perform their own inspections and may not even accept the inspection you have done.

Buyer's One-year Home Warranty

An insurance industry has grown up around insuring buyers against potential problems when they first buy a home. This type of insurance has become more and more popular. Home warranty plans cover the major components of the home that may break down in the first year. The plans cover the cost of repair or replacement (less a deductible of about $35) for the kitchen appliances, except the refrigerator, washer, and dryer, which are considered personal property. Most plans also cover the heater, water heater, plumbing and electrical systems, and, in some states, a limited amount of roof repair. The cost of these policies is in the $250 to $500 range and can be well worth it. Your agent probably works with one or two different home warranty companies.

If you do not have an agent or your agent does not work with these companies, you can check the Internet. Some of the most popular home warranty companies are Old Republic (*www.orhp.com*), First American Home

Warranty (*www.homewarranty.firstam.com*), and American Home Shield (*www.americanhomeshield.com*). Read all the fine print. Pre-existing conditions, incorrect modifications to appliances, and some other items are not covered under these plans.

FACT

After spending their life savings getting into a house, it is great for buyers to know that the major expenses are covered for the first year. As a seller, offering a home warranty to prospective buyers can also be a great selling feature. Mention it on your flyer and in the MLS. It will give the buyer peace of mind, especially with an older home.

As a seller, a home warranty policy provides the security of knowing the buyer will not come back to you six months after closing and ask for a water heater. You may also qualify for seller's coverage, usually for a small fee. This will put the policy in place while you are on the market. If any of the major components of the home fail during this time, repair or replacement can be handled by the home warranty company. Just as no one wants to put new tires on a car he is selling, no one wants to replace a dishwasher in a house he is selling.

Surveys and Rental Inspections

In some areas of the country, it is common to have a survey completed on the property in order to transfer ownership. It is less common in other areas, but it is often a good idea. Buyers may request a survey if there are numerous easements, there is a question as to the property lines, the buyer plans to expand the house in the future, or for a number of other reasons. Depending on the last time the property was surveyed and the schedule of the surveyor, a survey can take three weeks or more to complete. This contingency can run concurrently with the other contingencies to save time. The cost of a survey is dependent on the size and location of your property, as well as how much time the surveyor needs to complete it. On a quarter- or half-acre parcel, a typical survey will be in the $1,000 to $1,500 range in most areas of the country.

If it is customary in your area to have a survey, it is best to order it as soon as possible, even before you have a buyer. A surveyor's schedule may be busy, and it could take several weeks before he can even start the process.

If the house you are selling is a rental, the buyers will want to see the lease or rental agreement and an accounting of the rental history. They will need to know the amount of the security deposit, and they will need to see the tenants' move-in statement. If you have photos of the property before the tenant moved in, they will need those as well. They may even request to interview the tenants. The buyers may take these items to their CPA or financial adviser for approval, and this contingency can take time as well.

Title Arrangements

Most sellers and buyers have no experience with title companies. For this reason, they depend on their agent to find the company that will be best for them. If there is no agent involved, the seller and the buyer usually make the decision by mutual agreement. You may have found a title company to work with you when you were building your team. (See Chapter 8.) As long as the buyer is comfortable with the title company, you can move forward with the one you have chosen.

ALERT!

According to the Federal Real Estate Settlement Procedures Act (R.E.S.P.A.), 12 U.S.C. § 2608 provides that a seller or seller's broker may not require the buyer, as a condition of sale, to purchase title insurance from any particular title company if the buyer uses a federally related loan to help purchase the property, irrespective of who pays for the title insurance.

The change of title is accomplished with a signed grant deed from seller to buyer and recorded with the county recorder's office. In the western portion of the country, all the paperwork and signings are completed in advance of the close of escrow. The buyer's funds are wired to the escrow company the day before escrow closes. On rare occasions, the funds are wired the day of close. Once funds are received, the documents that need to be recorded, most commonly the deed and the loan documents, are sent by courier to the county recorder's office. When the courier submits them, the county recorder officially confirms receipt of the recordable documents, and the property changes hands.

In the eastern portion of the country, all the paperwork and signings are done at the closing table. The buyers and sellers and their agents and attorneys all come to the table together. If you cannot go to the closing, you can appoint your attorney to be at the closing in your stead, but being at the closing yourself is customary. The grant deed and any other paperwork are signed. Keys, money, and paperwork are exchanged. Loan funds are usually wired to the closing, but the buyers present their cashier's check at the closing table. It is at this time that the property changes hands. The attorney insures that the grant deed and loan documents are recorded with the county on that day or the following morning.

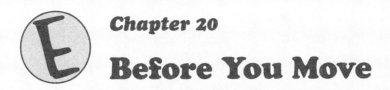

Chapter 20

Before You Move

The time between placing a home on the market and actually selling it can be a stressful one for most sellers. Each showing could mean a potential buyer. Did they like the house? Were they here long enough to see all the great features? The time between getting an offer on the house and actually closing escrow can be even more stressful. Are the inspections going well? Can they get the loan? Knowing what happens now and what happens next will eliminate some of the stress.

The Waiting Game

Once you have an accepted contract on your house, there is a period of time, usually between thirty and sixty days, where the buyer performs all the tasks necessary to complete the purchase. You spend the majority of this time waiting for answers, while the buyer or his agent coordinates all the tasks. You or your agent will have the timeline of events to keep tabs on the buyer. If you stay informed at each step in the process, it will make the waiting less painful.

ALERT!

Use the waiting time to continue packing. If you have been in the house a long time, packing will be the biggest task of the selling and moving process. Remember, it is easier to stack boxes if they are all the same size. Place them in one staging area so you can continue to live comfortably. Be sure to label them!

Check in with your agent if she does not check in with you. At the beginning of the escrow, there will probably be new information about once a week and more often as you move closer to the closing. Once the inspections are completed, you or your agent will be scheduling repairs and having them accomplished. When things are happening and you are not just waiting, the time will pass more quickly. Sometimes it actually goes too fast and projects like packing can get away from you.

After the Contract, Is Your House Still for Sale?

The answer is yes and no. Once you have a signed contract, it is up to the buyers to complete their due diligence, and it is up to you to permit that to happen. This means that the buyers need to have their inspections done, get their loan in place, and perhaps sell another house in a specified time frame.

During this time, you may continue to offer the property for sale to allow for backup offers. These offers would replace your buyer's offer in the event they falter during the contingency period or fail to go through with the sale. This does not mean you can break the contract with the existing buyer if a better offer comes along.

Backup offers can work if your current buyer has another house to sell. If another offer comes in, the current buyer is usually given seventy-two hours to remove the contingency on the sale of her other house. If she does not have a buyer for her house by then, the backup offer can take over first position.

If you are soliciting for backup offers, you may not actually get one. Don't be disappointed if no backup offers materialize. Chances are that you will have fewer showings as well. Most agents do not want to show a house that is under contract since their buyers may like it and be disappointed when they cannot have it. Savvy buyers don't want to present a backup offer. If they think an existing contract may fail, they just wait for the house to come back on the market. Savvy buyers know that a backup offer will make the current buyer stronger. Since the current buyer will follow the contract to the letter if they are worried that someone else can take over their position, a backup offer can be seen as a waste of time.

The Closing

When the buyer's loan funds and down payment are received at the escrow company or attorney's office, it is time for the close. At this point, the escrow officer or attorney will release the deed to record in the county recorder's office.

Customs vary from state to state as to what happens at the closing. In many states, traditionally in the eastern part of the country, everyone is present at the closing. All parties sit around a closing table and exchange money, keys, deed, and other paperwork. This includes the buyer, seller, their agents and the attorneys for the buyer and seller. In most areas of the western portion of the country, there is no closing table. All the paperwork is signed in advance, money is wired and the escrow company makes sure that everything is recorded properly. The seller gives the keys to her agent or the escrow company for delivery to the buyer.

Once all this has happened, your property is sold. Any loans, liens, or other costs you have are paid off, the expenses related to the transaction are paid, and the balance of the money is given to you or sent on to the escrow company or attorney who is handling the purchase of your new home.

ALERT!

There are times when the closing process is not enough to complete a sale, but these times are rare. If the buyer believes he has been sold the property under fraudulent circumstances, he may file a lawsuit to rescind the sale, requiring you to buy back the house. Be sure you have all agreements between you and the buyer in writing!

Occupancy Before Closing

The sellers moved out a few days before close of escrow, and the buyers wanted time to move in. They asked if they could just move items into the garage; they were not going to sleep in the house. The buyers were granted permission and began to move their belongings into the garage. During this time, they met the neighbor. This neighbor hated the seller and really wanted to make his life miserable. When the neighbor discovered the property had not actually changed hands, he told the buyer several lies about the house that made the buyer afraid to go through with the purchase. The buyers moved out of the garage and cancelled the contract. The seller attempted to keep the earnest money deposit, but the buyer threatened a lawsuit, which would prevent the seller from selling the property to someone else without settling with the buyers. The seller gave up the fight in order to place the home back on the market and get it sold quickly.

Although allowing the buyers to move in a few days before close of escrow does not always turn out to be a disaster, without some sort of monetary compensation for this extra time, you are setting yourself up for potential problems. Even if they only move into the garage, you will have the liability of a landlord with none of the protection or benefits.

In a lease option, the buyer does move in before close of escrow, but the seller has received monetary compensation. If you plan to allow the buyer to move in before close, have some of the funds released directly to you and/ or require the buyer to pay rent. Coordinating a move can be difficult, and it is helpful to accommodate people. Just be sure that you are protected.

Before you grant early access to your house, call your homeowner's insurance carrier and let them know you are allowing the buyer to move in early. Be sure that any accidents, fires, or injuries are covered under your policy. If not, get a binder for those few days and have the buyer pay for it.

You need to have an understanding of the tenant-landlord laws in your state. If you do not have an agent, you may be able to find this information at your local county court house or on the Internet. If the buyer does move in early and you end up with a problem, you want to be sure that you can get the buyer out of the house easily. In some states, it can take several months to get a tenant out of a piece of property. Up-front monetary compensation will make the wait less of an issue.

Occupancy After Closing

Some sellers just can't get out in time, and there are unforeseen things that can prevent the most organized person from moving as planned. Perhaps the buyers need to close escrow quickly for tax reasons, but you can't move out by that date. Suppose there is a big snowstorm; suppose the place you are buying isn't ready. There are many cases when a seller may want to stay on for a few days or more.

If you remain in the house after close of escrow, you become a tenant. Naturally, the buyer will want to be protected under the tenant-landlord laws of your state. You will want to compensate the buyer for the cost of you staying on the property. This is usually a daily amount, prorated to cover the buyer's principal, interest, taxes, and insurance on the property, or fair market rent, whichever is higher. You will still be responsible for utilities; so don't have them changed over until you move out.

Many sellers get upset about the idea of paying rent on their own home. After the close, it is no longer your home; it is the buyer's new home. If you are a tenant, you should pay rent.

ALERT!

The buyers should contact their insurance company to let them know that you are staying in the property for a period of time after the close of escrow. Since you are no longer the homeowner, your insurance company will not cover any losses to the structure. Since your personal belongings are not covered by the buyer's insurance, you should get a temporary renter's policy to cover your contents. These policies are usually under $100.

The buyers bought your house because they wanted it. Unless it is an investment and they are not planning to move in, your stay-over period will be very difficult for them. They have purchased a house, and now they want to be in it! Be gracious about allowing the buyers access to the property so that they can measure rooms or decide where things will go. If there is a way to avoid staying after close of escrow, you should.

Leave On, Turn Off, or Transfer?

Transferring a house is only a part of the process. You are moving and must also transfer utilities, mail, and other services. Once you receive an offer, make a list of the utilities and other services that you need to change. These may include:

- Electrical power
- Natural gas

- Propane
- Oil
- Sewer or septic service
- Water
- Trash
- TV and cable
- Rented satellite
- Telephone
- Internet
- Regular deliveries such as milk or bottled water
- U.S. mail

The processes required to transfer all these services can take some time. You will have a lot to do, and it is wise to start a little early. After you have reviewed the list to be sure you have included everything, call each service provider individually. Ask how much time they need to transfer the service into another person's name. Some may be able to do it in a day or less. Some will need time to read meters or collect other information to determine final billing, which could take a week or more. Once you know the time frames, add that information to the list. This will allow you to take care of the transfers as late as possible—hopefully, after all the contingencies are removed.

You may want to give this list to the buyers or their agent as a courtesy—to be sure they have everything turned on in their name as you turn it off. This can prevent downtime of the utilities. Downtime is a strong disadvantage in the winter with no heat (potential for frozen pipes) or in the summer with no air conditioning (potential for heat stroke).

In order to have your mail forwarded to your new address, you will need to fill out change of address forms with the U.S. Postal Service. These forms are available at your post office branch. You should also directly notify everyone who sends you a bill or a magazine and notify the people on your personal mailing list.

Even if you move out early, do not turn off the utilities before you close escrow. If there is a problem, such as frozen pipes, it will likely be your responsibility.

Tips for Moving with Children

In the process of moving, adults can put up with lots of things that are hard for kids to handle. A change of routine, lack of sleep, and too much pizza may be okay for an adult, but for a child, it can be a lot harder. With parents' nerves on edge during this time, children can sense the anxiety, and it makes them uneasy. A child will get unhappy and make the rest of the family unhappy if his regular schedule is disrupted. If you take some extra time to help your kids through this, it will be a more pleasant experience for all of you.

Ideally, the children should see your new place in advance of the move. Let them talk about their new rooms; make the idea fun and exciting. If they are not able to come with you to the new house, bring home pictures and show them how great it is going to be.

Here is a list of pointers to make the move easier on your kids.

- Bring a small box of their favorite toys with you in the car. Don't put them all in the moving van.
- Give each child a disposable camera, labeled with his name, to record the move. Get the pictures developed as soon as you get settled in the new house.
- Food helps. Be sure there are lots of healthy and fun snacks on hand. Cold bottled water is important, too. Kids' eating schedules will get messed up during a move, which can make them cranky.
- Relax for a few moments every hour or so and play with the kids.
- Whistle while you work, or play your children's favorite CD.
- A nap works wonders—for you and the kids.

Chapter 21

Special Sales Situations

Not all real estate transactions involve a primary home or a single-family house. There are many different types of real estate, and each type of property has unique qualities that need to be addressed when that property is for sale. This chapter will cover some of the most popular additional property types, including condo, co-op, inherited home, vacation home, time-share, and vacant land, and the intricacies involved with selling them.

Selling a Condo

When you are selling a condominium, you are not merely selling a unit. You are also selling ownership in an association. As the owner of a condominium, you are a partial owner of all the shared facilities, known as the common areas. That common area, such as driveways, roofs, shared and exterior walls, swimming pools, insurance, and other shared facilities, are maintained and paid for by the homeowner's association, of which each owner is a part. Each homeowner's association has documentation that explains the details of the association's duties.

FACT

There are freestanding condominiums where you own the airspace individually and the building and grounds in common. Sometimes these freestanding units are a part of a planned unit development (PUD). In a PUD, you own the airspace and the building plus a small portion of the land. You own the balance of the land and any facilities in common with other owners.

Each owner is required to pay association dues or fees to the homeowner's association to cover the costs of maintaining the common areas. A portion of that money is used for daily or weekly maintenance, such as pool chemicals and landscaping. A portion is also placed on reserve for long-term maintenance, such as driveway sealing or roof replacement. It is the seller's responsibility to make the buyer aware of all the documentation related to the association.

Bylaws

Bylaws are simply rules and regulations adopted by an association or corporation, which govern its activities. Condominiums often use bylaws to keep control of the property.

CC&Rs: Covenants, Conditions, and Restrictions

Covenants, conditions, and restrictions (CC&Rs) is a term used in some areas to describe the restrictive limitations that may be placed on property. In some areas, these are simply called restrictions. The CC&R document provides detailed information about the association's rules for maintenance and use and is distributed to all members of the homeowner's association (owners).

Budget

The expenses of the association or corporation determine the budget. Once those expenses are discovered, monthly dues are assessed, which reflect the amount needed to run the common areas and build a reserve account for long-term maintenance. If the monthly dues do not cover the expenses, it is possible that each property owner will be assessed a one-time fee to catch up on the costs. If dues continue to fall short of costs, it is possible to have additional assessments.

Lender Requirements

Lenders want to be sure that they are lending money on a property that has a value greater than that of their loan. As with all other homes, the lender will require an appraisal. When lending on a condo, they will also require the association documentation, including the budget. A condominium association with a weak financial position or with limited documentation can make it difficult for your buyer to get a loan. This could mean working with several different lenders before finding one that will loan on the property, or it could mean paying a higher interest rate. Some buyers will be concerned about this and decide not to purchase the property.

Some lenders will be concerned if there are more tenant-occupied units than owner-occupied units in your complex. Lenders view properties with high tenant- to owner-occupied ratios as investment properties and may require a higher down payment, charge a higher interest rate, or deny the loan.

If your association is in a weakened condition, you may want to shop for loans in advance of placing your property on the market so that you can direct buyers to the best sources. If this is not possible, consider paying some of the loan fees, which may allow the buyer to obtain a better interest rate. The lender may require that certain things be accomplished before they lend, such as a clear pest report. The association may be deemed responsible to meet some of the requirements, but it may not be in their budget. You could end up paying for them.

Selling a Cooperative or Co-Op

A cooperative, sometimes called a stock cooperative, is a structure of two or more units owned by a corporation. The right to occupy a unit is obtained by the purchase of stock in the corporation that owns the building. This right is similar to a lease—a lease that lasts for as long as the corporation exists.

Can the buyer of your co-op use the same lender you did when you purchased it?
Check with the lender you used to be sure they have not changed their lending guidelines and are still lending on cooperatives.

Because the building that houses a co-op is owned by a corporation (of which owners are a part), the corporation may require that any new owner be approved by the board of directors. Although approvals are more a matter of custom than an actual approval, it can be uncomfortable for a buyer to be interviewed before they are allowed to purchase.

Be aware that some lenders will not loan on co-ops because a co-op is not considered real property. As stated previously, it is ownership in a corporation that owns property, not in the actual property itself. Lenders who are willing to lend on co-ops will still want to see financial and other documentation relevant to the corporation. Sometimes a seller must finance, and sometimes it is necessary to find an outside lender. Some corporations own several co-op complexes and have the financial ability to lend the money on the sale of a unit in their corporation.

Staging a Condo or Co-op to Sell

Every homeowner's association or corporation has different rules and regulations regarding what can be done on the outside of a property. In some associations, no personal items can be left outside; others are less concerned about your individuality. If you are allowed a welcome mat, get one. If you are allowed flowerpots, place some outside your door with brightly colored flowers. If you are allowed a flag, hang one. It does not have to be a U.S. flag; it can be a decorative banner with an appliquéd picture. If you are allowed a wreath, hang a seasonal wreath on the outside of your door. It used to be that wreaths were only for Christmas, but now there are wreaths for every season and holiday. Be sure to keep your decorations current if your property is on the market for awhile. You don't want that Christmas wreath hanging on the door at Valentine's Day.

Interior staging for a condo or co-op is done in much the same manner as staging a single-family home, with one major exception. If the view from your windows is of a common walkway, another unit, or an unsightly feature such as the dumpster, leave the blinds closed. If you have sheers that let in light but are opaque enough to keep the view from being seen, all the better.

Signs and Mailers

If allowed by your homeowner's association, you or your agent should place a for sale sign in the window. This will inform your neighbors and passersby that you are selling. The next step is for you or your agent to send out a mailer to all other owners in the complex, letting them know your unit is for sale and at what price. It is possible that one of the owners has a friend who said, "If a place comes up for sale in your complex, let me know." If this is the case, you could have a buyer quickly. It is also a good idea to place an ad in the homeowner's association publication, if they have one.

Some condominium complexes and cooperatives have a directive in their bylaws that requires you to offer the property to the association and/or its other members before marketing to the general public, or they may allow their members a first right of refusal. Find out what your association's rules are before placing your property on the market.

Selling a House You Inherit

If you inherit a house, you will likely be responsible for taxes on the value of the property at the date of death. An appraisal or a comparative market analysis (CMA) usually determines the value of the property. Once that value has been established, the amount of inheritance tax can be determined. If the tax is more than you can afford to pay without selling the house, selling may be your best option. Consider the following facts.

- If you are able to sell for more than the value determined at the time of death, you may be responsible for additional taxes.
- If your sale price is less than the value at the time of death, you will likely be paying taxes on the value at death, a higher tax than the true value indicates.
- It is important to get a good, conservative opinion of value. You do not want to get stuck paying more tax than necessary if there is a downturn in the market.

Your Right to Sell

If you have inherited a piece of property, you may not have the right to sell it immediately. You will need to check with the attorney for the estate.

Although you may be the legitimate heir and there may be no one contesting that fact, you may not have any rights for a period of time. If the house is part of a trust, of which you are the beneficiary trustee, you do have the potential to sell immediately. If the house is included as part of a will in which you are named as the beneficiary, you may have to go through probate before having the right to sell the property. Probate is a court procedure that administers the estate of a deceased person. If there is no will in place at the time of death, the probate procedure can be very complicated and take considerable time. Get immediate assistance from the courts to be sure that the deceased's household bills will be paid, including the mortgage and utilities.

Staging a House You Inherit

When you put a house on the market, it is important that it look attractive. Putting an inherited house up for sale is no different. It is likely that a house you inherit was lived in for many years by the relative or friend who willed it to you. They may have been sick for a period of time, and they may have even passed away in the home. When this is the case, it is possible that maintenance has been neglected, windows have remained closed, and odors may need to be eliminated. As emotionally difficult as it can be, the house must be transformed. Buyers will become depressed if they enter a home and sense staleness or death. Do the following to cheer up a gloomy atmosphere.

- ✔ If there is a sick bed in the living room or elsewhere in the house, remove it. Remove all the accessories for the bed as well, such as rolling bedside trays and bars hanging from the ceiling that allow the bedridden to pull themselves into a sitting position.
- ✔ If there is an adjustable bed in the bedroom, lay it down flat.
- ✔ Remove any raised toilet seats and other accoutrements of a declining life.
- ✔ Remove personal items, such as clothing and photographs.
- ✔ Remove all food items and toiletries.
- ✔ If there are boxes of tissues, mothballs, and other conveniences that you would not see in a model home, remove them.

✔ Have the carpets and drapes professionally cleaned.
✔ Clean the windows.
✔ Air out the house.
✔ If you need to leave furniture, that is acceptable. If there is too much furniture, remove what you can. There should be wide areas for walking, and no doorway should be obstructed by furniture.

You will appeal to the largest pool of buyers by making the house as generic looking as possible. The goal is to have the buyer finish his tour unable to guess anything about the seller.

Selling a Vacation Home

If you are selling a vacation home, it is probably in a resort area. The possibility of finding another person who is purchasing the home for a vacation is quite high. Because of this, a vacation home is often sold in a condition called "turnkey furnished." This means that everything (except personal items, such as clothing, sporting equipment, and grooming aides) is included for the next buyer. Furniture, dishes, pots and pans, bedding, towels, and pictures will be included in the sale.

ALERT!

When selling a home in turnkey furnished condition, make an inventory of everything that is to be sold with the house. If there are some personal items that you are not going to leave, such as skis or a special piece of artwork, remove them from the property or place them in a locked closet.

Furniture is not considered part of the real estate; it is considered personal property, not real property. Lenders will not loan on the value of the furniture. Furnishings must either be left for convenience or the money paid for their value must be paid separately. No matter how nice, used furniture has very little financial value; so take that into consideration when pricing the property.

Even if you are not planning to use the vacation property, it is important to keep the utilities on for the showings. If you use the property in the summer and shut everything down for the winter or vice versa, you should still keep the house up and running while it is on the market. Buyers are turned off when they enter a house that has been shut down. If there is no power and no heat or air conditioning, the house will not be comfortable to view. If there is no water on at the property and someone needs to use the restroom, you can have a serious problem later.

If the vacation property is on a rental program, where other vacationers can use it for a fee, you may want to consider withdrawing from the program while it's on the market. Vacationers are not likely to cooperate by showing your property. They are on vacation. They came to relax, and they do not want the extra pressure. Even if they do allow it to be shown, they're liable to leave it a mess. If it is important for you to keep it on the rental program, be sure to have for sale flyers in the house. You may lose the buyer who wanted to see it, but you have the chance of converting the vacation tenant into a buyer, especially if they are having a good time and were considering a purchase anyway.

Selling a Resort Time-share

A time-share is not an investment; it is a toy. Just like the car or boat that loses value as soon as you buy it, a time-share loses value, too. Most people are excited when they first purchase a time-share. They anticipate using it every year or trading it for another resort. The fact is most people don't use their time-share, and most time-shares end up back on the market at a discounted price.

FACT

About 50 percent of the value of a new time-share is sales and marketing for the time-share company. This is why, if you purchased it new, your time-share may not be worth more than half of what you originally paid for it.

Time-share Clearinghouse

A time-share clearinghouse specializes in time-share resales. The majority of them charge an up-front fee, usually in the $500 range. Some of them charge no additional commission at sale, and some charge a commission at sale, most commonly a flat fee rather than a percentage. Most clearinghouses do a combination of both. These clearinghouses advertise your time-share on their Web site and in their mailings. If someone is looking for a time-share bargain, they look to the clearinghouses. If someone wants a time-share in a particular resort that has sold out, they look to the clearinghouses. You do have a chance of selling your time-share this way, although it may take several years. If you don't have the time to devote to the other methods, it may be worth the up-front costs to use a clearinghouse. Some of the clearinghouses also rent out units. If your unit does not sell, you at least have the chance of renting it for the week you are scheduled to use it.

Deciding which time-share resale company to use can be daunting. There are thousands of Web sites for time-share resales. Each of the following companies has its own style of selling, but they are established and a good place to start: *www.stroman.com* (since 1979), *www.holidaygroup.com* (since 1992), and *www.time-share-resales.net* (since 1994).

Selling Through the Resort

If a time-share has sold out at the resort where you purchased it, the resort will often keep a list of time-shares available for resale. The resort will not usually do this if they have not sold out because they do not want to compete with themselves. Some of the resorts will also put units that are for sale and have not sold in a rental pool. So, you have a chance of renting the unit if it doesn't sell right away. This is a good solution if you are in a popular resort but is less beneficial with a resort that is not well known.

For Sale By Owner

Attempting to sell a time-share yourself can work, too. For a fee, many of the time-share clearinghouses do the advertising for you and then hand the buyer over to you so that you can sell the time-share yourself. If you don't want to pay their advertising fees, you can go completely on your own. Advertise in the classified section of your local newspaper as well as the paper in the area where your time-share is located. You can also advertise in primary markets within four hours' drive of your time-share. You may also want to list your time-share on eBay or Yahoo Auctions. Chances are that you will have to take a considerable discount from what you paid, but you can get out from under the association dues and, if you purchased it with a loan, the monthly payments.

Trade

If you cannot find a buyer for your time-share, you may be able to trade it for something else that you are interested in owning. If you are interested in purchasing a piece of property, maybe the seller of that property will take your time-share in exchange for a portion of the down payment. If your time-share is in a desirable location or has good trading value for other locations, there will be sellers interested in accepting this trade.

The other items that may make a good trade with a time-share are collector cars or boats, airplanes, antiques, and other luxury purchases. People who sell these types of possessions are profiled to be the type of people who own time-shares as well.

Donate

There is a smaller pool of potential buyers for time-shares, and sometimes it is just not possible to sell them. If you have tried to sell your time-share without any luck, the next option may be to donate it to a local charity. This will give you a tax write-off. There are times when the tax write-off is higher than the value you would have received by selling it. If the time-share is within driving distance, your local charity may auction the week off each year to raise money. If it is not within driving distance, they may not want it since people are less likely to bid on something if it means they have to purchase transportation to use it. If driving distance is an issue, consider a larger charity that will be able to include airfare in the auction.

Selling Vacant Land

Perhaps you purchased land to build your dream house, and you have decided not to build. Perhaps you purchased it for the potential appreciation. No matter why you bought it, the buyer may have other motivations. Consider all of the potential plans a buyer may have for your land and be sure that you can address all the possible concerns, from zoning to utilities. This will help you sell your vacant land more easily.

ALERT!

If you have architectural plans that you would like to sell with the property, be sure that you first check with the architect who drew the plans. Architectural drawings are considered copyrighted material and may not be transferable without written permission or paying an additional fee.

Land Use Regulations

Governmental agencies that oversee land use are concerned with environmental or social issues, and regulations can be very restrictive in some areas. There may be restrictions regarding the allowable types of improvement (building a home or other structure) that were not on the property when you purchased it. You or your agent will need to do some research to be sure that your property can be improved in the manner you expect and in the manner you are advertising to potential buyers.

Check with your local building department or planning agency to find out which agencies have jurisdiction over your property. If your lot is located in a restrictive subdivision where certain architectural standards must be adhered to, this information needs to be passed along to the buyer as well.

Providing a potential buyer with a list of expected permit and related fees can help them make an informed decision and avoid future liability.

You don't want a buyer to come back to you saying that they expected the permit costs to be a part of the purchase!

Survey

A survey shows you where the property lines are located, topography of the land, where rocks and trees are located, and where the setbacks are. Most buyers find it in their best interest to get a survey. If you did not have one done when you purchased the property, you may want to get one now. If you already have a survey, it is wise to have it updated. A licensed surveyor for your state should perform the survey. You should have the corners and the borders marked on the property itself, and you should also have a map drawn up that can be presented to any potential buyer.

The corners of the property are marked with a combination of metal pins hammered into the ground, concrete posts, or other permanent markers. The surveyor should also mark the locations with a flagged wooden stake so that the permanent marker can be located quickly and easily. Be sure to ask if this is their standard procedure since not all surveyors will perform this additional task. Have them do this for you, even if it is not standard and there is an additional fee.

Depending on the location of your property, a surveyor may also create a path between the corner points (known in some areas as a cut-through) to allow you to see the lines between the corner points when vegetation is heavy or topography is irregular.

Chapter 22

Entering the Homestretch

Your house is sold. You have a check in your hand. You've packed up and moved out. You may have bought another house in the same community or perhaps you are renting for awhile. You may have moved far away from your familiar town. Is there anything else you need to do? Of course, but don't worry! Now is the time for recovery, settling in, and rec-reating a sense of normalcy for you and your family. This chapter will wrap up all you've learned throughout this book and leave you with some words of wisdom.

Physical Fatigue

Selling your house can physically wear you out. Packing and moving all of your belongings, including heavy furniture, can take a big toll on your body. While working off the adrenaline of preparing and selling your house, the strains may go unnoticed. Once the job is over, those strains can come at you with a vengeance.

Don't worry about unpacking every box and setting up the new house the minute you arrive. Just set up the beds. In midst of just-moved-in turmoil, the comfort of your own mattress will give you a peaceful place to rest.

You have been on the fast track for a while. Even if your house sold quickly, you have spent at least a month preparing your house for sale, showing the house, signing paperwork, packing, cleaning, and doing all the things it took to get sold. You are probably tired, not only from lack of sleep as "crunch time" came, but also from the stress of having your house on the market. Take some time to rest. True, you may have to go back to work. You may even have a new job, in a new community, which means long hours. You have things to unpack, and you want to get settled. Yes, there are a lot of things to do. The fact is that in order to take care of those things, you need to take care of yourself as well.

Start by taking care of your body. Take at least one day to do nothing except stare into space and nap. Your mind may be racing with thoughts of things you have to accomplish but try to set them aside for one day. If you can't shut off your brain, keep a notepad with you and jot down the things you need to do tomorrow and throughout the rest of the week. You are probably dehydrated; drink plenty of water and remember to eat well. Treat yourself to a nice dinner—not just another pizza. If you are in a community where you know people, ask a friend to cook you a meal. Home cooking is a great cure. If you are in a new community, some good comfort food (like a bowl of hearty soup) at a local restaurant will help restore you.

FACT

A massage can do wonders to help you feel refreshed and rested. The body aches from packing and lifting can be taken away with virtually no effort on your part. So that you have it to look forward to, book the massage when you book the movers.

On the next day, do some stretches when you first wake up. Take a walk and get to know your new neighborhood and revitalize your muscles at the same time. Aching, overworked muscles don't stop aching in one day; it can take up to a week to fully recover. Some good stretching and walking will speed up the recovery process.

If you made a to-do list while you were resting yesterday, you can look at it now and consider prioritizing tasks. Don't plan on crossing everything off that list today. Even if you feel great, you are still physically drained from the move and overexertion could lead to injury.

Emotional Exhaustion

Under stress, people often snap at the simplest things, get angry at the smallest incident, or even yell at someone who did nothing wrong. Things that would not normally bother people become extremely irritating when tiredness sets in. Chances are that everyone in your household has been on edge and some healing of the relationships needs to take place. Even if you think you weren't cranky and did nothing hurtful, start by apologizing. "I'm sorry" can go a long way toward restoring your family to the peaceful coexistence you had before the sale and move. If possible, plan a mini vacation. You don't need to travel far away or spend a lot of money. Just take a few days away from it all—to recuperate, renew, and leave the stress of moving behind.

Trade places with the kids for a day; you be the kids and let them be in charge. This exercise can be enlightening as you see yourself through your children's eyes. It can be a lot of fun, too. Usually, everyone learns about each other and decides they don't really want someone else's job.

Take time to relax together and enjoy each other's company. Most people, especially children, will go through a period of mourning after selling their home. Honor that time by having the children make up a "good-bye to the old house" song or poem. Perhaps everyone can do this, and you can share your creations over dinner.

Developing a new routine in the new place will help repair the psyche as well. Other than that, time is the psyche's greatest healer. Remember to be patient as you learn the idiosyncrasies of the new house. The mysterious night sounds or the fact that you turn left instead of right to the bathroom will soon become familiar.

Be aware that exhaustion can also bring on seller's remorse. In reality, you may not be disappointed that you sold your home, but you could feel regret if you're too tired to be reasonable. If seller's remorse does set in, focus on your initial reasons for the move. Make a list of all the great things about the new house and the new community. Read that list every day, and the seller's remorse will fade.

After a move, the most important step in restoring order and balance to your life is to make the new place feel like home. It is now time for the unpacking and organizing.

Settling In

If you placed the furniture in the correct rooms as you moved in and have already set up the beds, it's time to divvy up the boxes. Establish a staging area in each room to place the boxes for that room.

Tackle the kitchen first. Having a working kitchen will allow you to prepare meals and stop living on takeout. You won't be so hungry, and you'll be eating better, which means you won't feel as stressed.

ALERT!

Stop the vicious fast-food cycle. If you have moved far away, you may not have packed food. Even if you moved nearby, you probably used all the perishables at the old house in anticipation of the move. Make a list of staples and fresh food and do a big shopping trip in the first day or two.

Once you have unpacked the kitchen, move on to the bathrooms and then the linen closets. Unpacking is dirty work, and you'll be happy to have a functioning bath and know where your towels are. This is especially important if you've already gone back to work and school.

Tackle each subsequent room one at a time. There is nothing worse than half a dozen unfinished areas and no area that feels complete. Unpack the most necessary items first. In a bedroom, these might be clothes and shoes. In a family room, they might be the television set and other audiovisual equipment.

ESSENTIAL

Families should designate one brilliant person and individuals should set aside a specific time to set up audiovisual equipment. This task can get complicated, and it's easy to lose half a day or more trying to figure out all those connections. First things first. You don't want to wake up Monday morning without shampoo or underwear.

Once you have unpacked all the essentials, you'll notice that the room is shaping up and your box pile has shrunk considerably. You may be tempted to move on to the next room. If your remaining boxes contain nonessential things (such as knickknacks, books, videos, and music CDs), you can stack those final boxes in a corner or move them to the nearest closet so that the room feels useable. Just remember to deal with them soon.

Hanging pictures will make your new house feel fuller and more like home. Once you position the furniture, place the pictures on the floor against the wall where you think they should go. Move them around until you have the arrangement you like, hang them up, and take a moment to admire your work.

Revisiting Your Old Home

It is easy to get nostalgic about your old house and want to take one last peek. This is probably not a good idea. Don't even drive by. You don't want the new owners to think they are being stalked. It is no longer your house; it is someone else's new home. The new owners may be gracious and allow you to come in, but they might actually be uncomfortable. If they have made changes, they may be concerned that you won't like them or that your feelings will be hurt. The new owners may be quite private or quite friendly, but either way, it is their home now.

When you unpack, if you find an appliance manual or broiler pan that belongs to the old house, it is best to deliver it to your real estate agent rather than bring it by yourself. Likewise, if you forgot to take something when you moved, ask your agent to check on it for you. Don't get mad if the new owners can't find it, want to keep it, or threw it away.

Prepare yourself for a potentially upsetting scenario: Imagine that you drive by your old house for one last look. It was a beautiful place where you had raised three children and spent thousands of hours tending to the garden. As you drive slowly past, you see a huge hole in the ground where the house had been. There is heavy equipment on the property and a dumpster full of wood, bent metal, and broken tile that had once been your home. You are shocked. As the shock melts away, you become angry and hurt. This is certainly a hard reality to face.

Your house may have been a great home for you, but it may only be a location for the next owner. If you are afraid that you will be disappointed to see a hole instead of your home, driving by is a bad idea.

What if you want to take your yard ornaments but they are buried in snow at close of escrow?

This is something to address in the initial contract, with arrangements about who will be picking them up and when. It is important to state a specific date for the pickup, such as "March 15th," rather than "when the snow melts."

A New Adventure

You sold your house for a reason. Maybe you needed something bigger or smaller. You may have been transferred to another community. You may have gone through a divorce or lost someone through death. Whatever your reason for selling, you are now in a new house, and you face the exciting adventure of making it into a home.

In the Same Community

Buying a home near the house that you sold can keep your sense of roots intact. This part of the moving process is easy because you still have your friends and your favorite grocery store, hairdresser, doctor, and mechanic. Settling in may seem less like an adventure, but setting up your new home and learning the little things about it can be a pleasure.

Renting

Selling a home and moving into a rental can feel like a step backward to many people. Again, you had your reasons for making this decision. If you're renting temporarily, think of this as a time to regroup. If you've changed communities, you have a lot to discover. If you're looking for a new home to buy, that can be a lot of fun as well.

ALERT!

Check with your landlord about the rules for personalizing your rental. Are you allowed to paint one wall a decorator color? Can you put some potted plants on the patio? Find out what you can do to make your rental as homey as possible.

If you plan to rent long-term, enjoy the freedom of being able to pull up stakes and change your environment with just a month's notice. Whatever your reason for renting may be, you'll have new neighbors to meet and befriend and a new place to make your home.

In a New Community

While moving to a new community can be a little scary, it can also be inspiring. Hopefully, you checked out your new area before relocating. You know about the crime rate, school system, and type of people you might encounter. You have the stimulation of making your new house a home and the adventure of locating the new stores and services you need.

You also need to meet your new neighbors and friends. The best way to do that is to get involved. You can meet new people at work or through your children's school activities but also consider volunteering for a charity you believe in or taking a class to learn a hobby you've considered exploring. Attending local events and festivals can give you a sense of the place as well.

Taking part in activities you enjoy will acquaint you with like-minded people, give you a place in the community, and make your experience that much richer.

Moving Forward

You have nearly finished reading this book, and you now know what to do to get your house on the market and sell it. You know what to expect from your agent and from a potential buyer. Perhaps you are a little overwhelmed by all the knowledge you now possess. Don't worry! Now is the time to review what you've learned and rediscover your motivation for selling.

If you need to sell or if you just want to sell for a change of lifestyle, your motivation will affect everything you do to get ready. Feeling halfhearted about the idea of selling will make you halfhearted about getting ready. If you know you must sell but you really don't want to, the process will seem overwhelming. In this case, it's vitally important to find the benefit of selling your home and keep that in mind as you progress.

If you are excited about selling, you will be excited about getting the house ready and will do anything and everything necessary. Every project outlined in this book will seem easier because it is moving you toward your goal. As discussed earlier, things can get tough as the process moves forward, so keeping your goal in mind is always important.

Can You Avoid Mistakes?

In Chapter 3, you learned ten common mistakes that homesellers make. Be aware that there are also less common blunders too numerous to list. Chances are good that you will experience at least one or two of the less common mistakes. Hopefully, you won't commit any of the big ten now that you are aware of them. Because every transaction is different, your agent may make a mistake or two, the lender may make a mistake or two, and the title company, escrow company, and nearly everyone involved in the transaction can potentially make a mistake.

Consider this example: A man had been an agent for fifteen years and had read hundreds, if not thousands, of closing statements. This time he missed something. The escrow company missed something as well. They forgot to include a $250 repair bill for a plumbing leak that the seller had ordered and agreed to pay. Neither the agent nor the escrow officer noticed that the plumbing bill was missing—two humans, one little error. Escrow closed, and the seller's proceeds were forwarded on to the escrow company for the new house the seller was buying.

The following month, the plumber called the escrow company to ask when his check would arrive. The escrow company called the seller to let her know of the mistake and to request that she pay the plumber. The seller was mad at the escrow company and mad at the agent. She did not think she should pay the plumber's bill because someone had forgotten to put it on the closing statement. True, it didn't make the statement, but hadn't she agreed to pay the bill long before that? Once the seller calmed down, she realized she had promised to pay the plumbing bill, and she did take care of it.

ALERT!

Don't beat yourself up over the little mistakes, and don't beat up your team, including the agent and support staff who are helping to get your home sold. Remember, your team is made up of humans. These professionals don't like making mistakes and should repair the problems they create. Most mistakes are fixable; rather than pointing fingers, work together toward fixing any errors and don't look back.

With a small change though, this could have turned out differently. What if the agent had ordered the plumber and forgot to let the seller know? In this case, the agent would usually take care of the plumbing bill. Either way, small mistakes will happen. Expecting small glitches and handling them with ease will make the transaction smooth.

Pick and Choose

Go back to the beginning of the book and start crossing out things that do not apply to you. Treat this book like a textbook—don't be afraid to mark it up. Highlight the things you know you can accomplish. You may feel comfortable with putting some furniture in storage, but painting the house may sound overwhelming. Start with the things that feel comfortable.

Use a second color to highlight the things that you might want to accomplish but feel a little daunting right now. After you get rolling on the first highlighted list, you might be inspired to tackle the second list. Once the first list is finished and the second list is under control, you may even tackle a third or fourth list.

If you are working with an agent, have her look at your highlighted lists and any plan you have formulated from the different areas of this book. Get her opinion on how to prioritize and what is valuable for your area. Her advice could save you from a few setbacks.

Every market is different. In your area, you may have to paint the house to get it to sell; in another area, it is enough just to have things cleaned up. Ask your real estate agent for her opinion as to what really needs to be accomplished. She is likely to know just what you need to do to make your house stand out in your market. If you are selling on your own, tour some open houses and see what kind of preparation your competition has done. If you find that those houses sell quickly, try to emulate them. If they take forever to sell, those sellers may not have the answer.

To save time, mark the areas of this book that you will need to refer to repeatedly. Keep your plan for preparation in your mind by copying the lists you need and posting them on the refrigerator or the bathroom mirror so that you can refer to them regularly.

What Else Do You Need to Know?

Yes, this is *The Everything® Homeselling Book,* and virtually everything you need to know is here. However, real estate is a fluid business, and it changes every day. (This is one of the reasons this book is a second edition.) From market conditions to loan programs, from tax consequences to your own personal needs, nuances that apply to you may have to be gleaned from between the lines.

Trust your instincts and be prepared for anything. Mark up this book, add sticky notes, and basically do whatever it takes to learn the information given here. Armed with knowledge, selling your home will be a positive experience, and who knows, you may even want to do it again some day!

Appendix A

Phone Numbers for Real Estate Commissions by State

Each state has a real estate authority, which governs real estate transactions and administers the state's specific requirements and regulations. They are usually called the Real Estate Commission or Real Estate Division.

Your licensed real estate agent has received training and is well aware of your state's regulations and requirements. But if you are selling your home without an agent, it is important to contact the body that governs real estate transactions in your state. They can offer a wealth of information, tell you which forms you must complete, what disclosures you must provide, and a lot of other useful information to help ensure that your sale is legal and complies with all of your state's demands. They cannot give legal advice, however. You will need an attorney for those questions.

Following are the phone numbers for the Real Estate Commission or Real Estate Division for every state and the District of Columbia:

Alabama: 334-242-5544

Alaska: 907-269-8160

Arizona: 602-468-1414

Arkansas: 501-683-8010

California, Northern: 916-227-0864

California, Southern: 213-576-6982

Colorado: 303-894-2166

Connecticut: 860-713-6150

Delaware: 302-739-6150

District of Columbia: 202-442-4320

Florida: 407-245-0800

Georgia: 404-656-3916

Hawaii: 808-586-2643

Idaho: 208-334-3285

Illinois: 217-785-9300

Indiana: 317-232-2980

Iowa: 515-281-7393

Kansas: 785-296-3411

Kentucky: 502-425-4273

Louisiana: 225-765-0191

Maine: 207-624-8603

Maryland: 410-230-6200

Massachusetts: 617-727-2373

Michigan: 517-241-9288

Minnesota: 615-296-4026

Mississippi: 601-932-9191

Missouri: 573-751-2628

Montana: 406-444-2961

Nebraska: 402-471-2004

Nevada, Northern: 775-687-4280

Nevada, Southern: 702-486-4033

New Hampshire: 603-271-2701

New Jersey: 609-292-8280

New Mexico: 800-801-7505

New York: 518-473-2728

North Carolina: 919-875-3700

North Dakota: 701-328-9749

Ohio: 614-466-4100

Oklahoma: 405-521-3387

Oregon: 503-378-4170

Pennsylvania: 717-783-3658

Rhode Island: 401-222-2255

South Carolina: 803-896-4400

South Dakota: 605-773-3600

Tennessee: 615-741-2273

Texas: 512-465-3900

Utah: 801-530-6747

Vermont: 802-828-3228

Virginia: 804-367-8526

Washington: 360-664-6500

West Virginia: 304-558-3555

Wisconsin: 608-266-5511

Wyoming: 307-777-7141

Appendix B

Allowable Charges to FHA/VA Borrower

The FHA and VA have very strict guidelines for what fees and costs can be paid by the buyer, known by the FHA and VA as the *borrower*. The fees and costs that cannot be paid by the buyer (borrower) are usually the seller's responsibility.

The FHA borrower may be charged:

Home inspection: $200 or actual, whichever is less

Escrow fee: One-half of total, never more than the seller

Notary fee: $10 per person and no more than $40

Onetime MIP (mortgage insurance premium, to protect lender if mortgage isn't paid)

1 percent origination fee

Discount

$5 maximum payoff charge per bill, no liens

Beneficiary statement: $15

The FHA borrower is not allowed to pay:

Rent and interest on the same day

Tax service contract fee

Processing fee

Termite work

Charges for drawing additional documents

Homeowner's association transfer fee

Assignment fee

Interest prior to date of recording

Federal Express or messenger fees

Change of ownership

Document fee or redraw

Fee to record corporation assignment

Charges to other lenders

Subescrow fee

The VA borrower may be charged:

Recording fee: Actual fee charged by recorder's office

Credit report

Appraisal fee

Title insurance: ALTA

Tax proration to day of recording

Buyers protection policy if required by veteran

VA funding fee

1 percent origination fee

The VA borrower is not allowed to pay:

Escrow fee

Rent and interest on the same day

Appraisal fee if not in vet's name

Termite report and work

Notary fee

Charge for drawing additional documents

Homeowner's association transfer fee

Charge for other lenders

Processing fee

Tax service contract fee

Subescrow fee

Change of ownership

Federal Express or messenger fees

Document fee or redraw

Fee to record corporation assignment

Appendix C

To Do List: Preparing and Staging the House to Sell

To begin, make a copy of this list. Read the entire list. Add items that come to mind as you read, and cross off items that do not apply to your home or do not need to be completed. If there are things that you cannot afford to do or that you will not have time to do, highlight those items—but don't cross them out. You may be able to accomplish them later or you may find that they are not necessary. It is important to keep them on the list as reminders.

As you begin to show the house, you may become aware of things that buyers don't like or don't want to do after purchasing the house. It's better to eliminate objections by taking care of these items than to lose the chance of an offer or have the buyer ask you for a discount.

Now that you have personalized your list, it's time to start working. Keep track of your progress by checking off each item as you complete it.

1. Write your motivation for selling: _____

2. Take pictures of the house (as described in Chapter 11)

3. Exterior cleaning and preparation
   - ✔ Mow the lawn
   - ✔ Trim bushes
   - ✔ Remove any dead vegetation
   - ✔ Make sure no vegetation blocks access to the house, walkways, or the view of your front door
   - ✔ Sweep or wash down the driveway, walkways, front steps, patio, and decks
   - ✔ Make sure your front door lock is in good working order
   - ✔ Power wash the house
   - ✔ Check the driveway for cracks and wear
   - ✔ Hide or remove any exposed trash cans

✔ Remove any old, abandoned items (such as worn play equipment or old tires)
✔ Reseed or sod any bare spots in the lawn
✔ Clean and service the swimming pool
✔ Repair any cracks or broken tiles around the swimming pool or patio
✔ Add caution signs around the pool area
✔ Make sure all stair treads and handrails are secure
✔ Remove snow and ice during winter
✔ Replace torn or missing screens
✔ Repair siding or stucco
✔ Paint front door
✔ Paint exterior trim
✔ Paint or stain exterior
✔ Purchase pet carriers for showings
✔ Build outdoor pen for pets

4. Exterior staging
✔ Add potted or planted flowers near your front door
✔ Add a welcome mat or wreath
✔ Shine the lock set
✔ Paint siding
✔ Paint trim
✔ Reseal driveway
✔ Plant fresh flowers in the yard

5. Sorting and packing: Go through your house room-by-room. Approach each closet, drawer, storage area, and surface one at a time. Sort items into the following categories:
   • Keep for immediate use (items you need now)
   • Pack up for new house (items you will need after your move)
   • Pack up for storage (financial records and things you must keep, but barely look at)
   • Give away (useful items that you no longer need)
   • Throw away (items that have outlived their usefulness to anyone)

Note: As you empty each storage area, vacuum out debris and clean surfaces. Replace only the items you designated as "keep for immediate use."

Living Room
- ✔ Storage areas
- ✔ Surfaces

Entry Hall
- ✔ Closet
- ✔ Storage areas
- ✔ Surfaces

Dining Room
- ✔ Storage areas
- ✔ Surfaces

Kitchen
- ✔ Pantry
- ✔ Cabinets
- ✔ Drawers
- ✔ Counters

Family Room
- ✔ Closet
- ✔ Entertainment center
- ✔ Other storage areas
- ✔ Surfaces

Office
- ✔ Closet
- ✔ Other storage areas
- ✔ Surfaces

Master Bedroom
- ✔ Closet
- ✔ Drawers
- ✔ Surfaces

Master Bathroom
- ✔ Cabinets
- ✔ Drawers
- ✔ Counters

Bedroom #2
- ✔ Closet
- ✔ Drawers
- ✔ Surfaces

Bedroom #3
- ✔ Closet
- ✔ Drawers
- ✔ Surfaces

Bathroom #2
- ✔ Cabinets
- ✔ Drawers
- ✔ Counters

Bathroom #3
- ✔ Cabinets
- ✔ Drawers
- ✔ Counters

Garage
- ✔ Area: _____
- ✔ Area: _____
- ✔ Area: _____

Porch/Deck/Patio
- ✔ Area: _____
- ✔ Area: _____
- ✔ Area: _____

Other: _____
- ✔ Area: _____
- ✔ Area: _____
- ✔ Area: _____

What to do with all the stuff:
- Take your pack-up-for-storage items to a storage unit
- Take your packed up keep-for-new-house items to storage or stack neatly in garage
- Take give-away pile to the thrift store or have a garage sale
- Take throw-away pile to the dump (right away)

6. Interior cleaning and preparation
Throughout the house

- ✔ Scrub floors, baseboards, window and door trim
- ✔ Wash walls
- ✔ Vacuum carpeted floors
- ✔ Have carpet professionally cleaned
- ✔ Replace shabby, stained carpet
- ✔ Use area rugs where needed
- ✔ Wash windows, inside and out
- ✔ Have draperies professionally cleaned
- ✔ Wash window blinds and other window coverings
- ✔ Repair or replace broken blinds or outdated window coverings
- ✔ Wash walls in bathrooms and kitchen
- ✔ Check for dirty walls in other areas
- ✔ Repair or replace any broken or worn items
- ✔ Replace broken light fixtures
- ✔ Replace burned out light bulbs
- ✔ Repair latches and install stoppers on all doors
- ✔ Caulk chipped or damaged grout
- ✔ Remove any extra furniture (pieces that crowd the space)
- ✔ Have an honest friend visit your house for a "smell test"
- ✔ Clean animal cages and fish tanks
- ✔ Find a temporary home for pet reptiles
- ✔ Replace sagging closet rods
- ✔ Remove stacks of paper, magazines, books
- ✔ _____
- ✔ _____
- ✔ _____

Kitchen

- ✔ Wash down cabinet faces and doors
- ✔ Wash walls
- ✔ Clean out refrigerator and wash shelves
- ✔ Remove items from front sides and top of refrigerator
- ✔ Clean oven
- ✔ Clean stove top
- ✔ Clean sink
- ✔ Wash counters and backsplash
- ✔ Bleach stained grout
- ✔ Caulk around sink
- ✔ Remove most items from countertop
- ✔ Remove rugs from kitchen floor
- ✔ Hide trash bin
- ✔ Replace cracked or yellowed fluorescent light lenses
- ✔ _____
- ✔ _____

Master Bathroom

- ✔ . Wash down cabinet faces and doors
- ✔ Wash walls
- ✔ Wash all fixtures and counters
- ✔ Eliminate mold and mildew
- ✔ Clean all glass, mirrors, and shower door
- ✔ Remove any extraneous personal products from shower stall or tub
- ✔ Check bathtub stickers and remove or replace, as necessary
- ✔ Wash or replace shower curtain
- ✔ Remove most items from countertop
- ✔ Remove dusty decorative items
- ✔ Bleach stained grout
- ✔ Caulk around sink, tub, toilet
- ✔ _____
- ✔ _____

Bathroom #2

- ✔ Wash down cabinet faces and doors
- ✔ Wash walls
- ✔ Wash all fixtures and counters

✔ Eliminate mold and mildew
✔ Clean all glass, mirrors, shower door
✔ Remove any extraneous personal products from shower stall or tub
✔ Check bathtub stickers and remove or replace, as necessary
✔ Wash or replace shower curtain
✔ Remove most items from countertop
✔ Remove dusty decorative items
✔ Bleach stained grout
✔ Caulk around sink, tub, toilet
✔ _____
✔ _____

Bathroom #3

✔ Wash down cabinet faces and doors
✔ Wash walls
✔ Wash all fixtures and counters
✔ Eliminate mold and mildew
✔ Clean all glass, mirrors, shower door
✔ Remove any extraneous personal products from shower stall or tub
✔ Check bathtub stickers and remove or replace, as necessary
✔ Wash or replace shower curtain
✔ Remove most items from countertop
✔ Remove dusty decorative items
✔ Bleach stained grout
✔ Caulk around sink, tub, toilet
✔ _____
✔ _____

Master Bedroom

✔ Vacuum
✔ Dust
✔ Clean windows
✔ Address window coverings
✔ _____
✔ _____

Bedroom #2
- ✔ Vacuum
- ✔ Dust
- ✔ Clean windows
- ✔ Address window coverings
- ✔ _____
- ✔ _____

Bedroom #3
- ✔ Vacuum
- ✔ Dust
- ✔ Clean windows
- ✔ Address window coverings
- ✔ _____
- ✔ _____

7. Interior staging
- ✔ Check and trim or discard any sad-looking houseplants
- ✔ _____
- ✔ _____

Kitchen
- ✔ Add a colorful bowl of fruit
- ✔ Add new cabinet knobs
- ✔ _____
- ✔ _____

Bathrooms
- ✔ Add fresh new towels
- ✔ Add new cabinet knobs
- ✔ _____
- ✔ _____

Bedrooms
- ✔ Place a book and a lamp on your cleared bedside table
- ✔ Check closets to see that they are clean and presentable
- ✔ _____
- ✔ _____

Living Room

- ✔ Remove all excess decorative items
- ✔ Remove all excess furniture
- ✔ Add a flower arrangement and a coffee table book
- ✔ Lay a fire in the fireplace
- ✔ _____
- ✔ _____

Dining Room

- ✔ Set the dining table or use only a simple centerpiece
- ✔ _____
- ✔ _____

Other Rooms

- ✔ _____
- ✔ _____
- ✔ _____
- ✔ _____

8. Painting
   - ✔ Entryway
   - ✔ Hallway
   - ✔ Living room
   - ✔ Dining room
   - ✔ Kitchen walls
   - ✔ Kitchen cabinets
   - ✔ Family room
   - ✔ Office
   - ✔ Master bedroom
   - ✔ Bedroom #2
   - ✔ Bedroom #3
   - ✔ Master bathroom
   - ✔ Bathroom #2
   - ✔ Bathroom #3
   - ✔ Garage
   - ✔ Porch/Deck/Patio
   - ✔ Front door
   - ✔ Other _____

✔ Other _____
✔ Other _____
✔ Other _____

9. Staging an empty house
✔ Easel with interior photos of furniture placement
✔ Toilet paper in all bathrooms
✔ Keep utilities on
✔ Clean windows
✔ Clean carpets
✔ Remove picture hangers, patch and paint
✔ Remove speaker wires
✔ Remove all trash
✔ One bed and bedside table
✔ Table in dining room with tablecloth and chairs
✔ Towels in bathrooms
✔ New decorative soaps in bathrooms
✔ Keep landscaping tidy
✔ Keep property free of snow and ice

Index

R

THE EVERYTHING SERIES!

BUSINESS & PERSONAL FINANCE

Everything® Budgeting Book
Everything® Business Planning Book
Everything® Coaching and Mentoring Book
Everything® Fundraising Book
Everything® Get Out of Debt Book
Everything® Grant Writing Book
Everything® Home-Based Business Book
Everything® Homebuying Book, 2nd Ed.
Everything® Homeselling Book, 2nd Ed.
Everything® Investing Book, 2nd Ed.
Everything® Landlording Book
Everything® Leadership Book
Everything® Managing People Book
Everything® Negotiating Book
Everything® Online Business Book
Everything® Personal Finance Book
Everything® Personal Finance in Your 20s and 30s Book
Everything® Project Management Book
Everything® Real Estate Investing Book
Everything® Robert's Rules Book, $7.95
Everything® Selling Book
Everything® Start Your Own Business Book
Everything® Wills & Estate Planning Book

COOKING

Everything® Barbecue Cookbook
Everything® Bartender's Book, $9.95
Everything® Chinese Cookbook
Everything® Cocktail Parties and Drinks Book
Everything® College Cookbook
Everything® Cookbook
Everything® Cooking for Two Cookbook
Everything® Diabetes Cookbook
Everything® Easy Gourmet Cookbook
Everything® Fondue Cookbook
Everything® Gluten-Free Cookbook

Everything® Grilling Cookbook
Everything® Healthy Meals in Minutes Cookbook
Everything® Holiday Cookbook
Everything® Indian Cookbook
Everything® Italian Cookbook
Everything® Low-Carb Cookbook
Everything® Low-Fat High-Flavor Cookbook
Everything® Low-Salt Cookbook
Everything® Meals for a Month Cookbook
Everything® Mediterranean Cookbook
Everything® Mexican Cookbook
Everything® One-Pot Cookbook
Everything® Pasta Cookbook
Everything® Quick Meals Cookbook
Everything® Slow Cooker Cookbook
Everything® Slow Cooking for a Crowd Cookbook
Everything® Soup Cookbook
Everything® Thai Cookbook
Everything® Vegetarian Cookbook
Everything® Wine Book, 2nd Ed.

CRAFT SERIES

Everything® Crafts—Baby Scrapbooking
Everything® Crafts—Bead Your Own Jewelry
Everything® Crafts—Create Your Own Greeting Cards
Everything® Crafts—Easy Projects
Everything® Crafts—Polymer Clay for Beginners
Everything® Crafts—Rubber Stamping Made Easy
Everything® Crafts—Wedding Decorations and Keepsakes

HEALTH

Everything® Alzheimer's Book
Everything® Diabetes Book
Everything® Health Guide to Controlling Anxiety

Everything® Hypnosis Book
Everything® Low Cholesterol Book
Everything® Massage Book
Everything® Menopause Book
Everything® Nutrition Book
Everything® Reflexology Book
Everything® Stress Management Book

HISTORY

Everything® American Government Book
Everything® American History Book
Everything® Civil War Book
Everything® Irish History & Heritage Book
Everything® Middle East Book

HOBBIES & GAMES

Everything® Blackjack Strategy Book
Everything® Brain Strain Book, $9.95
Everything® Bridge Book
Everything® Candlemaking Book
Everything® Card Games Book
Everything® Card Tricks Book, $9.95
Everything® Cartooning Book
Everything® Casino Gambling Book, 2nd Ed.
Everything® Chess Basics Book
Everything® Craps Strategy Book
Everything® Crossword and Puzzle Book
Everything® Crossword Challenge Book
Everything® Cryptograms Book, $9.95
Everything® Digital Photography Book
Everything® Drawing Book
Everything® Easy Crosswords Book
Everything® Family Tree Book, 2nd Ed.
Everything® Games Book, 2nd Ed.
Everything® Knitting Book
Everything® Knots Book
Everything® Photography Book
Everything® Poker Strategy Book
Everything® Pool & Billiards Book
Everything® Quilting Book
Everything® Scrapbooking Book

All Everything® books are priced at $12.95 or $14.95, unless otherwise stated. Prices subject to change without notice.

Everything® Sewing Book
Everything® Test Your IQ Book, $9.95
Everything® Travel Crosswords Book, $9.95
Everything® Woodworking Book
Everything® Word Games Challenge Book
Everything® Word Search Book

HOME IMPROVEMENT

Everything® Feng Shui Book
Everything® Feng Shui Decluttering Book,
 $9.95
Everything® Fix-It Book
Everything® Homebuilding Book
Everything® Lawn Care Book
Everything® Organize Your Home Book

EVERYTHING® *KIDS'* BOOKS

All titles are $6.95

Everything® Kids' Animal Puzzle & Activity
 Book
Everything® Kids' Baseball Book, 3rd Ed.
Everything® Kids' Bible Trivia Book
Everything® Kids' Bugs Book
Everything® Kids' Christmas Puzzle
 & Activity Book
Everything® Kids' Cookbook
Everything® Kids' Crazy Puzzles Book
Everything® Kids' Dinosaurs Book
Everything® Kids' Gross Jokes Book
Everything® Kids' Gross Puzzle and
 Activity Book
Everything® Kids' Halloween Puzzle
 & Activity Book
Everything® Kids' Hidden Pictures Book
Everything® Kids' Joke Book
Everything® Kids' Knock Knock Book
Everything® Kids' Math Puzzles Book
Everything® Kids' Mazes Book
Everything® Kids' Money Book
Everything® Kids' Nature Book
Everything® Kids' Puzzle Book
Everything® Kids' Riddles & Brain Teasers Book
Everything® Kids' Science Experiments Book
Everything® Kids' Sharks Book
Everything® Kids' Soccer Book
Everything® Kids' Travel Activity Book

KIDS' STORY BOOKS

Everything® Fairy Tales Book

LANGUAGE

Everything® Conversational Japanese Book
 (with CD), $19.95
Everything® French Phrase Book, $9.95
Everything® French Verb Book, $9.95
Everything® Inglés Book
Everything® Learning French Book
Everything® Learning German Book
Everything® Learning Italian Book
Everything® Learning Latin Book
Everything® Learning Spanish Book
Everything® Sign Language Book
Everything® Spanish Grammar Book
Everything® Spanish Practice Book
 (with CD), $19.95
Everything® Spanish Phrase Book, $9.95
Everything® Spanish Verb Book, $9.95

MUSIC

Everything® Drums Book (with CD), $19.95
Everything® Guitar Book
Everything® Home Recording Book
Everything® Playing Piano and Keyboards
 Book
Everything® Reading Music Book (with CD),
 $19.95
Everything® Rock & Blues Guitar Book
 (with CD), $19.95
Everything® Songwriting Book

NEW AGE

Everything® Astrology Book, 2nd Ed.
Everything® Dreams Book, 2nd Ed.
Everything® Ghost Book
Everything® Love Signs Book, $9.95
Everything® Numerology Book
Everything® Paganism Book
Everything® Palmistry Book
Everything® Psychic Book
Everything® Reiki Book
Everything® Tarot Book
Everything® Wicca and Witchcraft Book

PARENTING

Everything® Baby Names Book
Everything® Baby Shower Book
Everything® Baby's First Food Book
Everything® Baby's First Year Book
Everything® Birthing Book
Everything® Breastfeeding Book
Everything® Father-to-Be Book
Everything® Father's First Year Book
Everything® Get Ready for Baby Book
Everything® Get Your Baby to Sleep Book,
 $9.95
Everything® Getting Pregnant Book
Everything® Homeschooling Book
Everything® Mother's First Year Book
Everything® Parent's Guide to Children
 and Divorce
Everything® Parent's Guide to Children
 with ADD/ADHD
Everything® Parent's Guide to Children
 with Asperger's Syndrome
Everything® Parent's Guide to Children
 with Autism
Everything® Parent's Guide to Children with
 Bipolar Disorder
Everything® Parent's Guide to Children
 with Dyslexia
Everything® Parent's Guide to Positive
 Discipline
Everything® Parent's Guide to Raising a
 Successful Child
Everything® Parent's Guide to Tantrums
Everything® Parent's Guide to the Overweight
 Child
Everything® Parent's Guide to the Strong-
 Willed Child
Everything® Parenting a Teenager Book
Everything® Potty Training Book, $9.95
Everything® Pregnancy Book, 2nd Ed.
Everything® Pregnancy Fitness Book
Everything® Pregnancy Nutrition Book
Everything® Pregnancy Organizer, $15.00
Everything® Toddler Book
Everything® Tween Book
Everything® Twins, Triplets, and More Book

All Everything® books are priced at $12.95 or $14.95, unless otherwise stated. Prices subject to change without notice.

PETS

Everything® Cat Book
Everything® Dachshund Book
Everything® Dog Book
Everything® Dog Health Book
Everything® Dog Training and Tricks Book
Everything® German Shepherd Book
Everything® Golden Retriever Book
Everything® Horse Book
Everything® Horseback Riding Book
Everything® Labrador Retriever Book
Everything® Poodle Book
Everything® Pug Book
Everything® Puppy Book
Everything® Rottweiler Book
Everything® Small Dogs Book
Everything® Tropical Fish Book
Everything® Yorkshire Terrier Book

REFERENCE

Everything® Car Care Book
Everything® Classical Mythology Book
Everything® Computer Book
Everything® Divorce Book
Everything® Einstein Book
Everything® Etiquette Book, 2nd Ed.
Everything® Inventions and Patents Book
Everything® Mafia Book
Everything® Philosophy Book
Everything® Psychology Book
Everything® Shakespeare Book

RELIGION

Everything® Angels Book
Everything® Bible Book
Everything® Buddhism Book
Everything® Catholicism Book
Everything® Christianity Book
Everything® Jewish History & Heritage Book
Everything® Judaism Book
Everything® Koran Book
Everything® Prayer Book
Everything® Saints Book
Everything® Torah Book
Everything® Understanding Islam Book
Everything® World's Religions Book
Everything® Zen Book

SCHOOL & CAREERS

Everything® Alternative Careers Book
Everything® College Survival Book, 2nd Ed.
Everything® Cover Letter Book, 2nd Ed.
Everything® Get-a-Job Book
Everything® Guide to Starting and Running
   a Restaurant
Everything® Job Interview Book
Everything® New Teacher Book
Everything® Online Job Search Book
Everything® Paying for College Book
Everything® Practice Interview Book
Everything® Resume Book, 2nd Ed.
Everything® Study Book

SELF-HELP

Everything® Dating Book, 2nd Ed.
Everything® Great Sex Book
Everything® Kama Sutra Book
Everything® Self-Esteem Book

SPORTS & FITNESS

Everything® Fishing Book
Everything® Golf Instruction Book
Everything® Pilates Book
Everything® Running Book
Everything® Total Fitness Book
Everything® Weight Training Book
Everything® Yoga Book

TRAVEL

Everything® Family Guide to Hawaii
Everything® Family Guide to Las Vegas,
   2nd Ed.
Everything® Family Guide to New York City,
   2nd Ed.
Everything® Family Guide to RV Travel &
   Campgrounds
Everything® Family Guide to the Walt Disney
   World Resort®, Universal Studios®,
   and Greater Orlando, 4th Ed.
Everything® Family Guide to Cruise Vacations
Everything® Family Guide to the Caribbean
Everything® Family Guide to Washington
   D.C., 2nd Ed.
Everything® Guide to New England
Everything® Travel Guide to the Disneyland
   Resort®, California Adventure®,
   Universal Studios®, and the
   Anaheim Area

WEDDINGS

Everything® Bachelorette Party Book, $9.95
Everything® Bridesmaid Book, $9.95
Everything® Elopement Book, $9.95
Everything® Father of the Bride Book, $9.95
Everything® Groom Book, $9.95
Everything® Mother of the Bride Book, $9.95
Everything® Outdoor Wedding Book
Everything® Wedding Book, 3rd Ed.
Everything® Wedding Checklist, $9.95
Everything® Wedding Etiquette Book, $9.95
Everything® Wedding Organizer, $15.00
Everything® Wedding Shower Book, $9.95
Everything® Wedding Vows Book, $9.95
Everything® Weddings on a Budget Book,
   $9.95

WRITING

Everything® Creative Writing Book
Everything® Get Published Book
Everything® Grammar and Style Book
Everything® Guide to Writing a Book Proposal
Everything® Guide to Writing a Novel
Everything® Guide to Writing Children's Books
Everything® Guide to Writing Research Papers
Everything® Screenwriting Book
Everything® Writing Poetry Book
Everything® Writing Well Book

Available wherever books are sold!
To order, call 800-258-0929, or visit us at *www.everything.com*
Everything® and everything.com® are registered trademarks of F+W Publications, Inc.